Nietzsche
and the
Promise of Philosophy

SUNY Series in Contemporary Continental Philosophy
Dennis J. Schmidt, Editor

Nietzsche and the Promise of Philosophy

Wayne Klein

State University of New York Press

Published by
State University of New York Press, Albany

Printed in the United States of America

For information, address State University of New York Press, State University Plaza, Albany, N.Y. 12246

Production by E. Moore
Marketing by Fran Keneston

Library of Congress Cataloging-in-Publication Data

Klein, Wayne, 1963–
Nietzsche and the promise of philosophy / Wayne Klein.
p. cm. — (SUNY series in contemporary continental philosophy)
Includes bibliographical references and index.
ISBN 0-7914-3549-0 (hardcover : alk. paper). — ISBN 0-7914-3550-4 (pbk. : alk. paper)
1. Nietzsche, Friedrich Wilhelm, 1844–1900. I. Title. II. Series.
B3317.K614 1997
193—dc21 97-3885
CIP

10 9 8 7 6 5 4 3 2 1

In memory of Reiner Schürmann

[. . .] for someone who thinks such things as I must think them, there is an ever present danger that he will destroy himself.
—Nietzsche, notebook entry, fall 1885

Do I contradict myself?
Very well then I contradict myself,
(I am large, I contain multitudes.)
—Walt Whitman, Leaves of Grass

Contents

Preface and Acknowledgments

Since the mid-1960s there has been a veritable explosion of interest in Nietzsche in the English-speaking world. By then almost twenty years had passed since the end of the Second World War and the influence of those who had tried to use Nietzsche's name and thought for ideological purposes had begun to fade. Today few would feel the need to assert, as Walter Kaufmann did in 1950, that Nietzsche is one of the most important thinkers in the Western tradition. Nietzsche's philosophical importance and the enormous influence he has had on the intellectual and cultural life of the twentieth century, whether one considers it to be positive or negative, can no longer be denied.

One consequence of this is that over the past thirty years a consensus has gradually evolved in the United States and Britain about where Nietzsche's importance lies and what his philosophy means. Although there is still substantial disagreement over the interpretation of particular passages and ideas, there is broad agreement over how Nietzsche's writings are to be approached. Most scholars would agree, for example, that Nietzsche's first book, *The Birth of Tragedy*, articulates a form of the metaphysical philosophy that he would spend much of the remainder of his life opposing, that the content of Nietzsche's thought is inseparable from its form, and that the collection of notes published under the title *The Will to Power* is an invaluable resource for understanding the often inscrutable writings of the late 1880s.

This volume is an attempt to critically examine certain aspects of this consensus and to reaffirm the importance of close reading as the foundation of interpretation. Although most scholars would now agree that all interpretation is conditioned by the beliefs and historical circumstances of the interpreter, there is too little recognition of the enormous influence that received ideas about a text or author have on shaping the way in which they are understood. To take a rather obvious example, most readers unquestioningly assume that Nietzsche was a disciple of Schopenhauer from his student days through 1876, the year he completed the last of the *Untimely Meditations*. There is, of course, a great deal of evidence in the texts Nietzsche had written up until that point to support this contention, particularly in *The Birth of Tragedy*, where Nietzsche seems to cite Schopenhauer approvingly and at great length. Little thought is given, however, to the effect that this assumption has on how we read the individual texts from this period. If we assume at the outset that *The Birth of Tragedy* is a neo-Schopenhauerian text, our interpretation cannot but be prejudiced in such a way as to predispose us to confirm this presupposition. The expectations produced by critical commonplaces such as this divert our attention away from the text, from reading how, for example, the influence of one author on another is inscribed or negated. Yet the test of whether Nietzsche did in fact write *The Birth of Tragedy* under Schopenhauerian influence must be a close reading of the text, and once we have undertaken this task, both the question of 'influence' and the text itself appear more complicated and less easy to circumscribe.

Each of the following chapters is concerned with an aspect of Nietzsche's thought. The Introduction begins by examining the attempts of two influential readers of Nietzsche, Martin Heidegger and Arthur Danto, to locate Nietzsche's philosophy within the mainstream of the Western tradition. I argue that Heidegger and Danto can only succeed in their task by imposing a particular understanding of what philosophy is on texts which explicitly resist conformity to this model. The source of this tension is found to lie in the understanding of philosophy held by both Heidegger and Danto. This understanding of philosophy can be traced back to Plato and the Introduction proceeds by undertaking a reading of several key sections of the *Republic* in order to examine the way in which the Platonic conception of philosophy shapes contemporary theories of interpretation. The Introduction concludes by contrasting this traditional understanding of the aims and methods of interpretation with a critical approach to reading, which contests some of the central assumptions underlying the traditional view.

Chapter 1 interrogates the claim that recent Anglo-American interpretations of Nietzsche, informed by the assumption that Nietzsche's style is an irreducible part of his thought, represent a real advance over previous interpretations which have paid little or no explicit attention to the question of style. While it is undeniable that Nietzsche's thought cannot be understood apart from his style, frequently style is conceived as a self-conscious semantic strategy, an understanding that necessarily remains caught within an intentionalist theory of meaning put into question by Nietzsche's texts. In this chapter I examine Alexander Nehamas' interpretation of Nietzsche's style as a means of creating a philosophical persona which would demonstrate, by example, that interpretation is necessarily perspectival. The limits of Nehamas' interpretation are explored through a reading of the concept of identity in *Ecce Homo*.

Chapter 2 undertakes a reexamination of Nietzsche's theory of language and rhetoric. In this chapter I argue that the text in which Nietzsche most fully articulates his view of language, the unpublished essay "On Truth and Lie in an Extra-Moral Sense," has largely been misunderstood because it has been read out of context and in isolation from the other writings on language from this period. One of these texts, a set of notes which Nietzsche wrote for a lecture course on ancient rhetoric, provides important clues as to how the seemingly idiosyncratic vocabulary of "On Truth and Lie" can be read in a philosophically fruitful manner. Rather than denying the possibility of truth, Nietzsche's essay argues for a reinterpretation of the traditional concept of truth. The last part of chapter 2 seeks to demonstrate that there is a continuity between the views on language and rhetoric Nietzsche develops in these early texts and those he held in the 1880s, the period of what is conventionally called Nietzsche's philosophical maturity. The consequence of this is that these writings should be read against the background of the early theory of language and not, as many today assume, as an implicit repudiation of this theory.

Chapter 3 considers the question of whether the theory of language and rhetoric Nietzsche develops in "On Truth and Lie" and in the course on rhetoric is not already operative in *The Birth of Tragedy*, a text, which as I have suggested, is usually assumed to uncritically reinscribe Schopenhauer's metaphysical valorization of music as the immediate expression of the will and concomitant devaluation of language. In this chapter I argue that the key to Nietzsche's theory of tragedy lies in a theory of signification which has important parallels to the theory of language and rhetoric he will subsequently develop. Rather than arguing that music provides privileged access to the essence of the world, access that is denied to language, the text demonstrates that music and language are grounded in a common system of signification. The difference separating music and language is shown to be rhetorical rather than ontological. The chapter concludes with an exploration of the implications of this reading for an understanding of the text as a whole and of its place within the Nietzschean corpus.

Chapter 4 examines Nietzsche's use of naturalistic and biologistic concepts in the writings of the mid- and late 1880s and asks whether there is not a conflict between Nietzsche's critique of the metaphysical concept of truth, which entails an interpretative pluralism opposed to the idea of a single correct interpretation, and his critique of morality, which seems to rest on an essentialistic understanding of the concepts of nature and life. This tendency is perhaps clearest in *Twilight of the Idols*, where Nietzsche contrasts two types of morality, an anti-natural morality which opposes the instincts of life, of which Christian morality is paradigmatic, and a natural morality which furthers the interests of life by codifying nature's own drives and demands. I argue that although the concepts of life and nature appear to function as essentialist categories for Nietzsche, a close reading of these texts demonstrates that this essentialistic rhetoric is incompatible with the ways in which these concepts function within the texts in which they are inscribed.

The Appendix argues for a radical reappraisal of *The Will to Power*. Originally published in 1901 and presented as Nietzsche's magnum opus, it has long been acknowledged that this text is in fact a selection of notes culled from Nietzsche's notebooks of the 1880s by his friend and assistant Heinrich Köselitz and his sister Elisabeth Förster-Nietzsche. In spite of the misleading circumstances surrounding the publication of *The Will to Power*, there was little reason to suspect that notes included in this volume were not, as Förster-Nietzsche insisted, faithful reproductions of Nietzsche's manuscripts. The number of notes collected, their thematic arrangement and seemingly representative quality, all made *The Will to Power* an invaluable resource for scholars and, since its translation into English in 1967, it has de facto been regarded as one of Nietzsche's books in the Anglophone world. In the Appendix I argue that there is compelling philological evidence that *The Will to Power* does not in fact present us with a faithful transcription of notes selected from Nietzsche's notebooks, and that the published text is philologically corrupt and should, in contrast to current practice, be regarded as largely apocryphal and not as a genuine or reliable source.

Although the chapters of this volume were written as parts of a single critical project, it is possible to approach them separately since each essay examines a distinct problem in the field of Nietzsche studies. Both the essay form itself and the overlapping nature of some of the inquiries pursued here necessitated a certain amount of repetition. I have attempted to avoid this wherever possible, but those instances in which I have failed will, I hope, be accompanied by a sense of recognition, not reiteration.

This book would not have been possible without the support of many individuals and institutions. The German Academic Exchange Service provided me with two grants that enabled me, at critical junctures in the course of my studies and research, to spend two summers in Germany. The Fulbright Commissions of the United States and Germany generously financed a year of doctoral research at the University of Tübingen during the 1991–1992 academic year. I take this opportunity to thank both organizations for their generous financial support.

The long apprenticeships demanded of academics mean that a great number of people have influenced and helped me on the way to completing this book. I would particularly like to thank my teachers Raymond Geuss, Agnes Heller, Harvey Goldman, Günter Figal, and the late Reiner Schürmann, each of whom, in different yet equally significant ways, kindled and encouraged my work in philosophy. Babette Babich and the other participants in a seminar on Nietzsche and Heidegger held in Trieste in April, 1992, provided crucial support and encouragement, then and since. I would also like to express my gratitude to two anonymous readers for SUNY Press, whose criticisms helped me make this a better book than it would otherwise have been. My greatest debts, however, are to my parents, who believed that I could learn to read even when others did not, and to my wife, Madeleine Dobie, who taught me how.

Portions of this book have previously appeared in print. "Truth and Illusion in *The Birth of Tragedy*" and "Tragic Figures," which contain material now incorporated into chapter 3, were published in *International Studies in Philosophy*, vols. XXVI/3 (1994) and XXVIII/3 (1996), respectively. The final section of chapter 4 appeared, in somewhat altered form, as a review essay under the title "Forgetting Nietzsche: Maudemarie Clark's *Nietzsche on Truth and Philosophy*," *Graduate Faculty Philosophy Journal*, vol. 16, no. 1 (1992). I would like to thank the editors of these journals for their kind permission to reproduce this material.

Note on Texts and Abbreviations

References will be given, whenever possible, parenthetically in the text. References to Nietzsche's *Nachlaß*—the notes, plans, and fragments drawn from Nietzsche's notebooks—are indicated by the appropriate volume, notebook, and fragment number of Giorgio Colli and Mazzino Montinari's critical edition of Nietzsche's writings: Friedrich Nietzsche, *Sämtliche Werke, Kritische Studienausgabe* (Berlin: de Gruyter, 1980). References to Nietzsche's letters are indicated by the volume and letter number of the companion edition of the letters: Friedrich Nietzsche, *Sämtliche Briefe, Kritische Studienausgabe* (Berlin: de Gruyter, 1986) Letters to Nietzsche, none of which are included in the *Studienausgabe*, are cited according to Friedrich Nietzsche, *Kritische Gesamtausgabe Briefwechsel* (Berlin: de Gruyter, 1975 ff.). References to Nietzsche's other writings, those published during his lifetime and those which fall under the heading of posthumous writings, are indicated by the initials of their English titles followed by a section number, or in the case of the essays, a page number. Additional references also follow this form.

In most cases citations from Nietzsche's writings are taken from existing English translations, occasionally modified. In all other cases the translations are my own. In contrast with the practice of most translators, I have attempted to maintain, as much as possible, Nietzsche's own punctuation, including his frequent use of dashes or *Gedankenstriche* and his practice of often using ellipses rather than periods at the ends of sentences and paragraphs. Although this may prove distracting to some readers, it seemed to me to be the best way of preserving the character of Nietzsche's texts, with their frequent pauses and interruptions. It is also important to remember that Nietzsche's punctuation appears as idiosyncratic to German readers as it does to

English readers. Italics are Nietzsche's unless otherwise indicated, and are always based on the German text.

In order to keep the number of footnotes to a minimum, I have listed the writings by Nietzsche referred to in the text along with the abbreviations used. These abbreviations will also be used in the footnotes whenever possible. Bibliographical information about these texts—and their English translations—appears in the bibliography.

Kritische Gesamtausgabe Briefwechsel = KGB
Kritische Gesamtausgabe Werke = KGW
Sämtliche Briefe, Kritische Studienausgabe = KSAB
Sämtliche Werke, Kritische Studienausgabe = KSA
Nietzsches Werke (Großoktavausgabe) = GA
Nietzsches Werke (Taschenausgabe) = TA
Historisch-kritische Gesamtausgabe, Werke = HKGW
The Birth of Tragedy = BT
Beyond Good and Evil = BGE
The Case of Wagner = CW
"Description of Ancient Rhetoric" = Rh
Ecce Homo = EH
The Gay Science = GS
"Homer's Contest" = HC
Human All-Too-Human = HH
Human All-Too-Human, vol. 2 = HH II
Nietzsche Contra Wagner = NCW
On the Genealogy of Morals = GM
"On Truth and Lie in the Extra-Moral Sense" = TL
"Philosophy in the Tragic Age of Greeks" = PTA
Twilight of the Idols = TI
The Untimely Meditations = UM
The Will to Power = WP
Thus Spoke Zarathustra = Za

Introduction

The Historical Foundations of the Question of Style: Plato and the Determination of Philosophy

It is that ascent to what is which we shall truly affirm to be philosophy.

—*Plato,* Republic

With Plato something entirely new begins.

—*Nietzsche,* Philosophy in the Tragic Age of the Greeks

SETTING LIMITS

Nietzsche scholarship has, since its inception, persistently grappled with the question of how to reconcile the literary character of Nietzsche's writing with the philosophical importance of his texts. This concern over the hybrid quality of Nietzsche's thought has not been confined to the English-speaking world, which, in contrast with continental Europe, has been slow in accepting Nietzsche as a thinker worthy of serious philosophical consideration. Towards the beginning of his lecture course "The Will to Power as Art," delivered in 1936, Heidegger observes that "for a long time it has been declaimed from chairs of philosophy in Germany that Nietzsche is not a rigorous thinker but a 'poet-philosopher' . . . who has at long last quashed abstract thought."[1] Such an approach, Heidegger asserts, is in error because it prevents a confrontation with the thought of Nietzsche, which can only occur if his place within the history of Western philosophy is correctly acknowledged. This means recognizing that in "Nietzsche's thinking the prior tradition of Western thought is gathered and completed in a decisive respect."

Rather than being a confrontation with a poet-philosopher who bears only a tangential relationship to the philosophical tradition of the West, the confrontation with Nietzsche is "one with all Western thought hitherto" (N I, 13/N 1, 14).

Writing from a radically different perspective, the American philosopher Arthur Danto has expressed similar concerns about the desires of philosophers working in the Anglo-American tradition to exclude Nietzsche from the philosophical canon. In contrast with those who would see Nietzsche as a poet, madman, or proto-fascist, in short as a figure not worthy of the name philosopher, Danto insists on the importance of putting aside such prejudices and considering Nietzsche as a serious thinker. Writing in 1979, fourteen years after the initial publication of his influential study *Nietzsche as Philosopher*, Danto reflects back on what he hoped to accomplish in his book:

> I wanted to show that whatever else he was or was not, Nietzsche was certainly a philosopher in just the way that everyone who is one is one: that he thought systematically and deeply about each of the closed set of questions which define what philosophy is, and that he gave serious, original, and coherent answers to them all.[2]

In spite of his conviction that Nietzsche is a thinker of some importance, Danto suggests that if we are to be successful in our attempt to treat Nietzsche seriously as a philosopher, it may be necessary to edit his texts and translate his ideas into an acceptable philosophical idiom, so as to be able "to see his analyses in terms of the logical features which he was unable to make explicit, but toward which he was unmistakenly groping." This is necessary, Danto continues, because Nietzsche had not always "known what he was trying to say."[3]

Despite the great differences in their philosophical orientations, Danto's and Heidegger's remarks form a common brief for Nietzsche to be taken seriously as a philosopher. And since the 1960s, when the books by Danto and Heidegger appeared, Nietzsche has come to be regarded in most quarters as one of the most important thinkers of late modernity. There are, to be sure, still dissenters, notably among Danto's intended audience of analytic philosophers, but judging by the number of recently published books and articles on Nietzsche authored by philosophers working in the Anglo-American tradition, a significant shift of opinion has occurred. In Germany, where Nietzsche's importance was recognized sooner than elsewhere,[4] interest continues to grow, as the founding this past year of a second German journal devoted to Nietzsche studies attests.[5]

These developments have, no doubt, been welcomed by those long convinced of Nietzsche's importance. Nevertheless, significant questions remain as to whether the basis upon which Nietzsche has been accepted into the pantheon of Western philosophy provides a foundation for a genuine appreciation of his thought. The reason for this can be gleaned by returning briefly to Danto's remarks cited above.

The first thing to notice about Danto's remarks is that they begin with the assertion that Nietzsche was not just a philosopher, in the same way as was Kant, for example, for Danto quite plainly asserts that Nietzsche was also something other than a philosopher. His concern, however, is not with these other things that Nietzsche was, but rather with the fact that "whatever else he was or was not, hc was certainly a philosopher." The point of this remark is not to exclude banal qualities such as being a man or a German, which are certainly compatible with one's being a philosopher, but other qualities, which, in Danto's view, cannot easily be reconciled with the concept of the philosopher. It is appropriate here to speak of *the* philosopher because it is clear that Danto believes that the label philosopher can only be applied to a single kind of thinker.

Thus when Danto says that Nietzsche was certainly a philosopher, what he means is that he fits this mold, for Nietzsche was a philosopher "in just the way that everyone who is one is one." The philosopher is a singular figure because he is concerned with the unique set of questions or concerns which define philosophy. Nietzsche is a philosopher like any other because "he thought systematically and deeply about each of the closed set of questions which define what philosophy is." This is not the place to examine Danto's claim that Nietzsche is a systematic thinker. Of more immediate concern is his assertion that philosophy is defined by a several "closed" sets of questions. What is striking about this statement is that Danto makes no effort to defend or explain it, but rather seems to assume that his claim is self-evident. However, the dubiousness of this assumption is illustrated by the fact that people have been philosophers in many different ways and that philosophy has, historically speaking, meant quite different things to different thinkers over time. To take an obvious example, it is only relatively recently that gender and race have become topics of discussion for philosophers. What is one to make of this? Following Danto's statement that the parameters of philosophical discourse are in some sense fixed, one is left to choose between two horns of the following dilemma: either one can maintain that race and gender have always formed part of one of the closed sets of questions which defines philosophy, an assertion which seems patently false, or one can maintain that questions of race and gender are not genuinely philosophical questions being concerned with particular rather than universal characteristics of human beings, which also seems quite false. Danto's characterization of philosophy remains caught in this dilemma because of his insistence that the parameters of philosophy can be determined ahistorically without regard for the content or historical quality of thought itself. Such an approach seems particularly unsuited to a thinker such as Nietzsche for whom "only that which has no history is definable" (GM, II.13).

It is not difficult to see that, whatever its merits, Danto's interpretation can only succeed by artificially limiting the scope and parameters of Nietzsche's thought. By claiming to be able to define philosophy and the questions that belong to it, Danto enforces a normative structure on the Nietzschean corpus which is alien to it. If Danto is to make sense of Nietzsche, if he is going to make Nietzsche respectable as a philosopher, he must do this at the expense of the Nietzschean text which refuses, which must refuse, to be forced into the Procrustean bed of analytic philosophy. As Karsten Harries has observed, 'translating' Nietzsche's texts in the way Danto suggests

> may well help us grasp what Nietzsche has written, but we should ask ourselves whether such appreciation is not also a defense against a style and thinking that puts the philosophy guarded by professional philosophers into question.[6]

This, of course, is precisely what is at stake when Danto distinguishes, at the head of the passage cited above, between Nietzsche the philosopher and "whatever else he was." For it may not be too much of an exaggeration to say that it is only when we glance behind the curtain separating philosophy from its other and see what is hidden there that we will find Nietzsche.[7]

THE SELF-UNDERSTANDING OF PHILOSOPHY

Danto's attempt to translate Nietzsche's texts into the conceptual language of analytical philosophy is grounded less in the exigencies of contemporary philosophy than in the historical determination and self-understanding of philosophy itself. As we shall see, virtually since its inception philosophy has been preoccupied with defining itself in contradistinction to other modes of discourse, particularly literature. Whatever philosophical texts have been about, they have always been explicitly concerned with demonstrating that the questions, concepts and language of philosophy are *sui generis* to it, belonging to philosophy alone. This is the promise of philosophy. This tendency, which is contemporaneous with the beginnings of Western philosophy in Greece in the fifth and sixth centuries before the common era,[8] reaches it full expression in the writings of Plato, the first thinker to attempt to systematically define philosophy and distinguish it from other forms of discourse, such as poetry and rhetoric, to which it is closely related. The argument against poetry found in the *Republic*, which culminates in the expulsion of the poets from the city, is Plato's attempt to put an end to the "old quarrel between philosophy and poetry" (607b).[9] It is my contention that this is a decisive moment in the history of philosophy. For irrespective of whether one accepts that the *Republic* represents Plato's definitive and final view of this matter, it would be difficult to deny that almost all philosophy after Plato is Platonic philosophy in the sense that it assumes, as established fact, the definition of philosophy set forth in the *Republic* and the view of poetry and poetic language that follows from it.[10]

Nietzsche's texts, I want to suggest, can be read as a reply to Plato and the Platonic tradition. They represent an attempt to rethink critically the tradition of Western philosophy, and, crucially, the self-understanding of philosophy as an autonomous discourse distinct from poetry and rhetoric. It is often assumed that Nietzsche's texts, which explicitly combine characteristics usually identified with literary and philosophical discourse, represent an exception in the history of philosophy, a special case that needs to be treated with special means. It is for this reason that so many books on Nietzsche, particularly those published for an Anglo-American audience, begin with a chapter on Nietzsche's style. Frequently, however, these discussions of Nietzsche's style amount to nothing more than pragmatic strategies for separating Nietzsche the writer from Nietzsche the philosopher.[11] In this regard, the result is fundamentally no different from Danto's translation of Nietzsche's writing into the language of analytical philosophy. If Nietzsche's texts are anomalous, it is not because they are 'literary' in the way in which most other philosophical writing is not, but rather because they explicitly and inexorably force us to question our assumptions about meaning, understanding and writing in a way that few other philosophical texts have. What is at stake here is not merely the question of style, viewed as the understanding of how an author writes, but the very content and method of philosophy. Nietzsche's work poses the question of whether the traditional way of understanding philosophy, namely, as a set of abstract problems of logic, ethics, and ontology, is not at root mistaken because it ignores the fact that the statement and solution of all such problems cannot be separated from the materiality of language itself. For Nietzsche, philosophical thought is a type of writing, a kind of text that is produced by the same forces, and needs to be read in the same way, as other kinds of texts. A striking example of this point, which we will have occasion to return to in detail in chapter 2, is Nietzsche's assertion that the Platonic ideas are the products of a tropological exchange of an effect and its cause. We perceive an effect, and as a means of making sense of it, project a cause behind it: "The *abstracta* evoke the illusion that *they* themselves are these essences which cause the qualities, whereas they receive a figurative reality only from us, because of those characteristics. The transition from the *eidē* to *ideai* by Plato is very instructive; here metonymy, the substitution of cause and effect, is complete." (Rh, 59). What for Plato is ontological is for Nietzsche rhetorical.

Just how such a statement is to be understood and what implications it has within the context of Nietzsche's thought can only be shown by a detailed reading of his texts. However, if Nietzsche's philosophy can be understood as a response to Plato's determination of philosophy and critique of poetry, as we have suggested, an appropriate preliminary to a detailed consideration of Nietzsche's texts would be to undertake a reading of the relevant sections of the *Republic*. This undertaking has a twofold purpose: first, to clarify Plato's definition of philosophy and his understanding of what it means for one to be a philosopher; and second, to elucidate the connections linking Plato's understanding of philosophy and philosophical discourse to contemporary theories of interpretation. We will endeavor to show that a continuity exists from Plato's conviction that empirical objects are imitations of ideas which alone represent true being, to the assumption which grounds most contemporary theories of interpretation, namely, that the meaning of a text can be understood in abstraction from the form or manner in which it is expressed. Such an approach, we will argue, can only succeed by doing violence to the letter of the text. In contrast, deconstructive theories of interpretation, because they reject the assumption that meaning and form are independent of one another, afford a more adequate means of approaching philosophical texts, particularly Nietzsche's, which pointedly demonstrate that there is no clear divide between meaning and rhetoric or philosophy and literature.

PLATO'S DETERMINATION OF PHILOSOPHY

Although the beginnings of speculative thought in ancient Greece can be traced back as far as Homer,[12] there is general agreement that philosophy, as we understand the term today, begins with Plato. Not only does the vocation of the philosopher as personified by the figure of Socrates receive its definitive description in Plato's dialogues,[13] but the parameters of philosophical discourse are circumscribed by Plato in a manner that is both novel and paradigmatic for the subsequent development of Western philosophy.[14]

Broadly speaking, the innovations of Platonic philosophy are three-fold. The first innovation concerns form. The Platonic dialogue, as Nietzsche suggests, is a new kind of writing (BT, 14). Although Plato's prose is highly stylized and to this extent continuous with literary tradition, it is clear that the dialogues are neither works of poetry nor dramas in any sense that would have been recognizable to Plato's contemporaries. In part this is because Plato's texts contain explicit criticisms of poetry and drama, which would have been a clear indication to the readers of the dialogues that they are not to be understood in the same way as these other texts. More important, however, is the fact that the dialogues have a specific and explicit pedagogical function. While it is true that epic poetry, most notably the Homeric epics, and tragic drama also played a recognizably pedagogical role in Greek culture,[15] in the Platonic dialogue we find that the burden of the teaching is displaced away from myth and replaced by argument. Myths perform their pedagogical function indirectly by means of illustration; the fates of Achilles, Oedipus, and Antigone are meant to have an exemplary status for members of the the audience, who can draw lessons for their own lives from what they have seen. In the case of tragedy, its pedagogical function is inseparable from its avowedly political significance. Tragedies were public in the dual sense that they were performed before an audience and that their performance at the Great Dionysia, held each March, constituted an important part of the life of the *polis*.[16] The Platonic dialogues, on the other hand, do not teach in this way. The dialogues were meant to be read, not acted out. Very often there is little or no action to speak of, and the lessons to be drawn from the dialogues are not gleaned indirectly from the exemplary status of the tragic hero, but directly from the arguments of the texts themselves. Even in a dialogue such as the *Apology* whose plot seems perfectly suited to be presented as a traditional drama, most of the action of the trial takes place outside of the parameters of the dialogue, while the majority of the text itself is devoted to the presentation of Socrates' speeches to the jury. By constructing the dialogue in this way, Plato directs the reader's attention away from the action to the arguments presented by Socrates.

The second innovation is the separation of religious and philosophical discourse. Among the changes wrought by the enlightenment in fifth-century Greece was the emergence of new scientific and philosophical ways of thinking against the background of traditional religious beliefs and practices. As one might expect, the emancipation of the scientific and philosophical discourses from their religious background was a gradual process. The texts of Parmenides and Heraclitus, which contain well thought out and recognizably philosophical views, remain within an explicitly religious context to the extent that both texts begin with descriptions of divine revelation. In contrast, Plato's dialogues can be read as an explicit attempt to establish the autonomy of thought and rational argument against religious authority. Unlike the hegemony of the poets, which is explicitly criticized by Plato, religious authority is not so much criticized as marginalized and subordinated to the force of argument. In the *Apology*, for example, Socrates refuses simply to accept the oracle, told to him by Chaerephon, that he is the wisest man in the city, but seeks to put its truth to the test by engaging the citizens of Athens in conversation (21b–23c). Although he eventually accepts the truth of the oracle and goes on to describe his philosophical calling as a "service to the god" Apollo, patron of the temple at Delphi, Socrates' reasons for accepting are rational rather than religious. This conclusion is supported by Socrates' own description of just what his service to Apollo entails. In contrast with what one might expect, Socrates does not exhort his fellow citizens to religious devotion, but rather to philosophical virtue: "For I go around and do nothing but persuade you, both younger and older, not to care for bodies and money before, nor as vehemently as, how your soul will be the best possible. Not from money does virtue come, but from virtue comes money and all of the other good things for human beings both privately and publicly" (30a–b).[17] Perhaps the clearest symbol of Plato's desire to effect a separation between philosophical and religious discourse is to be found at the beginning of the *Republic*, where the elderly Cephalus, who wears a wreath during the entire conversation, leaves Socrates and his interlocutors to look after the sacrifices (331d). The traditional justifications for the social order that Cephalus represents belong to the past, while the future can only be established through rational dialogue with the young. In this regard Plato is the true antipode of Sophocles, whose tragedies can be read as pleas on behalf of traditional religious wisdom in opposition to rationally grounded knowledge.[18]

The third Platonic innovation is the transformation of philosophy from a general desire to observe the world into a distinctive way of knowing, namely, a form of knowledge grounded in rational argumentation. Usually translated as "the love of wisdom"—a compound noun formed by the verb *phileîn*, to love, and the noun *sophia*, wisdom—the originary meaning of *philosophia* was less specific and technical than this translation suggests. As Wolfgang Schadewaldt has shown, the etymological roots of the term philosophy go back to Homer, where the verb *phileîn* describes a process of propriation, "to pursue something one wishes to make one's own."[19] In Herodotus, the word philosophy achieves a more general sense akin to, but still somewhat removed from, the Platonic definition. Herodotus describes Solon undertaking a series of journeys "in pursuit of *theoria*." Solon does this, writes Schadewaldt, "freely, not with some purpose in mind, as a merchant might, but rather simply in order to observe things. This he did *philosophéon*, as a friend of knowledge."[20] Philosophy here does not describe a specific way of knowing that can be distinguished from others, but rather a concrete striving for knowledge and cultivation undertaken for its own sake. Philosophy is less a form of knowledge—one could hardly speak of philosophical knowledge in this context—than the expression of curiosity with respect to the world, a desire to see and observe. Solon undertakes his journeys not as a craftsman, but as a wanderer.

With Plato the term *philosophy* takes on a much narrower, more technical meaning. No longer understood as a general desire for knowledge or aimless observation, philosophy for Plato becomes the pursuit of a definite kind of knowledge, to which he gives the name wisdom or *sophia*. In the *Republic*, Socrates describes wisdom as "that knowledge [*epistēmē*] which alone among the various kinds of knowledge ought to be called wisdom [*sophia*]" (429a). What distinguishes wisdom from the other forms of knowledge is that it represents the knowledge of things as they are in themselves, rather than as they appear. The philosopher does not seek merely a general knowledge of things in the world, but rather desires to know the eternal and immutable forms that constitute the way things are in themselves and on which their appearances depend. Philosophy, Socrates tells Glaucon, produces a "turning of a soul around from a day that is like night to the true day; it is that ascent to what is [*tou ontos ousan epanodon*] which we shall truly affirm to be philosophy" (521c). To be a philosopher is to "delight in each thing that is itself" (480a).

The philosophers' peculiar conception of knowledge distinguishes them from the sophists, with whom, at least superficially, they have the most in common. Although both are adept at speaking well, the philosopher engages in conversation in order to understand the true nature of things, while the sophist speaks in order to please the clients on whose patronage he depends.[21] For the philosopher there is an intimate connection between the search for knowledge and living well. As Socrates famously asserts in the *Apology* "the unexamined life is not worth living" (38). By contrast, the sophist aims to entertain his clients, and it is therefore a matter of complete indifference to him whether what he says is true or not, as long as his speech produces the desired result in his audience. In a series of well-known passages from the *Republic*, Socrates distinguishes the philosopher from the sophist in the following terms. It is in the nature of the philosopher,

> the real lover of learning to strive for what is; and he does not tarry by each of the many things opined to be but goes forward and does not lose the keenness of his passionate love nor cease from it before he grasps the nature of each thing. . . . And once near it and coupled with what really is, having begotten intelligence and truth, he knows and lives truly. (490b)

In contrast, the sophist does not pursue truth. His opinions are dictated by the whims of those he serves. Socrates compares the sophists, whom he calls "private wage earners," to

> a man who learns by heart the angers and desires of a great, strong beast. . . . Knowing nothing in truth about which of these convictions and desires is noble, or base, or good, or evil, or just, or unjust, he applies all these names following the great animal's opinions—calling

> what delights it good and what vexes it bad. He has no other argument about them but calls the necessary just and noble, neither having seen nor being able to show someone else how much the nature of the necessary and the good really differ. (493a–b)[22]

Because the sophist is guided by external forces, there can be a gap, perhaps even an opposition, between the content of an argument and its rhetoric, and accordingly, between the justness of the argument and the result it produces. Socrates' objection to the sophists is that the gap between content and rhetoric, which is permitted when one focuses exclusively on the effect produced by an argument, ignores the crucial question of truth and leads to a situation in which appearances are valued over the real nature of things.[23]

Since poetry, like sophistry, also values appearances over truth, it is open to many of the same objections Socrates raises against the sophists. These objections generally touch on two central points. The first is that poetry, as a mimetic art form, values imitation and the effects it produces in the soul of the observer over the truth of things as they really are. "The maker of the phantom [*eidōlon*], the imitator [*mimētes*]," Socrates tells his audience, "understands nothing of what is but rather of what looks like it is" (601b–c). The poet's ignorance of what is, is not a failure on his part but belongs to the very nature of what it is to be a poet. Poets do not concern themselves with how things truly are, but rather with how they appear. Socrates illustrates this point by comparing the poet with a painter, also an imitator and maker of phantoms. In order to paint an object—Socrates uses the example of a couch—the painter need not know how it is produced, or in the case of a musical instrument, how it is played. The painter's task is not explanatory or didactic, but simply imitative. If the painting is judged to be beautiful, however one might wish to determine this, it must be because it reproduces the appearance of its subject. Socrates expresses this point by asking his interlocutors whether painting is directed "toward imitation of the being as it is or toward its looking as it looks?" More simply put, "is it imitation of looks [*phantasmatos*] or of truth [*alētheias*]?" (598b) The answer Socrates seeks is, of course, that painting is imitation of looks, and he concludes that imitation "is surely far from the truth."

The distinction Socrates draws in this passage between imitation of looks and of truth can be grasped by examining the relative positions of the craftsman and the imitative artist with respect to objects in the world. According to Socrates, both the craftsman and the imitative artist require an object to perform their respective tasks, neither is capable of creation *ex nihilo*. The craftsman looks to the idea of the thing itself for a model of what it is that he or she is to create. It is, Socrates says, "in looking to the idea of each implement that the one craftsman makes the couch and another the chairs we use . . .

for presumably none of the craftsmen fabricates the idea itself" (596b). The idea constitutes the template on the basis of which the chairmaker or couch-maker is able to build a chair or couch. If the idea of a couch did not in some sense already exist, the craftsman would be unable to produce it. In this regard, the craftsman, too, engages in a kind of imitation, since he doesn't produce "the being but something that is like the being, but is not being" (597a). Although the couchmaker can also be considered an imitator, there is a crucial difference separating this kind of imitation from that practiced by the poet or painter. Whereas the couch produced by the craftsman is a copy of the idea itself, the imitative artist can at best only produce a copy of a copy. Rather than working from the idea of the objects he imitates, the painter and the poet merely copy what others have already produced. The imitative artist is "an imitator of that which these others are craftsmen" (597e). Since his creations are twice removed from being, mere copies of copies, they can communicate nothing of what an object truly is, but merely how it appears.

The second principal objection that Socrates raises against poetry, and imitative art in general, is that the poetic work, arising out of a concern for appearances alone, is morally neutral. Since the artist's creative process is not tied to the ideas of how things truly are, he is free to depict the world in a manner that takes no account of the moral worth of the things represented. In the following exchange with Glaucon from Book X, Socrates makes it quite plain that imitation and a concern for what is right and good are mutually exclusive activities:

> And will the imitator from using the things that he paints have knowledge of whether they are fair and right or not, or right opinion due to the necessity of being with the man who knows and receiving prescriptions of how he must paint?
>
> Neither.
>
> Therefore, with respect to beauty and badness, the imitator will neither know nor opine rightly about what he imitates.
>
> It doesn't seem so.
>
> . . .
>
> Then it looks like we are pretty well agreed on these things: the imitator knows nothing worth mentioning about what he imitates; imitation is a kind of play and not serious; and those who take up tragic poetry in iambics and in epics are all imitators in the highest possible degree. (602a–b)

Because the imitative artist knows nothing worth mentioning about what he imitates, his creations can only have a deleterious effect on those who experience them. This is because the images produced by the imitative artist nourish the "ordinary" and "irrational" [*alogistos*] tendencies of the soul at the expense of its deliberative and "calculating part" [*tò logistikon*] (604d–605b). Near the beginning of Book X Socrates warns Glaucon about the danger poetry poses to those who cannot easily distinguish between appearance and truth. "Between us," Socrates begins, "and don't denounce me to the tragic poets and all the other imitators, all such things seem to maim the thought of those who hear them and do not have knowledge of how they really are as a remedy" (595b). Later Socrates identifies precisely where the danger lies. The poet should be excluded from the city because he

> awakens [the irrational] part of the soul and nourishes it, and by making it strong, destroys the calculating part, just as in a city when someone, by making wicked men mighty, turns the city over to them and corrupts the superior ones. Similarly, we shall say the imitative poet produces a bad regime in the soul of each private man by making phantoms that are very far removed from the truth and by gratifying the soul's foolish part. (605b–c)

Rather than cultivating the harmony which is paradigmatic of the healthy soul, imitative art destroys the balance between the parts of the soul and consequently of the city itself. Paradoxically, the better the artist, the more destructive the impact on the viewer.[24] Socrates' response is to ban poetry from the city until such time that its protectors are able to demonstrate "that it's not only pleasant but also beneficial to regimes and human life" (607d).

On the terms of the argument developed in the *Republic*, however, poetry can never be beneficial to either the regime of the individual or the regime of the city. By valuing appearance over the true being of things, the imitative arts undermine the very foundation of the just regime, namely, the principle that each individual is naturally suited to practicing one craft and that justice consists in he or she practicing this craft and not another. The just regime is one in which each citizen is

> brought to that which naturally suits him—one man, one job—so that each man, practicing his own, which is one, will not become many but one; and thus, you see, the whole city will naturally grow to be one and not many. (423d)

Accordingly, the just city is a harmonious whole which is produced when each member of the city practices the task which is his or hers according to nature. In such a city the couchmaker will make couches and not chairs, while the chairmaker will make chairs, and not tables, because each is best suited to grasp the one idea that provides the template for their respective craft. "There is," Socrates says, "no double among us since each man does one thing" (397e). In fact, Socrates believes that this functional determinacy is so rigid and the need for harmony in the city so great, that it would be a perversion of the natural order for a single craftsman to produce several different kinds of instruments or for the musician to attempt to master more than a single musical genre.

Whereas the just man promotes the harmony of the city by vigilantly practicing the one task given to him by nature, the imitative artist promotes disorder by imitating many different things. "For example, the painter, we say, will paint for us a shoemaker, a carpenter and other craftsmen" (598b). One might object that while the painter takes different subjects for his pictures he is really engaged in one task, namely, imitation, but Socrates argues that by depicting different kinds of craftsmen he gives the impression that he possesses knowledge of their tasks, whereas "he doesn't understand the arts of any one of them." The artist seems to produce everything, but in actuality he merely "lays hold of a certain small part of a thing, and that part is itself only a phantom" (598b). Hence the imitative artist is not merely unjust in his own regime, but promotes disharmony within the regime of the city.

The imitative artist is expelled from the city, then, not simply because he values appearances over the truth of things as they are, but more important, because he is unable to live a just life. In this sense, he is the antipode of the philosopher, who eschews the world of appearances and particular things for the sake of a knowledge of the good. It is in virtue of this knowledge that the philosopher is esteemed as the most just of men and as the one who can best legislate the justice of the entire city. The Socratic philosopher acts philosophically by pursuing that which is most proper to his nature, a knowledge of that which truly is, while the imitative artist is the most unphilosophical of men because it is inherent to his vocation to act against nature, pursuing both what belongs to him and that which is most proper to others.

PURIFYING PHILOSOPHY

Although Plato certainly was neither the first nor the only ancient philosopher to criticize poetry in the name of philosophy—one might recall that Heraclitus ridicules Homer, the wisest of the Greeks, by suggesting that he "was deceived by boys killing lice"[25]—the critique of poetry articulated in the *Republic* is the most influential and far reaching of these texts. This state of affairs is not without some irony, since the tradition tells us that Plato was active as a tragic poet in his youth (BT, 14).[26] While he is said to have destroyed his poetic writings after coming under the influence of Socrates and taking up philosophy, the remarkable artistry and wit of the dialogues suggests that this break with poetry was not complete. Nevertheless, it is quite clear that Plato's decision to turn away from poetry and express his own views and those of his teacher, Socrates, in an entirely different form was motivated by a belief that philosophical thought should be expressed in a style particularly suited to the development and expression of its ideas, namely, the dialogue.

The idea that philosophy should have a style or genre unique unto itself follows from the relative epistemological status of philosophy and poetry. As we have seen, Socrates criticizes poetry because of its valuation of appearances over truth and the pernicious effects this has on the regime of the individual and the city. Whereas the artist is concerned with the many, particular things and their appearances, the philosopher seeks knowledge of the one, the unchangeable immutable idea of how a thing actually is. Because philosopher and artist are concerned with quite different aspects of the world, their mode of access to it and the type of knowledge this yields will be substantially different. In the case of the imitative artist, the principal mode of access to the world is by way of the senses. In a passage cited in the previous section, Socrates remarks that the imitative artist is not concerned with the being of his subject, the way it actually is, but is directly solely toward its appearance, "its looking as it looks" [*hōs phaínetai*] (598b). Knowledge of appearances, how things look, sound, smell, feel and taste, is acquired not by means of intellection, but through the senses. The imitative artist learns by observation and experience. In Socratic terms, an acquaintance with the appearances of things remains ineluctably removed from the idea of what truly is and, not being grounded in rational argument, cannot properly be called knowledge, but opinion or *doxa.*

Because an acquaintance with the world by means of the senses can only produce opinion, not knowledge, the philosopher must have another means of access to the world which allows him to know the true nature of things. The method which grants the philosopher access to the world of true being is dialectic [*dialegein*]. In the exegesis of the allegory of the cave which occupies the second half of Book VII of the *Republic*, Socrates elucidates the concept of dialectic by means of a contrast with the power of sight. Whereas sight is able to perceive those objects which are illuminated by the sun and hence belong to the realm of the visible, dialectic is directed towards that which can be known by means of intellection alone, that is, towards the ideas which constitute the intelligible realm. Just as the sun illuminates all things which belong to the visible realm and is the last and highest thing to be seen within this domain, so the idea of the good, "the cause of all that is right and fair in everything" (517c), is the peak towards which all intellection strives. Although the two realms, the visible and the intelligible, are distinct with regard to their objects and methods, they share a similar structure in virtue of the fact that the visible realm owes its existence to the intelligible idea:

> The sun is the offspring of the good I mean—an offspring the good begot in a proportion with itself: as the good is in the intelligible region with respect to intelligence and what is intellected, so the sun is in the visible region with respect to sight and what is seen. (508b–c)

It is against this background that Socrates contrasts dialectic with sight. "Dialectic," he avers,

> . . . is in the realm of the intelligible, but it is imitated by the power of sight. We said that sight at last tries to look at the animals themselves and at stars themselves and then finally at the sun itself. So, also, when a man tries by discussion, by means of argument without the use of the senses [*aneu pasōn aisthēseōn*], to attain to each thing itself that is and doesn't give up before he grasps by intellection itself that which is good itself, he comes to the very end of the intelligible realm just as that other man was then at the end of the visible. (532a–b)

On this account, dialectic is distinguished from sight principally in virtue of the means and method it employs to reach its goal. Like dialectic, sight seeks to ascend the ladder of being incrementally until it reaches that object which constitutes the end of its realm. The end of the visible realm is that object which produces light and allows for the very possibility of sight, namely, the sun. The complementary relationship which exits between the sun and sight is replicated with respect to the intelligible realm with one important difference. Whereas it belongs to the nature of the sun to produce light and allow for physical objects, including itself, to be seen, it belongs to the nature of the idea to be grasped not by sight, but by intellection. The idea of the good is to be sought by "discussion," that is, "by means of argument without the use of the senses." Dialectic is the method most proper to philosophy because it is only by this means that one get beyond appearances and can seek the truth of things as they truly are.

This conclusion has important implications for an appreciation of Plato's style. For it should now be clear that for Plato the question of content, what constitutes the proper subject of philosophy, is inseparable from the question of form, or the proper way to philosophize. If the goal of philosophy is to know the idea of the good and dialectics constitutes the path to this idea, it follows that the method which is most proper to philosophy is dialectic. And when one realizes that in Greek the word for dialectic and discussion are the same—*dialegein*—it becomes clear why Plato chose to write dialogues rather than the more poetic texts characteristic of Heraclitus and Xenophanes.[27] This also goes some way towards explaining why Plato launches such a vigorous attack on poetry in the *Republic*. As we noted above, Plato was not the first ancient philosopher to criticize poetry. The enormous impact which his critique of poetry has had on Western philosophy can be attributed to the way in which he defines philosophy in contradistinction to poetry and the other imitative arts, attributing to it a distinctive domain and method. It is in this sense that Plato represents a historical event of the highest order, for he, more than any other thinker before him, understood that philosophy is not simply the love of wisdom, but a way of making that wisdom one's own.

THE RHETORIC OF TRUTH

Although few philosophers today would accept the distinction between appearance and reality that lies at the heart of Platonic philosophy, the vestiges of this division are still apparent in a conviction that is a central tenet of modern philosophy, namely, that linguistic meaning is independent of form. Just as for Plato the idea of a chair can be instantiated in an almost infinite number of individual chairs, each of which is "like the being, but is not being" (597a), it is often assumed that the meaning of a word or sentence is distinct from its manner of expression. This idea is supported by the powerful intuition that the same thought can be produced by a variety of different words. The seeming incontrovertibility of this intuition is demonstrated by the following rather simple case of translation. The thought expressed in the English sentence "I have a piece of bread" can be articulated in a variety of different ways. In French, one says "*J'ai un morceau de pain*," in German, "*Ich habe ein Stück Brot*," yet each statement apparently means the same thing, which would be impossible if meaning were tied to form. The fact that concepts such as bread and possession can be expressed across many different languages demonstrates the meaning is not dependent on the material resources of any single language, but constitutes a type of "information" that can be encoded in an infinite number of ways.

This view that linguistic meaning is independent of its manner of expression has important implications for the way in which philosophers approach and interpret philosophical texts. For if meaning is independent in this way, it follows that the interpreter of a philosophical text should be concerned first and foremost with grasping what a given text means, that is, what a texts says rather than how it says it. The goal of interpretation is then to reproduce the meaning of a text, its ideas, theses, and statements, that is, precisely those parts of the text which could, in principle, be translated into other languages. On this view, the language and form of a text are extraneous to and necessarily subordinate to its meaning, which can only be culled by abstracting from those "literary aspects" of the text that are a mere vehicle for its ideas. So conceived, the task of scholarship is to effect just this kind of abstraction.

This tendency is exemplified in Margaret Wilson's well respected interpretation of Descartes. For Wilson, the question of style in the writings of Descartes is an "almost incidental point of interpretation,"[28] which needs to be addressed for the sole reason of alerting readers to the danger of ceding too much importance to the narrative form of Descartes' most central texts at the expense of their philosophical content. Although Descartes' use of first-person narrative might be considered an important aspect of his thought, in the following passage Wilson argues for a strict separation of the form and style of Descartes' texts from their properly philosophical import.

> The first sentence of the *Meditations* has already made clear that Descartes' exposition of his mature philosophy will be presented in the style of colloquial autobiographical narrative, This style can lead to the assumption that Descartes is directly concerned . . . with the facts of his own intellectual development, his private mental history. It seems to me, however, that we should guard against such an assumption. . . . The main point is just that the work must be read primarily as the presentation of a philosophical position having some claim to general relevance, and not as a history or autobiography at all.[29]

However in the *Discourse on Method*, published four years earlier and also narrated in the first person, Descartes explicitly suggests that this text should be read as a personal history from which others might derive some benefit. "I shall," Descartes writes,

> be delighted to show in this Discourse what paths I have followed and to represent my life as it were in a picture [*un tableau*]. . . . I offer this work only as a history, or, if you like, a fable, [*une histoire, ou, si vous l'aimez mieux, que comme un fable*] in which there may perhaps be found, besides some examples that may be imitated, many others that it will be well not to follow.[30]

Many readers of the *Discourse* have rightly pointed to passages such as this as evidence of Descartes' fear of persecution at the hands of Church authorities. The news of Galileo's condemnation by the Inquisition in 1633 had a profound effect on Descartes, as evidenced by his decision, taken the following year, to suppress the text of his treatise *The World*. The fear which this event provoked was certainly still in evidence in 1637, when he published the text of the *Discourse*, along with essays on optics, geometry, and meteorology. Nevertheless, it would be a mistake to dismiss passages such as these as examples of a mere prophylactic rhetoric, which can harmlessly be separated from the text's philosophical meaning. For this ignores the obvious connection between the first person narrative form of these texts and the tradition of spiritual and philosophical autobiography, of which Augustine's *Confessions* stands out as the prime example.[31] Although the significance of the relationship between these two thinkers can only be hinted at here, it is important to note that there are not simply stylistic and formal similarities between the *Confessions* and both the *Discourse* and *Meditations*, but the solution to the problem of radical doubt that is the foundation of these two Cartesian texts was first formulated by Augustine in his dialogues *On Free Choice of the Will*.[32] This suggests that the similarities in style between these texts cannot be dismissed as a mere coincidence, and that an investigation into the question of style in Descartes which made reference to the history of spiritual autobiography might well produce a richer understanding of Cartesian philosophy and the relationship between religious and philosophical discourse.[33]

Similar tensions emerge in the interpretations of Wittgenstein essayed by most Anglo-American scholars, who show an almost uniform disregard for the fragmentary nature of his texts. Wittgenstein himself calls attention to the question of style in the Preface to the *Philosophical Investigations*, where he describes his first intention regarding the form which his book will take:

> It was my intention at first to bring all this together in a book whose form I pictured differently at different times. But the essential thing was that the thoughts should proceed from one subject to another in a natural order and without breaks [*in einer natürlichen und lückenlosen Folge*]. After several unsuccessful attempts to weld my results together into such a whole, I realized I should never succeed. The best I could write would never be more than philosophical remarks; my thoughts were soon crippled if I tried to force them on in any *single* direction against their natural inclination [*natürliche Neigung*].—And this was, of course, connected with the very nature of the investigation.[34]

In this passage Wittgenstein draws attention to the fact that there is an essential connection between his thought and style. The fragmentary style of the *Investigations* is not incidental or arbitrary, but was dictated by the force and structure of his thoughts, which were crippled if forced to conform to the strictures of conventional philosophical prose. That the influence exerted by the nature of his thoughts was in fact decisive in determining the form of the text is confirmed by Wittgenstein's description of the structure of conventional prose in which thoughts follow a linear path as a "natural order." It is precisely this natural order that conflicts with the "natural inclination" of his thoughts. In the end, the demands of thought proved the more urgent.

While Wittgenstein explicitly states that it is the nature of his thoughts which makes it impossible for him to write a book in which his remarks would follow a linear structure, commentators have tended to treat this admission quite skeptically, interpreting it as a sign of failure on Wittgenstein's part. Thus G. P. Baker and P. M. S. Hacker, two of the leading Anglo-American interpreters of Wittgenstein, write in their analytical commentary on the *Investigations* that

> Wittgenstein blames the nature of the investigation of his repeated failure to fulfill this requirement of a sequential ordering. (In 1937 he blamed himself rather than his material.) It is difficult to believe that it is impossible to represent the material in sequential exposition. Waismann's *The Principles of Linguistic Philosophy*, which attempted to do just that for Wittgenstein's work at the stage of BT, is not defective in the organization of the material. . . . *Philosophical Investigations* is, as it were, a sketchbook of a master-artist who could not produce a finished canvas.[35]

Leaving aside the question of whether we should regard Wittgenstein's only published book, the *Tractatus Logico-Philosophicus*, also composed of remarks rather than naturally ordered prose as a finished canvas or not,[36] it is noteworthy that Baker and Hacker seek to play down the importance of Wittgenstein's reflections on the question of style. Rather than conceding the possibility that there is an essential incompatibility between his thought and the exigencies of conventional prose, Baker and Hacker interpret Wittgenstein's style as a mark of failure and incompleteness. In addition, they dismiss the claim, made in the last sentence of the passage cited above, that his need to compose philosophical remarks is connected with the nature of his investigation.[37]

However, the note from 1937 to which Baker and Hacker obliquely refer makes it perfectly clear that Wittgenstein was unable to think and write otherwise than in remarks which are necessarily nonsequential. "When I think for myself," he writes, "without wanting to write a book, I circle around a theme; that is the only natural manner of thinking for me. To be compelled to think in sequence is a torture."[38] Rather than attributing this to a failing on Wittgenstein's part, it might be more fruitful to ask what implications Wittgenstein's style has for an understanding of his philosophy.

The interpretative strategies pursued by Wilson and Baker and Hacker, which seek to recover the meaning of a text in abstraction from it manner of meaning, could be seen to be guided by the principle of charity, first formulated by Quine.[39] Donald Davidson, who has sought to develop this conception while pursuing the problems of radical translation and understanding first broached by Quine, has argued that interpretation is only possible if we assume that what others say and do is both meaningful and essentially rational.

> Making sense of the utterances and behavior of others, even their most aberrant behavior, requires us to find a great deal of reason and truth in them. To see too much unreason on the part of others is simply to undermine our ability to understand what it is they are so unreasonable about. If the vast amount of agreement on plain matters that is assumed in communication escapes notice, it's because the shared truths are too many and too dull to bear mentioning.[40]

An example of how the principle of charity aides the process of understanding can be found in cases where we are reading a book in a language other than our own and come across an unfamiliar word in a sentence of otherwise familiar words. More often than not, we are able to guess the meaning of the unknown word in virtue of the fact that, if the sentence is to be meaningful and not nonsense, then given the other words in the sentence there are only a limited number of possible meanings which the unfamiliar word can have. Sometimes, of course, we are wrong. However, this is not because we have misconstrued the other words in the sentence, but rather because usually more than one possible meaning of the unknown word is compatible with the other words; context is a important guide to meaning, but by itself it is not a determining factor. This process does not only apply to foreign languages, presumably many of the words of our native language are also learned this way.

Although this approach provides a reasonable explanation of how we come to understand and learn words previously unknown to us, it is unclear whether it provides a useful model for the interpretation of philosophical texts. The question is not whether this model of interpretation allows us to make the best possible sense of a given text, for there is little doubt that it does. Rather, the issue is whether sense, or in Davidson's terms, reason and truth, should necessarily be sought at the expense of those elements of a text, such as its form or mode of expression, which are generally considered to be extraneous to meaning. For it is open to question whether interpretations guided by the principle of charity can do justice to a text. Might not such interpretations amount to a form of hermeneutic violence by imposing, a priori, a coherent and rational meaning onto a text in complete independence of the way in which that meaning is constituted by the text itself?

We can answer this question by returning to Plato and examining a passage from the famous allegory of the sun from Book VII of the *Republic*. In this passage, Socrates is attempting to explain to Glaucon how it is that the true philosopher comes to know the idea of the good.

> This is the way the phenomena look to me: in the knowable the last thing to be seen [*horasthai*], and that with considerable effort, is the idea of the good; but once seen, it must be concluded that this is in fact

> the cause of all that is right and fair in everything—in the visible it gave birth to light and its sovereign; in the intelligible, itself sovereign, it provided truth and intelligence—and that man who is going to act prudently in private or in public must see it. (517c)

The first thing to notice about this text is that the rhetoric of Socrates' statement, the manner in which he says what he does, appears to conflict with the intended meaning of what he says. Since the middle books of the *Republic*, books V–VII, are in large part devoted to demonstrating that there are two realms of being—the realm of sensible things, which one comes to know through the senses, and the realm of intelligible things, which one comes to know by means of intellection—it is quite clear that Socrates is here using the metaphor of sight as a mere figure of speech. Surely Socrates is not suggesting that the philosopher actually sees the idea of the good, as in the allegory of the cave he is said to emerge from the cave and see the sun. It would be absurd to see, in Davidson's phrase, "too much unreason" in this passage and assume that Socrates is naively—and blissfully—contradicting himself. However, if we do not assume that, then what are we to make of this passage? The question we must ask is whether the meaning Socrates intends, which is that one does not, literally speaking see the idea of the good, but that the process of intellecting the good is like looking up and seeing the sun, is unaffected by the fact that this assertion is couched in language which blatantly contradicts it? To answer this question, we must first determine why it is that Plato chooses this simile rather than one which might prove less problematic.

To begin, we might recall that like the idea of the good, which is the highest being within the intelligible realm, the sun rules the domain of the visible. As a symbol of the sun's position is the fact that it is only in virtue of the sun's light that other beings in the visible realm can be seen at all. In order to help Glaucon grasp its importance, Socrates draws an analogy between the sun and the good. "The sun," he says, "is the offspring of the good I mean—an offspring the good begot in a proportion with itself: as the good is in the intelligible region with respect to intelligence and what is intellected, so the sun is in the visible region with respect to sight and what is seen" (508b–c). Since the sun is here elucidated by means of an analogy with the good, it seems perfectly consistent that later in Book VII, when the idea of the good is being explained to Glaucon, that the analogy is turned around so that the good can be elucidated by means of the image of the sun. The difficulty which arises is that in the latter passage it is not merely the role of the good that is being explained, but the manner in which the good can be known by the philosopher, and it is here that the analogy begins to break down. For while the sun is like the good in the role it plays relative to the other beings within the visible realm, it is fundamentally unlike the good in the manner in which it is known. This is not a minor point, because, as we have noted, the distinction between genuine knowledge and opinion, which is central to the text, assumes that there is a way of knowing things as they truly are without the senses. Furthermore, when Socrates explains what this other way of knowing is, intellection, he does so by contrasting it with sight. The following exchange from Book VI is quite typical:

> We both assert that there are and distinguish in speech many fair things, many good things, and so on for each kind of thing.
>
> Yes, so we do.
>
> And we also assert that there is a fair itself [*auto kalon*], a good itself [*auto agathon*], and so on for all the things that we set down as many. Now, again, we refer them to one idea of each as though the idea were one; and we address it as that which really is.
>
> That's so
>
> And, moreover, we say that the former are seen but not intellected, while the ideas are intellected by not seen [*ideas noeisthai men, horasthai d'ou*]. (507a–b)

However, it is just this distinction between intellection and sight which is threatened by the fact that in the passage we are considering Socrates asserts that the good, like the sun, is the last thing to be seen. Far from supporting the meaning which Socrates intends, the analogy between the sun and the idea of the good threatens to undermine the distinction between appearance and reality which constitutes the foundation of this text.

Yet is clear that this is not what Socrates meant to say. The analogy with the sun is intended merely to illustrate how it is that the philosopher comes to know the idea of the good, and is therefore extraneous to the philosophical point which Socrates is making. Such an interpretation, which follows the principle of charity, allows us to provide the most rational and consistent interpretation of the text. While the advantages of a hermeneutic organized around the principle of charity are not to be dismissed lightly, it is unclear whether it can do more than simply assimilate the analogy between the sun and the idea of the good into a set of literal meanings in which figurative language is excluded a priori. This is, in fact, the motivation behind Davidson's theory of metaphor, which assumes that there is no such thing as a metaphorical or figurative meaning outside of and addition to its literal meaning. Thus in the essay "What Metaphors Mean," Davidson asserts that "metaphors mean what the words, in their most literal interpretation, mean, and nothing more."[41] Davidson's claim that metaphors mean what they say is based on a resistance to the suggestion that metaphoric language possesses a "hidden second meaning," which, if accepted, would result in a form of semantic dualism. Davidson's reservations are not specific to metaphor, but apply equally to other forms of figurative language. "In the case of simile," he writes,

> we note what it literally says, that two meanings resemble one another; we then regard the objects and consider what similarity would, in the context, be to the point. . . . But having appreciated the difference between what the words meant and what the author accomplished by using those words, we should feel little temptation to explain what has happened by endowing the words themselves with a second, or figurative, meaning. (255)

On Davidson's view, the function of a simile is to draw our attention to similarities between two objects. Rather than being something out of the ordinary that requires us to postulate a second, figurative meaning, the simile's function is merely an extension of its literal meaning, and should be understood accordingly. But if a simile is to be understood in terms of its literal meaning, then figurative meaning loses all explanatory value. As Davidson puts it, "the supposed figurative meaning . . . explains nothing" (255).

However, in the analogy Socrates draws between the sun and the good, the concept of figurative meaning retains at least a modicum of explanatory force. The problem we identified above was that the sun is an unsuitable metaphor for the good because the ways in which each is said to be known are fundamentally different. We come to know the sun through sense experience, whereas the good can only be known by means of intellection, without any contribution from the senses. We can make sense of the analogy only if we ignore the fact that it threatens to disrupt the distinction between intellection and sense experience and interpret it in terms of what we believe Socrates actually meant to say rather than in terms of what he actually says. This is consistent with Davidson's view that the function of an analogy is to draw our attention to similarities between things that are analogous. The difficulty arises when we follow the logic of the analogy in the literal way suggested by Davidson, for it then becomes clear that the analogy does not simply draw our attention to observable features of things in the world, but at least one part of the analogy depends on an additional metaphor.

For although Socrates suggests that the power of sight imitates dialectic in its upward movement to the sun, the opposite cannot be said to be true. Dialectic, which is "argument without the use of any of the senses," cannot imitate sight. If it did, dialectic would fall back into the realm of opinion and cease to be the science of being, of that which truly is. Nevertheless, this is precisely what occurs in the passage under consideration. There, we recall, the idea of the good is described as "the last thing to be seen" in the intelligible realm. How is the idea of the good seen? Plato tells us it is seen with "the eye of the soul" [*tò tēs psychēs omma*] (533d). And it is here that the analogy between the sun and the idea of the good ceases to make sense in Davidsonian terms. For when we consider the power of sight and the intellect in order to see what similarity would be to the point, we are at a loss. According to the logic of the text, there cannot be a similarity of this kind between the soul and the eyes. Dialectic is, per definition, argument without use of the senses and cannot be thought of in terms of a sensual model. When we speak of the eye of the soul or the mind's eye we are, of course, talking figuratively. In this case, the figure is a metaphor, but a particular kind of metaphor, a catachresis, which by definition has no literal referent. In the *Poetics*, Aristotle identifies four types of metaphor, which he defines as "the application to one thing of the name belonging to another" (1457b).[42] The last type of metaphor is metaphor by analogy, which describes a situation when "among four things the second is related to the first as the fourth is related to the third, one may substitute the fourth for he second or the second for the fourth." Metaphor by analogy proceeds by means of a substitution of one name for another with which it stands in an analogous relation. However, in some cases one of the terms has no particular name. This is the situation Socrates finds himself in when he seeks to describe the way in which the philosopher intellects the idea of the good. In the course of his discussion of metaphor by analogy, Aristotle considers a case in which he seeks to describe the process by which the sun gives its rays, a situation, like that facing Socrates, for which there is no special name. "It may be," writes Aristotle,

> that some of the terms thus related have no special name of their own, but for all that they will be metaphorically described in just the same way. Thus to cast forth seed corn is called 'sowing'; but to cast forth its flame, as said of the sun, has no special name. This nameless act, however, stands in just the same relation to its object, sunlight, as sowing to the seed-corn. Hence the expression in the poet 'sowing around a god-created flame.' (1457b)

Socrates follows this exact procedure when he asserts that the idea of the good, like the sun, is *seen*. However, rather than endowing the metaphor of sight with a determinate, that is, literal sense, this act of naming reveals that the meaning of this metaphor is necessarily suspended between the literal and the figurative. Since there is no name for the act by means of which the philosopher comes to know the idea of the good, Socrates is forced to seek a name based on a perceived similarity between this act and another. However, because the mind does not, strictly speaking, have eyes, it cannot see the good in the same way as the eyes see the sun. In fact, outside of the metaphor employed by Socrates, there is no basis for believing that the mind does anything which remotely resembles sight. The meaning of this metaphor cannot then be accounted for by appealing to a referent or literal sense which the metaphor names, because in a catachresis there is no discernible difference between its literal and figurative senses. As Andrzej Warminski has observed in a remark on the expression "the face of a mountain," since the figurative use of catachresis

> does not take the place of an already existent, established literal use but rather replaces the lack of the literal, the lack of the proper expression, it is not just figurative; it can often become the proper, the only way to say the *x* of a mountain. But it would be a mistake to call it 'literal' . . . for catachresis is less a matter or the relation between literal and figurative, proper and transferred, sense, than it is a question of naming, marking, putting a word and imposing a sense where there is neither word nor sense.[43]

Because catachresis creates a sense where none previously existed, this sense cannot be reduced to a referent or prior, literal sense. The meaning imposed by a catachresis is both figurative and literal, and yet, precisely because of this, neither strictly figurative nor strictly literal, but exists in a undecidable space between these two poles. The undecidability inscribed within the catachresis of the mind's "sight" necessarily extends to the other members of the analogy. If the mind can be said to see, this is not because this metaphor represents an exception to the otherwise determine and literal meaning of this verb. On the contrary, the fact that sight can be ascribed to the mind means that the possibility of this meaning is always already inscribed in the literal and conventional meaning of the term. The metaphor of sight used by Socrates does not then represent an exception to the rule of literalness, but is paradigmatic of the kind of transfer or exchange of sense which makes language a radically open, tropological economy.

Contrary to Davidson's assertion that metaphors mean nothing more than the literal meaning of their words, catachreses such as the mind's eye, the face of a mountain or the leg of a table have no literal meaning that is prior to and separable from their figurative meaning. Catachresis gives something a name which was hitherto nameless. It does not simply supplement the name of an object by directing our attention to some previously unrecognized feature, but rather creates the very thing which it names. What makes catachresis unique among tropes is that it functions both as a figure and as a literal expression. On the one hand, it is a figure because it effects a transfer or *metaphorein* of sense from one place, the eye, to another, the mind. On the other hand, the catachresis is not merely a figure because it does not replace a literal expression, but becomes the only way of expressing the *x* to which we give the name "the mind's eye." Hence there is, from the very beginning, no possibility of reducing the figurative element in catachresis back a literal meaning in the manner suggested by Davidson.

In the logic of a hermeneutics based on the principle of charity, figurative language must be regarded as something outside the boundaries of meaning proper. It is for this reason that such a hermeneutics can do nothing more than attempt to assimilate or reduce the metaphor, which is the manner in which metaphor has always been treated within the confines of philosophy.[44] Davidson's insistence that figurative language must be tamed, returned to the foundation of the literal, is an extension of the program elaborated by Plato in the *Republic*, whereby poetry and the other imitative arts are regarded as secondary, irrelevant and, rather like the teaching of Socrates himself, seductive and dangerous.

READING AND NON-SENSE

Roughly speaking, the distinction between meaning and rhetoric, between what Benjamin calls "what is meant" [*das Gemeinte*] and the "manner of meaning" [*die Art des Meinens*],[45] gives rise to two distinctive approaches to the interpretation of philosophical texts. The first, which includes Davidson and a majority of philosophical approaches to understanding, focuses on meaning at the expense of rhetoric. Perhaps the most extreme example of this approach is provided by the nineteenth-century German theologian and translator Friedrich Schleiermacher, for whom the task of hermeneutics is to understand a text as the author himself understood it. Hans-Georg Gadamer, paraphrasing Schleiermacher, writes that "what should be understood is now not merely the text and its objective sense [*objektiver Sinn*], but equally the individuality of the speaker, that is, the author."[46] Interpretation, for Schleiermacher, "is ultimately a divinatory process, a placing oneself within the mind of the author [*ein Sichversetzen in die Verfassung des Schriftstellers*], an apprehension of the "inner origin" of the composition of a work, a recreation of the creative act" (191/164). Or, as Schleiermacher himself puts it: "What is the most beautiful fruit of all aesthetic criticism concerning discursive works of art if not an elevated understanding of the inner process of the poets . . . [and] the entire process of composition from the first outline to its final realization."[47] Although Gadamer rejects this model of understanding for being overly subjectivist, his own conception of understanding as a fusion of two perspectives or horizons, that of the reader and that of the text itself, is nevertheless directed towards producing a coherent meaning of the text. In a passage which bears a striking resemblance to Davidson's elucidation of the principle of charity, Gadamer compares the process of understanding to how we learn ancient languages. In reading an ancient text,

> we learn that we must 'construe'[48] a sentence before we attempt to understand the complete sense [*gesamten Sinn*] of the sentence in its linguistic meaning [*sprachliche Bedeuting*]. But this process of construing is itself already governed by an expectation of meaning that follows from the context of what has gone before. It is also necessary for this expected meaning to be adjusted if the text calls for it. . . . The movement of understanding is constantly from the whole to the part and back to the whole. Our task is to extend in concentric circles *the unity of the understood meaning* [*verstandenen Sinn*]. *The harmony of all the details with the whole is the criterion of correct understanding.* The failure to achieve this harmony means that understanding has failed. (296/259; emphasis added)

This passage shows that, for Gadamer, the process of interpretation is guided by a principle of coherence. The expectations which we bring to bear on a text necessarily project a coherent and unitary meaning. Although the details of the expected meaning are open to modification if they are found to conflict with the specifics of the text, the coherence of the interpretation can never be fully dispensed with. Gadamer's justification for insisting that interpretation obey a principle of coherence is that understanding can never be anything other than the understanding of a whole. For it is "plainly a formal condition of understanding . . . that only what really constitutes a complete unity of meaning is intelligible" (299/261). When this method, which is operative whenever we read a text, fails to make the text comprehensible, the fault lies not in the assumption of coherence, but rather in the text which the tradition has handed down to us.

The second approach, which has been practiced principally by poststructuralist critics such as Paul de Man and Jacques Derrida, questions the principle of coherence which governs hermeneutic theories of interpretation. Rather than assuming that interpretation should aim to produce a complete unity of meaning, deconstructive critics look to what the text actually says, its manner of meaning, to determine whether the meaning it produces is a coherent unity or not. This requires that the critic depart in two fundamental ways from the manner in which philosophical texts have conventionally been read. The first is that the reader can no longer accept the self-ascriptions of authors as an infallible guide to interpretation. Of course the descriptions that authors give of the nature of their projects, the means by which the investigation is pursued and the results they predict will be produced—and are produced in most cases, at least if authors are to be believed—will play an important part of any interpretation and cannot capriciously be tossed aside. However, rather than merely accepting these statements at face value and, by comparing them with what the text actually says, attempting to provide the most coherent interpretation possible, the attentive reader will examine the ways in which texts may in fact breakdown or turn against themselves and the explicit statements of the author about what they mean. The aim of such a procedure is not to engage in the pointless exercise of identifying inconsistencies for the sake of proving one's critical acumen, but rather to determine when certain texts do become inconsistent, and why this has less to do with mere linguistic or "performative contradictions," than with the unavoidable tension between meaning and the manner of meaning, linguistic exigencies beyond the control of any author or speaker.

If follows from this—and this is the second way in which the reader must depart from traditional methods of interpretation—that interpretation must no longer attend solely to what texts mean, but also to how they mean. It requires a recognition on the part of the reader that the what and the how, the meaning and the manner of meaning, cannot be sundered from one another in the interests of philosophical truth. The rhetoric of a text, its manner of meaning, must be seen as an integral part of the text, one that cannot simply be subordinated to meaning and passed over, "much as one might . . . tear out an illustrated leaf or allegorical representation in a more serious volume."[49]

In the course of an investigation of Locke's theory of words and language, de Man emphasizes the need to distinguish between a text's meaning, construed as the expression of the author's intentions (or the reader's expectations), and its manner of meaning. In reading Locke

> one has to read him, to some extent, against or regardless of his own explicit statements. . . . He has to be read not in terms of explicit statements (especially explicit statements about statements) but in terms of the rhetorical motions of his own text, which cannot be simply reduced to intentions or to identifiable facts.[50]

As de Man emphasizes, such a practice is not willfully contrary, but seeks out those moments in the text which exceed the boundaries of meaning defined by concepts such as intention and hence cannot be accommodated within traditional interpretative schema. In most cases this will mean that one's reading of a text, particularly one as well known as Locke's *Essay Concerning Human Understanding*, will run up against what de Man calls the text's "canonical reading," which seeks to interpret the text in terms of the author's intentions and explicit statements. In a reply to Raymond Geuss, de Man defends his reading of Hegel's *Aesthetics* by appealing to the necessity of attending to the ways in which Hegel's text challenges the canonical interpretation:

> Geuss' stance throughout his commentary, is to shelter the canonical reading of what Hegel actually thought and proclaimed from readings which allow themselves, for whatever reason, to tamper with the canon. Such an attitude, I hasten to add, is not only legitimate, but admirable. . . . There is no merit whatever in upsetting a canonical interpretation merely for the sake of destroying something that may have been built with considerable care. . . . The commentator should persist as long as possible in the canonical reading and should begin to swerve away from it only when he encounters difficulties which the methodological and substantial assertions of the system are no longer able to master. . . . The necessity to revise the canon arises from resistances encountered in the text itself (extensively conceived) and not from preconceptions imported from elsewhere.[51]

Earlier in his response, de Man attributes the differences separating his and Geuss' readings of Hegel to perceived differences between "philosophical" and "literary" readings of a text. Although de Man contends that such labels are ultimately of little value—the rigor of his reading of Hegel demonstrates that this is in fact so—it is a commonly held view among philosophers that a decisive difference does exist between the critical enterprises of philosophers and literary critics. On one level this is, of course, simply a territorial dispute. As we have seen, philosophy, perhaps more than any other avenue of inquiry, is concerned with distinguishing itself from other disciplines, particularly those such as literature and rhetoric which most closely resemble it. Literary critics are thus seen to be academic poachers, not satisfied with the game within their own preserves. On another level, however, serious differences in methodology and aims separate philosophers and literary critics. In large part these differences can be traced back to the philosophers' tendency to equate meaning with literal meaning and to regard texts as vehicles for propositions that present either a true or false picture of the way the world is. Wittgenstein expresses what is most essential to this tendency when, in the overtly positivistic mode of the *Tractatus*, he writes that a proposition "is a picture of reality" which restricts it "to two alternatives: yes or no."[52] On this view, philosophical interpretation as such depends on the possibility of deciding between the figurative and literal senses of statements, without which their truth value cannot be determined.

The naive opposition between literal and figurative meaning which this view assumes is untenable for the reason that language combines structures which cannot be construed as either exclusively referential or figurative. As we have seen, the possibility of catachresis, an exchange of sense without literal or referential foundation, ineluctably disrupts the boundary separating literal and figurative language. Since words can be exchanged without regard for their referential underpinnings, it is vain to hope that one could ever contain language within the confines of the strictly literal. This does not mean that language should be regarded as purely figurative with no literal sense whatsoever. Rather, what the foregoing consideration of catachresis demonstrates is that it is naive to believe that one can arbitrarily decide in favor of one of these two poles, privileging philosophic over aesthetic sense or inverting this relationship in favor of the strictly figurative. What is essential is to recognize the undecidability of this boundary separating the realm of the literal from the figurative, and the necessity that the suspension of language between these two poles threatens to undermine any order that seeks to exclude one or the other.

This conclusion bears directly on the project of self-definition that has occupied philosophy since its inception. If the figurative and literal dimensions of language cannot definitively be separated from one another, then the task which has been central to philosophy, namely, to exclude the figurative dimensions of language from its own discourse so as to distinguish itself from literature and rhetoric, with which it shares some obvious features, cannot succeed. We have noted that even in the case of the *Republic*, which is paradigmatic of philosophy's attempt at self-definition, at the moment in which this demarcation seems most secure, when Socrates elucidates the philosopher's relationship to the idea of the good, Plato must resort to an impossible metaphor, a catachresis, which undermines the distinction between appearance and reality that is central to this text. The collapse of this distinction is not the sign of a failure on the part of the author Plato, but a necessary consequence of any attempt to reduce language—and meaning—to either its literal or figurative dimensions.

Consequently, reading philosophical texts cannot simply be a matter of separating form and content, reducing a text to a series of propositions or arguments which are then evaluated with regard to their truth value, while concurrently dismissing the text's style and manner of meaning as mere ornamentation. Rather, one must attend to the way in which the text's meaning and its manner of meaning overlap, conflict, and are generally implicated in one another. This requires that the reader suspend some of the assumptions that have traditionally governed the interpretation of philosophical texts, for example, that there is a decidable opposition between figurative and literal meaning, assumptions that are necessarily imposed from outside the body of the text, and attempt instead to trace the semantic and rhetorical strategies which are inscribed within a particular textual economy. It follows from this that one can no longer continue to separate fully, on methodological grounds, the ways in which one reads philosophical texts in contradistinction to other kinds of texts. Since we have demonstrated that there is no discourse that is proper to philosophy alone, there is no reason to believe that there is a method that is uniquely suited to interpreting its texts and no other.

No doubt there is something disturbing, even paradoxical, about this conclusion. For it follows from this that the readings of Nietzsche collected here can make no a priori claim to be more truthful or more faithful to his texts than any other. While this might seem to be a gesture of humility on the part of the author, and a rather disingenuous one at that, for no one actually believes that his or her reading is just as good as any other, it is a gesture demanded by our inability definitively to distinguish literal from figurative meaning. If these two poles of language are always inextricably imbricated in one another, then one can no longer assume that there is a stable text or set or meanings to which a reading can or cannot ultimately be faithful to. And since the essays collected here are themselves texts, subject to the same forces as any other, there is no reason to believe that their meaning can be circumscribed and determined with any greater success.

Chapter 1

The Philosopher as Writer: Form and Content in Nietzsche

> *This book is intended for the placid reader [. . .]. Such a person has not yet forgotten how to think while he reads; he still understands the secret of how to read between the lines.*
>
> *—Nietzsche, "On the Future of Our Educational Institutions"*

> *This dual series of experiences, this access to apparently separate worlds, is repeated in my nature in every respect—I am a* Doppelgänger, *I have a 'second' face in addition to the first. And perhaps also a third . . .*
>
> *—Nietzsche, from a draft for* Ecce Homo

MISUNDERSTANDING NIETZSCHE

Nietzsche's writings have, from the very beginning, provoked misunderstanding among readers. His first book, *The Birth of Tragedy*, published in January 1872, was greeted with scornful silence by the philological community. Even Friedrich Ritschl, who three years earlier had recommended Nietzsche for a professorship in classical philology at Basel University with the greatest enthusiasm, could not bring himself to write to his former pupil and reveal his true feelings about the book. In private, however, Ritschl's judgment was all too clear. In a diary entry recorded shortly after receiving an advance copy of *The Birth of Tragedy*, Ritschl describes it as a piece of "ingenious dissipation."[1] Nietzsche, quite shaken by the lack of positive response from Ritschl and others, confesses to his close friend Erwin Rohde to being "seized by a terrible seriousness . . . because in such voices I divine the future of all that I have planned. This life will be very hard" (KSAB, 3/192).[2]

The failure of *The Birth of Tragedy*, which was openly ridiculed by some of Nietzsche's contemporaries, was to confirm his worst fears for the future, and in the following years Nietzsche's writings were to receive little, if any, positive attention. The silence was to continue almost without exception until the decade following Nietzsche's breakdown, when his fame quickly began to spread. The change in fortune was so great that by 1936 Heidegger could speak of the "enormous and varied secondary literature surrounding Nietzsche" (N I, 19/ N 1, 10).

A glance at the secondary literature, which since Heidegger's time has grown even more substantial, reveals a thinker whose work has been the subject of the most diverse interpretations imaginable. Rarely has a philosopher been read in such incompatible ways. As R. Hinton Thomas has documented in his study of Nietzsche's influence on German politics and social thought from 1890–1918, Nietzsche was read by nationalist and anti-Semitic thinkers as well as by leading socialist and feminist activists.[3] A similar split could be observed in Europe and the United States after the Second World War, between critics who viewed Nietzsche as a major intellectual force behind National Socialism and defenders who emphasized the potentially liberating aspects of Nietzschean thought. Even today, when scholars need not defend Nietzsche against the charge of being a fascist thinker, there is a surprising lack of agreement about the meaning of Nietzsche's philosophy and just where his importance lies. An example among many of this phenomenon is the oftentimes polemical debate over Nietzsche's relationship to poststructuralism which has taken place over the last decade.[4] The disagreement surrounding Nietzsche is not only unusual with respect to the diversity and incompatibility of the interpretations essayed, but there is a genuine lack of consensus regarding basic methodological questions such as what importance should be accorded to Nietzsche's unpublished writings, particularly the writings on language and rhetoric from the early 1870s, and whether a text such as *The Will to Power*, a posthumous collection of selections from Nietzsche's notebooks, is to be considered "an integral part of Nietzsche's literary and philosophical work"[5] or a philologically corrupt text of little or no scholarly value.[6] If Nietzsche's writings are no longer provoking the shocked silence displayed by Ritschl, they are, so it appears, still the subject of much disagreement.

One reason for this has to do with the character and texture of Nietzsche's writing. As has often been observed, anyone who has sat down with one of Nietzsche's books knows that the usual set of assumptions which normally govern the reading of philosophical texts does not apply. To begin with, there is a general lack of an obvious organizing principle, thematic or text around which an interpretation of Nietzsche's writings can be constructed.

Nietzsche's books, as Danto has observed, "do not exhibit any special structure as a corpus" (19). Although there may be compelling reasons to reject the rather extreme conclusion Danto draws from this fact, namely, that Nietzsche's "writings may be read in pretty much any order, without greatly impeding the comprehension of his ideas" (19), there can be little doubt that the question which, if any of Nietzsche's texts can be considered the magnum opus around which the other texts in the corpus can be organized, has no clear answer. Even if we limit ourselves to the texts written after 1881, Nietzsche's so-called mature period, the search for a central text raises more questions than it solves. The most obvious candidate to play such a role is *Thus Spoke Zarathustra*, which Nietzsche at one time thought of as the prolegomena to his mature philosophy. In a letter to his long time friend Franz Overbeck composed shortly after completing the third—and at that time final—part of *Zarathustra*, Nietzsche writes of his desire to undertake a wholesale revision of his "metaphysica" and "epistemological views." "I must," he writes,

> go though a whole series of disciplines, step by step, for I have now decided to use the next five years to work out my 'philosophy' for which I have, through my *Zarathustra*, constructed a vestibule. (KSAB, 6/504).

However, the published text of *Zarathustra* bears only the most indirect relationship to the books which follow. Not only is it radically different in form from these texts, but two of the concepts at the heart of this text, the will to power and the eternal recurrence of the same, play a relatively minor role in subsequently published texts,[7] while the figure of the *Übermensch* disappears completely from Nietzsche's writings. Although Nietzsche was, in the years which follow, to continually refer to *Zarathustra* as his most important book—in *Ecce Homo* he calls it the "greatest gift that has yet been given to humanity"—there is no obvious path from this text to the writings of the late 1880s.

A further, albeit related problem is that Nietzsche continually revised and enlarged his texts in such a way as to make it difficult to judge where one text ends and another begins, and hence to understand how the individual books relate to one another. Consider the case of *The Gay Science*. First published in 1882, the text initially had four major subdivisions or books. When the second edition appeared almost five years later, the text had a substantially different appearance. Whereas the first edition was published without a preface, beginning instead with a poetic "Prelude in German Rhymes," the second edition had both a preface and a new, concluding set of poems, the "Songs of Prince Vogelfrei." More important than these changes, however, was the addition of a fifth book, which radically altered the structure of the entire text. The dramatic denouement of book four, with its introduction of the idea of the eternal recurrence and the figure of Zarathustra in its concluding two sections (341–342), no longer serves as the end of the book itself. These changes raise important, though often unasked questions concerning how the second edition is to be read and the relationship between the new and old material. In addition to the internal changes the text underwent in this period, it is also important to consider external events, namely, the fact that in the roughly five-year period between the first and second editions, Nietzsche had published two additional books, *Thus Spoke Zarathustra* (1883–1885) and *Beyond Good and Evil* (1886). This raises the following question: Should the fifth book of *The Gay Science* be read in conjunction with the first four books originally published in 1882, or is it perhaps better read in the context of *Beyond Good and Evil*, with which it is roughly contemporaneous? The situation is further complicated when we consider that the title page of the first edition of *On the Genealogy of Morals*, published in November 1887, contains a note asserting that the text is meant to "supplement and clarify my most recently published book, *Beyond Good and Evil*."

The complicated textual history of *The Gay Science* is the rule rather than the exception. Rather than regarding his books as discrete works, Nietzsche seems to have considered them to be part of a larger, continuous project with no definite beginning or end. Returning to *Zarathustra*, we find that the "vestibule" of Nietzsche's philosophy, had, as it were, a vestibule of its own. In the conclusion to the letter to Overbeck cited above, Nietzsche writes that

> while reading through *The Dawn* and *The Gay Science* I found that there is practically no line contained in these books that cannot serve as an introduction, preparation and commentary to the above named *Zarathustra*. It is a *fact* [*eine* Tatsache] that I wrote the commentary *before* the text— —.

In light of this, it comes as no surprise that turning to the individual texts themselves provides little comfort to the philosophically inclined reader. Rather than fitting neatly into one of the recognized categories of philosophical writing, with few notable exceptions Nietzsche's texts appear to have little or no thematic continuity or purpose. Punctuated by rhymes, riddles, and irreverent asides and couched in a language which combines passages of great lyricism and irony, Nietzsche's texts seem joyfully to mock the pretensions and expectations of his readers. Even a text such as *On the Genealogy of Morals*, which Walter Kaufmann has described as the book of Nietzsche's that "comes closest, at least in form, to Anglo-American philosophy,"[8] could hardly be called a work of ethics or moral theory in the way in which these terms are usually understood. Rather than seeking to defend a particular moral theory, Nietzsche hopes to lay the groundwork for a critique of morality and of moral values in general. Such a task, Nietzsche says, requires a new kind of knowledge,

> a knowledge of the conditions and circumstances in which [moral values] grew, under which they evolved and changed (morality as consequence, as symptom, as mask, as tartufferie, as illness, as misunderstanding; but also morality as cause, as remedy, as stimulant, as restraint, as poison), a knowledge of a kind that has never existed or even been desired (GM, P.6).

In spite of the obvious cognitive aim of Nietzsche's task, the three essays that make up the *Genealogy* contain little of the argument and demonstrative intent usually found in philosophical texts. Theses are advanced, but often not defended, and when arguments are mustered in defense of particular assertions, they are usually of the rhetorical, rather than logical, variety.

Consider, for example, Nietzsche's analysis of the origin of bad conscience in the second essay. Having analyzed the relationship between punishment and the fundamental economic relationships of exchange and barter, which rest on the ability to assign a value to a particular ware or transgression, Nietzsche puts forth his own hypothesis as to how human beings first acquired the capacity to feel guilt:

> I regard the bad conscience as the serious illness that human beings were bound to contract under the stress of the most fundamental change they ever experienced—that change which occurred when they found themselves finally enclosed within the walls of society and of peace. The situation that faced sea animals when they were compelled to become land animals or perish was the same as that which faced these semi-animals, well adapted to the wilderness, to war, to prowling, to adventure—suddenly all their instincts were devalued and 'suspended.' From now on they had to walk on their feet and 'bear themselves' whereas hitherto they had been borne by the water; a dreadful heaviness lay upon them. They felt unable to cope with the simplest undertakings; in this new world they no longer possessed their former guides, their regulating, unconscious and infallible drives—they were reduced to thinking, inferring, reckoning, coordinating cause and effect, these unfortunate creatures; they were reduced to their 'consciousness,' their weakest and most fallible organ! I believe there has never been such a feeling of misery on earth, such a leaden discomfort—and at the same time the old instincts had not suddenly ceased to make their usual demands! Only it was hardly or rarely possible to oblige them: as a rule

> they had to seek new and, as it were, subterranean gratifications [. . .]. Those fearful bulwarks with which the political organization protected itself against the old instincts of freedom—punishments belong, first and foremost, among these bulwarks—brought about that all those instincts of the wild, free, prowling human being turned backward *against human beings themselves.* Hostility, cruelty, joy in persecuting, in attacking, in change, in destruction—all this turned against the possessors of such instincts: *that* is the origin of the 'bad conscience.' (GM, II.16)

The argument Nietzsche makes in this passage on behalf of his hypothesis, that the origin of bad conscience can be found in the exigencies of socialization which forced the instincts of primordial human beings to turn against these creatures themselves, is clearly not a logical proof, but an allegorical argument.[9] For there is no obvious way in which Nietzsche's hypothesis can be proved, in the logical sense of the word, true or false, and because this point is so obvious, there is good reason to think that this hypothesis should not be read as an empirical claim at all, as a statement which avails itself of "proof" in the traditional sense. In this respect, one misreads the passage if the word hypothesis is taken too literally.[10] To be sure, Nietzsche's intent in this passage and in the text as a whole is a cognitive one: he aims to illuminate the foundations and origins of moral values, and insofar as this is the case a passage such as this one cannot be dismissed as mere "rhetoric." However, both the manner in which Nietzsche's presents his hypothesis and his claim that the kind of knowledge he seeks has never existed or even been sought before, suggest that texts such as this need to be approached otherwise than by means of the criteria which have governed and determined philosophical knowledge hitherto.[11]

Nietzsche's rejection of traditional philosophical methods and procedures finds expression in the eschewal of linear narrative structures. Rather than the first person narrative voice we find in texts such as Augustine's *Confessions* and Descartes' *Meditations* or the seemingly neutral, undeclared narrator characteristic of most other philosophical writing, in Nietzsche's texts we are confronted with a variety of voices, personae and registers which, taken together, have the result of making it extraordinarily difficult to identify and definitively attribute any view to Nietzsche at all. Ironically enough, the one author Nietzsche most resembles in this respect is Plato, who never 'speaks' for himself, but only through the mouths of others. Nietzsche's observation that Plato was forced "by sheer artistic necessity to create an art form that was intimately related to the existing art forms repudiated by him" (BT, 14), could be applied equally well to Nietzsche himself. One is left with the impression that reading Nietzsche the way one reads Aristotle or Kant is analogous to reading Shakespeare and asking whether a particular soliloquy is true or false; the text and the evaluative criteria being brought to bear upon it appear utterly at odds with one another.[12]

In response to these challenges, recent scholarship, particularly in the United States, has focused on the possibility that paying sufficient attention to Nietzsche's style—seemingly one of the prime obstacles to understanding—is one way of making sense of his otherwise hermetic texts. Rather than viewing Nietzsche's style as something to be overcome, there is a growing consensus that his style is an integral part of his thought. In an introductory essay on Nietzsche written in 1988, Michael Gillespie and Tracy Strong describe how scholars have altered their approach to Nietzsche as a result of this recognition: "In the past decade, we have witnessed yet another rebirth of this apparently most protean of thinkers." Unlike previous approaches, this rebirth "does not start with the assumption that we we should look first at the 'content' of what Nietzsche says . . . [but] begins rather with the claim that we can best understand the meaning of what Nietzsche says by coming to terms with how he says it, that the meaning of Nietzsche's enigmatic utterances can best be understood by examining the style or structure of his thought."[13] The recognition that style and content, like the face and obverse of a single coin, cannot be prised apart from one another has led to a greater appreciation of Nietzsche in the Anglophone world. The fact that some of the more inscrutable and politically charged aspects of Nietzsche's texts are now seen to be parts of conscious philosophical or rhetorical strategies, has allowed scholars to more easily and convincingly draw connections between Nietzsche's thought and conventional philosophical discourse and thus to integrate Nietzsche into the philosophical canon in a way that seemed unimaginable fifty years ago. An example of this is the popularity and influence of Alexander Nehamas' study *Nietzsche: Life as Literature*, which has probably legitimated Nietzsche and the new approach to his writings more than any other recent work of scholarship. Another sign of Nietzsche's increasing legitimacy within the larger philosophical community is the number of recent studies authored by philosophers working within the Anglo-American tradition, who, historically speaking, have shown the greatest resistance to Nietzsche.[14]

In spite of the obvious success and influence of the new approach described by Gillespie and Strong, doubts remain as to whether the emphasis on style has truly altered our understanding of Nietzsche. The question is important because of the implicit assumption that by attending to the intrinsic interconnectedness of style and content, the new approach achieves something missed by previous approaches, that, to cite Henry James, the question of style is the figure in Nietzsche's carpet, "the very string . . . that [his] pearls are strung on."[15]

THE DISCOVERY OF STYLE

We have seen how the way in which Nietzsche composed his texts and his rejection of argumentative form and linear narrative structures force readers to self-consciously reflect upon the question of how these texts are to be read. This is a rare accomplishment, for unlike their literary counterparts, philosophers are generally inclined to view reading and interpretation as relatively perspicuous and unproblematic procedures. Before style became a significant concern for readers of Nietzsche, the most common reaction to the difficulties posed by Nietzsche's texts was to assume that his thought could only be understood properly if it were in a certain respect abstracted from the texts in which it was expressed. Thus in his ground breaking study of Nietzsche, first published in 1950, Kaufmann suggests that the inadequacies of Nietzsche's presentation of his ideas can be overcome if we project them on to a larger, systematic whole. Although he offered "many fruitful hypotheses, Nietzsche failed to see that only a systematic attempt to substantiate them could establish an impressive probability in their favor." The meaning of Nietzsche's individual thoughts and concepts, Kaufmann continues, "cannot possibly be grasped except in terms of their place in Nietzsche's whole philosophy."[16]

Kaufmann was well aware of Nietzsche's aversion to systematic philosophy and any form of system building. In a well known passage cited by Kaufmann, Nietzsche writes "I mistrust all systematic thinkers and avoid them. The will to a system is a lack of integrity" (TI, I.26). However, the openly unsystematic manner in which Nietzsche presented his thought possess a dilemma for Kaufmann who wants to maintain that, all appearances to the contrary, Nietzsche's thought constitutes a unity whose "coherence in organic" (91). Kaufmann's solution to this problem is twofold: to explain the unsystematic and discontinuous quality of Nietzsche's thought by means of an appeal to the deeply seated skeptical impulse in Nietzsche's thought, and concurrently, to criticize Nietzsche for taking this skeptical attitude to such a length that it had a deleterious effect on his thought as a whole. The skeptical impulse in Nietzsche is reflected in his insistence that beliefs must continually be subjected to doubt and questioned. Beliefs which one has accepted and ceased to question become convictions, which have a restraining effect upon oneself: "convictions are prisons. A spirit who wants great things, who wants the means to them, is necessarily a skeptic. The freedom from every kind of conviction *belongs* to strength, the *ability* to see freely. . . ." (A, 54). For Kaufmann, the motility and protean character of Nietzsche's thought are consequences of this need to continuously subject his beliefs to the most vigilant questioning. This method, which Kaufmann dubs Nietzsche's "experimentalism," is an attempt to "get to the bottom of problems" without being encumbered by the demands of systematization (87). Nietzsche's mistake, in Kaufmann's view, was to underestimate the extent to which "the insights which he tries to formulate in his aphorisms will have to be accounted for in any comprehensive explanatory system, just as an honest scientific experiment cannot be ignored by any comprehensive scientific system" (87). Nietzsche's experimentalism can only succeed, Kaufmann argues, if the results of previous experiments are codified and only questioned if they conflict with "new experiences and ideas. In this sense, a new insight in not exploited sufficiently, and the experiment is, as it were, stopped prematurely, if systematization is not eventually attempted" (94).

Similar presuppositions to these govern Heidegger's interpretation of Nietzsche. Like Kaufmann, Heidegger argues that Nietzsche's text must be read against the background of a systematic and coherent whole. As is well known, Heidegger locates this whole, Nietzsche's "philosophy proper," not in the published works, but in the notes, drafts and fragments left behind. In an infamous passage from the lecture course "The Will to Power as Art" offered in 1936, Heidegger writes that

> Nietzsche's philosophy proper, the fundamental position on the basis of which he speaks in these and in all the writings he himself published, did not assume a final form and was not itself published in any book, neither in the decade between 1879 and 1889 nor during the years preceding. What Nietzsche himself published during his creative life was always foreground. . . . His philosophy proper [*die eigentliche Philosophie*] was left behind as posthumous, unpublished work. (N I, 17/ N 1, 9)

In this lecture course Heidegger identifies Nietzsche's philosophy proper with the unity and coherence of the three concepts of eternal recurrence, will to power and revaluation of values. The task which Heidegger sets himself is to grasp "in a unified way the doctrines of eternal return of the same and will to power, and these two doctrines in their most intrinsic coherence as revaluation" (N I, 25/ N 1, 17). In later lecture courses, when the problem of nihilism began to figure more prominently in Heidegger's thinking, the list of concepts grows to five. In the lecture course on "European Nihilism" offered in the fall of 1940, Heidegger asserts that the totality of Nietzsche's philosophy is captured in five fundamental concepts or rubrics: "The five rubrics "nihilism," "revaluation of all values hitherto," "will to power," "eternal recurrence of the same," and "Overman"—each portrays Nietzsche's metaphysics from just *one* perspective, although in each case it is a perspective that defines the whole. Thus Nietzsche's metaphysics is grasped only when what is named in these five headings can be thought . . . in its primordial and heretofore merely intimated conjunction" (N II, 40/ N 4, 9–10).

Although Kaufmann's and Heidegger's interpretations differ in important and substantial respects, they share a common conviction that Nietzsche's thought can only be understood properly if it is abstracted from its context and read against the background of his philosophy as a whole. This leads both interpreters to regard Nietzsche's writings as vehicles of communication, rather than as books requiring interpretation. However, if Heidegger and Kaufmann do not read Nietzsche's texts as texts, it is not because they do not take Nietzsche seriously as a thinker, but rather because they fail to take him seriously as a writer, and in this respect they unquestioningly privilege content over form; the 'what' of Nietzsche's writings is thoroughly divorced from the 'how.' The new approach to Nietzsche outlined above aims to remedy this situation by insisting that form and content cannot be separated in this way, that Nietzsche's writing is, in a rather direct way, an integral part of his thought. If this characterization of the new approach to Nietzsche is correct, then one would expect that the interpretations essayed by the practitioners of the new approach would reflect a deeper appreciation of Nietzsche the writer, and that this would broaden our understanding of his philosophy as a whole. Rather than essaying a detailed survey of the recent scholarship, we might do well to briefly focus on an interpretation which perhaps best represents the potentials of the new approach, that of Alexander Nehamas.

Although he observes that one of Nietzsche's achievements was to show "that writing is perhaps the most important part of thinking" (41), Nehamas has a rather traditional view of the ends of interpretation. The task of the interpreter is to understand what Nietzsche thought, "the content of his work . . . his view of the will to power, the eternal recurrence, the nature of the self and the immoral presuppositions of morality" (1). In order to accomplish this aim, one must also consider Nietzsche's style, because his writing "puts the very effort to understand him, to offer an interpretation of his views . . . into question" (1). The dilemma that Nietzsche's writing poses is that in his texts we find him putting forth views that he claims are not truths in the traditional sense of the word, but only interpretations. The problem with this is that it seems to undermine the possibility of ever distinguishing between competing interpretations, hence doing away with any reason for believing one view to be truer or more correct than any other. In Nehamas' view, Nietzsche's style is an attempt to get around this problem, to put forth views as interpretations that cannot then be said to be *mere* interpretations, no better or worse than any other:

> Nietzsche uses his changing genres and styles in order to make his presence as an author literally unforgettable and in order to prevent his readers from overlooking the fact that his views necessarily originate with

> him. He depends on many styles in order to suggest that there is no single, neutral language in which his views, or any other, can ever be presented. (37)

According to Nehamas, style and content are thus related in only the most general way. Style is constitutive of meaning merely in the rather abstract sense that it determines the general form of what is said, namely, that what is meant to be understood is a contingent interpretation rather than a kind of absolute truth. Accordingly, Nehamas is less concerned with the style or rhetoric of a particular passage or book, than he is with the stylistic variation Nietzsche employs from book to book. Although he allows that questions such as why Nietzsche employs a particular style in one text rather than another might be important, he states that his "interest in Nietzsche's style is much more general and abstract . . . [and concerns] not the style of individual works or passages but the fact that he shifts styles and genres as often as he does" (19–20).

However, elevated to this level of abstraction, the question of style loses most of its significance.[17] The assumption made by Nehamas, that the function of interpretation is to offer a coherent and plausible account of Nietzsche's views, implies a privileging of content over style and begs the question of what role, if any, style plays in the production of Nietzsche's texts. Like Gadamer, Nehamas insists that the rhetoric of a text, its manner of meaning, must remain subordinate to its semantic content, which is itself subject to the demands of the principle of coherence. For Nehamas, the question of style is of interest because it allows us to read Nietzsche in such a way that he is neither a philosophical dogmatist, who presents his views as universally true, nor a radical relativist, who gives us no reason to prefer one view to another. Accordingly, style can tell us very little about the content of Nietzsche's views other than how they are to be understood with respect to dogmatism and relativism. The materiality of Nietzsche's texts, the specificity of his writing, is of little or no importance, and it is because Nietzsche's writing as such is overlooked that Nehamas is able to avoid the types of questions which threaten to undermine the distinction between content and style on which his interpretation depends.[18]

One such question that has been raised by recent readings of Nietzsche concerns the relationship between intentionality and meaning. Simply put, the question can be formulated as follows: Is the meaning of a text determined by the intentions of the author or, in addition, by semantic and syntactic structures that are, in principle, beyond the control of a single speaker or author? Although this question might appear to have very little to do with the issues at hand, its importance becomes apparent if we consider that Nehamas' interpretation of Nietzsche's style as a self-conscious strategy, "one of his essential weapons in his effort to distinguish himself from the philosophical tradition . . . and to offer alternatives to it" (20), commits him to an intentionalist view of meaning. It is because Nehamas views meaning as the product of authorial intention that he can maintain a distinction between form and content, between Nietzsche's views and the texts within which these views are expressed. If, however, style is viewed not as a self-conscious strategy but as one part of a larger, non-intentionalist textual economy, then the end of interpretation ceases to be the articulation and elucidation of an author's views as such, but rather a reading of the texts themselves. Such a reading must begin with the *factum* of the texts as texts, rather than with a set of concepts that are said to represent Nietzsche's views or the content of his work. The limitations of Nehamas' view of Nietzsche's style can be established more concretely if we consider one important element of his interpretation, namely, the relationship between writing and the self.

For Nehamas there is a clear relationship between the questions concerning the nature and constitution of the self and the question of style. If Nietzsche's style is an integral part of his attempt to combat philosophical dogmatism, to present his views as interpretations rather than as truths, one of the ways his texts can accomplish this task is by making it clear to the reader that the views being expressed are not in any sense those of a neutral and objective narrator, but that there is an essential connection between what is being said and who is doing the saying: "Nietzsche uses his changing genres and styles in order to make his presence as an author literally unforgettable and in order to prevent his readers from overlooking the fact that his views necessarily originate with him" (37). However, more is at stake than simply locating the origin of the views one finds in Nietzsche's texts, for Nehamas argues that there is an identification between the personality of the writer and his thought: "Nietzsche's varying self-conscious writing enables the practical reader always to be aware of who it is whose views are being presented, what personality these views express and constitute" (37). Nietzsche's writing "never lets his readers forget that the argument they are getting is always in more than one sense personal" (27).[19]

If Nietzsche's writing is essentially personal, for Nehamas it is also true that the self is at root a construction of the text and the act of writing. Nehamas rightly sees Nietzsche's critique of traditional philosophical conceptions of the self as an incorporeal, rational, thinking substance to be one of the central themes of his philosophy. However the sheer radicalness of Nietzsche's critique seems to undermine the very possibility of talking about a subject in any sense at all. In *Beyond Good and Evil*, Nietzsche criticizes the assertion, which is at the heart of the traditional, which is to say, Cartesian conception of the subject, that the existence of the self can be established by introspection as a mere consequence of the process of thought. "It is," Nietzsche writes,

> a *falsification* of the facts of the case to say that the subject 'I' is the condition of the predicate 'think.' It thinks: but that this 'it' is precisely the famous old 'ego' is, to put it mildly, only a supposition, an assertion and assuredly not an 'immediate certainty'. After all, one has even gone too far with this 'it thinks'—even the 'it' contains an *interpretation* of the process and does not belong to the process itself (BGE, 17).[20]

However, if Nietzsche wants to do away with the traditional conception of the self as a rational substance, it does not follow from this that he rejects the concept of the self altogether. Earlier in the same text he writes that the critique of the traditional concept of the self opens the way "for new versions and refinements of the soul-hypothesis: and such conceptions as 'mortal soul', and 'soul as subjective multiplicity,' and 'soul as social structure of the drives and affects' want henceforth to have citizens' rights in science" (BGE, 12).

In spite of the appeal of such hypotheses, it is not entirely clear that it makes much sense to talk of the self having done away with the idea that the self is a substance. For if the self is something which develops over time or is created, as this passage suggests, just precisely what is it that is created? How can one speak about the soul at all if there seems to be nothing substantial about which one is talking? The paradoxes inherent in Nietzsche's critique of the subject are poignantly illustrated by his numerous references to the Pindarian idea that "you ought to become who you are" (GS, 270). As Nehamas observes, this expression leave us inexorably suspended between the concepts of being and becoming, between thinking of the self as something that exists over time and conceiving of the self as something whose existence is essentially temporal, being created in time: "We are therefore faced with the difficult problem of seeing how that self can be what one is before it comes into being itself, before it is itself something that is. Conversely, if that self is something that is, if it is what one already is, how is it possible for one to become that self?" (175)

As we suggested above, Nehamas' solution to this paradox lies in the idea that the self is created gradually over time by a complicated process of action and integration: "the self-creation Nietzsche has in mind involves accepting everything that we have done and, in the ideal case, blending it into a perfectly coherent whole" (188–189). This is accomplished, in Nietzsche's case, by means of writing. It is no mere coincidence, Nehamas suggests, that the subtitle to Nietzsche's philosophical autobiography, *Ecce Homo*, is a variation of the Pindarian theme, one that is no longer couched in the imperative voice as the citation in the previous paragraph, but is both declarative and illustrative: "How One Becomes What One Is." For it is in *Ecce Homo* that Nietzsche provides a demonstration, as it were, of just how one might go about become what one is:

> One way, then, to become one thing, one's own character, what one is, is, after having written all these other books, to write *Ecce Homo* and even to give it the subtitle "How One Becomes What One Is." It is to write this self-referential book in which Nietzsche can be said with equal justice to invent or discover himself, and in which the character who speaks to us is the author who has created him and who is in turn a character created by or implicit in all the books that were written by the author who is writing this one. (196)

One of the cornerstones of Nehamas' understanding of this process of self-creation that we have not explicitly remarked upon is the idea that, for Nietzsche, the self that is created in this way is necessarily coherent and unified. This is one of the most surprising parts of Nehamas' interpretation of Nietzsche, but it is an idea which he expresses and defends with great vigor. We have already noted, in a passage cited in the previous paragraph, that Nehamas sees the Nietzschean process of self-creation ending, in the ideal case, in a "perfectly coherent whole."[21] It is important to emphasize that the unity which Nehamas has in mind is far removed from the conception of self-as-substance, which Nietzsche quite clearly rejects. Rather, the unity of the self Nehamas refers to develops over time and is produced by means of a conscious strategy of integration and synthesis:

> The unity of the self, which therefore also constitutes its identity, is not something given but something achieved, not a beginning but a goal. And of such unity . . . Nietzsche is *not at all suspicious*. . . . [T]he process of dominating, and thus creating, the individual, the unity that concerns us, is a matter of incorporating more and more character traits under a constantly expanding and evolving rubric. (182–183; my italics)

On Nehamas' reading, Nietzsche's style is the complement to his theory of the self, which in turn is illustrated or exemplified by his writings.[22] Just as the motivation behind Nietzsche's multifarious styles is to emphasize the irreducibly personal character of his ideas, so the self which Nietzsche came to create is brought into being by his texts, the very last of which describes the process in retrospect and presents a model for others to follow, not by imitating his path, but by urging others to create themselves and their own way (234).

Nehamas substantiates his surprising claim that the self should, as far as possible, be a coherent, unified whole by referring to passages such as this one from *Zarathustra*:

> I walk among men as among the fragments of the future—that future which I envisage. And this is all my creating and striving, that I create

> and carry together into One what is fragment and riddle and dreadful accident. And how could I bear to be a man if man were not also a creator and guesser of riddles and redeemer of accidents? (Za, II.20)

More direct evidence that Nietzsche sees self-creation as a process of integration and unification can be found in the *Genealogy*, where we read the following:

> For this alone is fitting for a philosopher. We have no right to *isolated* acts of any kind: we may not make isolated errors or hit upon isolated truths. Rather do our ideas, our values, our yeas and nays, our ifs and buts, grow out of us with the necessity with which a tree bears fruit—related and each with an affinity to each, and evidence of one will, one health, one soil, one sun.—[23]

For Nehamas, passages such as these are an essential part of his attempt to demonstrate that the picture of Nietzsche as an advocate of polysemy and interpretative indeterminacy that one finds in poststructuralist readings is quite mistaken.[24] Although Nietzsche was a radical and highly non-traditional thinker, his radicalness does not lead to a rejection of the concepts of unity, totality, and coherence, but rather consists in an effort to reinterpret these concepts in a fundamentally new way. Nietzsche's thinking, like his conception of the self, has "a determinate structure, form [and] meaning" (20).

While the evidence cited by Nehamas appears to be rather decisive, there are reasons to believe that Nietzsche's texts are less coherent and determinate than Nehamas suggests. Consider a third passage cited by Nehamas in support of his view that, for Nietzsche, the unity of the self is achieved and maintained by means of a conscious strategy of integrating one's character traits into a coherent whole. Here Goethe is apparently held up as a model of one who has achieved true selfhood:

> What he wanted was *totality* [Totalität]; he fought the mutual extraneousness of reason, senses, feeling, and will [. . .] he disciplined himself to wholeness [*Ganzheit*], he *created* himself. (TI, IX.49)

Near the end of the aphorism Nietzsche pays Goethe the highest compliment possible by describing him as ennobled with a Dionysian faith:

> Such a spirit who has *become free* stands amid the cosmos with a joyous and trusting fatalism, in the *faith* that only the particular is loathsome, and that all is redeeemed and affirmed in the whole—*he does not negate anymore. . . .* Such a faith, however, is the highest of all possible faiths: I have baptized it with the name of *Dionysus.*—

Now it is fairly clear that the whole mentioned in this last passage is an existential rather than an individual totality, and the faith to which Nietzsche refers is none other than an acceptance of the eternal recurrence. This is made explicit in the penultimate section of *Twilight of the Idols*, where Nietzsche links the Dionysian, here once more characterized as a form of affirmation, of "saying Yes to life even in its strangest and hardest problems," with the eternal recurrence by describing himself as "the last disciple of the philosopher Dionysus [. . .] the teacher of the eternal recurrence" (TI, X.5).

Yet what is striking about the characterization of Goethe as Dionysian is not the connection with the eternal recurrence as such, but rather with an earlier and somewhat different description of Dionysus that we find in the same chapter of *Twilight.* Here Nietzsche returns to the concepts of the Apollinian and the Dionysian introduced in *The Birth of Tragedy* and he gives the following account of the Dionysian:

> In the Dionysian state [. . .] the whole affective system is excited and enhanced: so that it discharges [*entladet*] all its means of expression at once and simultaneously emits [*heraustreibt*] the power of representation, imitation, transfiguration, transformation, and every kind of mimicking and acting. The essential feature here remains the ease of metamorphosis [. . .]. The Dionysian type [. . .] enters into any skin, into any affect: he constantly transforms himself. (TI, IX.10)

By itself, of course, this passage is not incompatible with the view of subjectivity Nehamas attributes to Nietzsche. In the spirit of Nehamas' reading one could say that it is a sign of great and exemplary strength for one to be able to control and unify the disparate elements that constitute the Dionysian state as Nietzsche here describes it. Goethe would then be, as Walter Kaufmann has put it, "the passionate man who is the master of his passions" (363). Yet this passage also gives us reason to pause. For if the essential feature of the Dionysian type is an ease of metamorphosis and constant transformation, if he can enter into *any* skin, how is it that this most protean figure can claim any or all these personae as his own? Could it not be the case that in order to be himself the Dionysian man must transcend himself and become someone else?

An answer to this question is suggested by Nietzsche's description of the Dionysian type as an actor. This description is certainly not incidental, for the figure of the actor and the related themes of the mask and dissimulation achieve something like emblematic status in Nietzsche's writings. In one of the more important of these texts, section 361 of *The Gay Science*, Nietzsche considers the "problem of the actor" which, he opines, might provide the only means of approaching the concept of the artist. It is a problem, Nietzsche says, that

> has troubled me for the longest time. I felt unsure (and sometimes still do) whether it is not only from this angle that one can get at the dangerous concept of the 'artist'—a concept that has so far been treated with unpardonable generosity. Falseness with a good conscience; the delight in simulation exploding [*herausbrechend*] as a power that pushes aside one's so-called 'character,' flooding it and at times extinguishing it; the inner craving for a role and mask, for *appearance* [. . .] all of this is perhaps not *only* peculiar to the actor?[25]

Read from the perspective provided by this passage, the initial description of Goethe takes on a different light. For if Goethe is a truly Dionysian figure, an artist and an actor, then the wholeness that he created for himself is at best a simulacrum for the kind of coherent, unitary subjectivity that Nehamas attributes to Nietzsche. The mechanical, impersonal, vocabulary of these passages underscores the extent to which one's identity is hostage to forces and procedures not wholly under one's conscious control: the affective system "discharges" its means of expression; the powers of representation and dissimulation are "emitted"; the delight in simulation "explodes," flooding and extinguishing the character of the actor. An analogous structure underlies Nietzsche's description of Dionysian rapture from *The Birth of Tragedy*, in which "everything subjective vanishes into complete self-forgetfulness" (BT, 1). Dionysus is the symbol of the essentially fractured structure of identity and the prototypical actor and artist: "until Euripides [. . .] all the celebrated figures of the Greek stage—Prometheus, Oedipus, etc.—are mere masks for this original hero, Dionysus" (BT, 1). On the terms of Nietzsche's text, the concept of identity functions as a synecdoche, in which a part of an essentially fragmentary and provisional self is taken for the whole. Rather than supporting Nehamas' interpretation, these passages suggest that the concepts of wholeness and totality are at bottom nothing more than rhetorical masks.[26]

Although the foregoing raises serious doubts that a close reading of Nietzsche's texts can support the conclusion that he regards the self as a coherent and unified whole, it might be objected that we have ignored the most obvious piece of evidence in support of Nehamas' interpretation, namely, the life and work of Nietzsche himself. For as we have already noted, Nehamas views Nietzsche's writings as prime examples of how one can create oneself in a unified and coherent manner. One way of achieving the "perfect unity" which Nehamas regards as the ideal of self-creation

> might be to write a great number of very good books that exhibit great apparent inconsistencies among them but that can be seen to be deeply continuous with one another when they are read carefully and well.

> Toward the end of this enterprise one can even write a book about these books that shows how they fit together, how a single figure emerges through them. (195)

The question which we must now pursue is whether a single figure, an *autos*, does emerge from these pages. Might it not be the case that, on the contrary, *Ecce Homo* is a book about the indeterminacy or suspension of identity which confirms, rather than contradicts, the reading of the self we have offered above? Nehamas' interpretation leaves this question open because he does not undertake a reading of this or any other of Nietzsche's books. Since the aim of his interpretation is to determine the "content" of Nietzsche's thought, he is principally concerned with discovering thematic connections and continuities among Nietzsche's writings, without attempting to take the texts on their own terms as texts.[27] In an effort to examine Nehamas' claim that a single figure emerges out of Nietzsche's texts, let us briefly turn to *Ecce Homo* itself.

WRITING THE SELF

At first glance, this short, rather striking book opens as one expects any autobiography to begin, namely, with a statement of the book's subject. The opening words of the foreword attest to the seeming conventional character of Nietzsche's undertaking: "Seeing that before long I must confront humanity with the most difficult demand ever made of it, it seems indispensable to me to say *who I am.*" The nature of Nietzsche's demand requires that he tell us who he is; in order to understand it, we must first understand him. Nietzsche emphasizes this point at the end of the first section of the foreword with the following words: "*Hear me! For I am such and such a person. Above all, do not mistake me for someone else!*" Nietzsche's emphatic exhortation not to mistake him for another betrays a suspicion that the reader might be mislead, and like Nietzsche's contemporaries, neither see nor hear him. Perhaps in an effort to forestall this possibility, Nietzsche inserts a short exergue between the foreword and the first chapter of the text. The exergue says that the story begins on a particular date, October 15, 1888, Nietzsche's forty-fourth birthday, and that it will be both retrospective and proleptic: "I looked back, I looked forward, and never saw so many good things at once [. . .]. And so I tell my life to myself." In what follows Nietzsche recounts the story of his life, beginning with the well-known description of his parents, his illness, his tastes in matters of literature, food, drink, climate, and peoples, followed by a consideration of his writings, including an account of each of his hitherto published books. The last and shortest chapter, "Why I am a destiny," is principally prospective in character. Having told the reader who he is, Nietzsche then returns to the real matter at hand, the revaluation of values. In a text remarkable for its apocalyptic tone, Nietzsche claims that the destiny of humanity will have been his destiny as well: the wars waged in his writings are precisely those that will be waged on the spiritual battlefields of Europe in the coming century.[28]

Although the form of Nietzsche's text suggests that it adheres to the prescriptions governing the genre of philosophical autobiography, a genre whose history extends at least back to Augustine, a close reading of both the title and the subtitle of this text indicate that the situation is rather more complicated than it first appears. Most readers will recognize that the title, *Ecce Homo*, is a quotation from the New Testament. The source of the quotation is the Gospel of John, where we read that Pilate, having listened to Jesus' claim to be a king, turns to the largely Jewish audience and says "ecce homo," behold the man.[29] In its original context, the expression is explicitly not auto-referential, but directs the reader's attention to someone other than the author himself. Written about oneself, therefore, the phrase *ecce homo* produces a paradoxical effect, and points to an internal duality or "contradicting duplicity,"[30] which will be echoed throughout the book in pairs such as male/female, death/life, decadent/beginning and identifications with dualities, for example, father/mother, Nietzsche/Wagner, Nietzsche/Oedipus, and Nietzsche/Socrates. Nietzsche underscores this point in a letter to Meta von Salis when he writes: "I myself am this *homo*, the *ecce* included" (KSAB, 8/1144). The duality suggested by the title is echoed in a series of identifications and counter-identifications which run throughout the entire book. The first of these is established by the title, which identifies Nietzsche with Pilate, the speaker of the phrase *ecce homo*. It is not a coincidence that Nietzsche should wish to identify himself with Pilate, since it was Pilate who, according to Nietzsche, enriched the New Testament "with the only saying *that has value*—one which is its criticism, even its *annihilation*: 'What is truth!'" (A, 46). And this is precisely what is at stake in the text of *Ecce Homo* itself, where Nietzsche, like Pilate, questions the value of all that has thus far been taken for the truth: "everything that has hitherto been called 'truth' has been recognized as the most harmful, insidious, and subterranean form of lie" (EH, IV.8).

The subtitle of the book, "How One Becomes What One Is," is also a quotation, namely, from Pindar's Second Pythian Ode.[31] Although this phrase seems at first to run contrary to the sense of the title by emphasizing the unity and stasis of identity, of what one is, the juxtaposition of being and becoming in the subtitle actually produces the opposite effect. Echoing the duality implicit in the expression "ecce homo," the juxtaposition of being and becoming deepens the attentive reader's suspicions that rather than affirming the coherence of the author's identity, the text's title and subtitle serve to place this identity into question. The subtitle does not merely reiterate the duality hinted at in the title but actually sharpens it by attributing to this duality a specifically temporal character, namely, by suggesting that being, what one is, is inseparable from from becoming, the process of how one becomes what one is. One way in which the implication of being in becoming manifests itself in Nietzsche's text is in the assertion that one's identity is something that can only be established retrospectively.[32] The knowledge of what one is, is always in some sense deferred; self-knowledge is mediated by this temporal gap between being and becoming, present and past.[33] One consequence of this is that self-knowledge is predicated on ignorance, on not knowing what one is. Nietzsche says precisely this in section 9 of the chapter entitled "Why I Am So Clever." Yielding to the inevitable, Nietzsche admits that

> the genuine answer to the question, *how one becomes what one is*, can no longer be avoided [. . .]. Assuming that the task, the fate [*Bestimmung*], the *destiny* of the task [Schicksal *der Aufgabe*] transcends the average very significantly, there would be no greater danger than catching sight of oneself *with* this task. That one becomes what one is, presupposes that one does not have the faintest notion *what* one is [*dass man nicht im Entferntesten ahnt*, was *man ist*].

To become what one is, one must forget and misunderstand oneself. Self-knowledge, Nietzsche suggests, is necessarily fragmentary and incoherent, because it rests on that which is other than itself, on ignorance, not having the faintest notion what one is. It is vain to hope that the fragmentary nature of self-knowledge can ever be overcome by introspection and greater efforts at self-integration, as if it were a matter of circumstance, rather than necessity, that one is constantly "in the dark" about one's self.

Nietzsche is quite explicit that the ignorance that is imbricated within self-knowledge is there by necessity, not chance. In the opening section of the second essay of the *Genealogy*, Nietzsche argues that the phenomenon of self-consciousness presupposes the existence of an active and opposing force, namely, forgetfulness. Reversing the traditional negative valuation of forgetfulness as a passive force that produces an unintentional and unwanted lack of knowledge, Nietzsche claims that

> it is rather an active and in the strictest sense positive faculty of repression that is responsible for the fact that what we experience and absorb

> enters our consciousness as little while we are digesting it [. . .] as does the thousandfold process involved in physical nourishment, so-called 'incorporation' [. . .] so that it will be immediately obvious how there could be no happiness, no cheerfulness, no hope, no pride, no *present* [Gegenwart], without forgetfulness.

Here again we see that knowledge—of the external world and of ourselves—is only possible on the basis of ignorance or forgetting. Just as knowing what one is would prevent one from actually becoming what one is, so, too, if forgetfulness did not stand before consciousness as a filter, only letting a fraction of the stimuli confronting one actually be experienced, the very possibility of experience as such would be undermined. What one experiences of the world and of oneself is always mediated by the absence of that which is not filtered out, forgotten, repressed.

Elsewhere in the *Genealogy*, the dependence of knowledge on an active and antecedent faculty of forgetfulness described in this passage is generalized into a principle of identity, where self-identity is said to necessarily presuppose ignorance of just who and what one is:

> as one divinely preoccupied and immersed in himself into whose ear the bell has just boomed with all its strength the twelve beats of noon suddenly starts up and asks himself: 'what really was that which just struck?' so we sometimes rub our ears *afterward* and ask, utterly surprised and disconcerted, 'what really was that which we have just experienced?' and moreover: 'who *are* we really?' and, afterward as aforesaid, count the twelve trembling bell-strokes of our experience, our life, our *being*—and alas! miscount them.—So we are necessarily strangers to ourselves, we do not comprehend ourselves, we *have* to misunderstand ourselves, for us the law 'Each is furthest from himself' applies to all eternity—we are not 'men of knowledge' with respect to ourselves. (GM, P. 1)

Ignorance about oneself is not a lack which can be fully remedied, but is a necessary condition of self-knowledge. To seek to bridge the gap between ignorance and knowledge is, like Oedipus, to run the risk of exchanging one form of blindness for another.[34]

Against the foregoing it might be argued that we have underestimated the importance which Nietzsche assigns to the unity of the self. If the aim of self-creation is to create a unified and coherent self, then perhaps these divisions can be reconciled by means of ever increasing efforts of integration? As we have seen, there is a certain amount of textual evidence to support this claim. Recall Zarathustra's statement that he strives to "create and carry together into One what is fragment and riddle and dreadful accident" (Za, II.20). An example of how such a process of integration might proceed is provided in *Ecce Homo*, where Nietzsche reinterprets his youthful enthusiasm for Schopenhauer and Wagner as a necessary step on the way to becoming what he is. In his remarks on the *Untimely Meditations* Nietzsche claims that the two essays devoted to Wagner and Schopenhauer do not really concern them at all, but "at bottom speak only of me." The names Wagner and Schopenhauer are signs for the name Nietzsche, employed "in order to to express something, in order to to have at hand a few more formulas, signs, means of language [. . .] in the same way that Plato used Socrates as a semiotic for Plato" (EH, 'UM'.3).[35] Nietzsche's retrospective recognition that the names Wagner and Schopenhauer are figures for the name Nietzsche does not, however, imply a progressive pattern of self-identification that would yield a determinate, albeit postponed, subject or 'I'. The logic of such a pattern in this text is undermined by Nietzsche's multiple self-identifications which preclude the possibility of a direct substitution of names, one that would affirm that the meaning of the most proper of words, the proper name, remains delimited and determinate. Nietzsche precludes precisely this possibility in an earlier remark on "Richard Wagner in Bayreuth":

> A psychologist might still add that what I heard as a young man listening to Wagnerian music really had nothing to do with Wagner[. . . . In] my essay "Wagner in Bayreuth" [. . .] I alone am discussed—and one need not hesitate to put down my name or the the word 'Zarathustra' where the text has the word Wagner [*man darf rücksichtlos meinen Namen oder das Wort 'Zarathustra' hinstellen, wo der Text das Wort Wagner gibt*]. (EH, 'BT'.4)

The name Wagner, Nietzsche says, can be exchanged at will for the name Nietzsche or Zarathustra.[36] This means, however, that the substitution remains inextricably suspended between Nietzsche and Zarathustra, and if one exchange is possible, then the field of possible exchanges can never be closed. Hence the meaning of the proper name Nietzsche, under whose signature this book appears, must remain indeterminate, both proper, signifying that which belongs to Nietzsche and enables him to sign his texts, and improper, that which remains other and unrecognizable within the parameters of the classical definition and logic of "the proper."[37]

If the names Nietzsche or Zarathustra can be substituted for the name Wagner, it is because the identity of the author Nietzsche, the *ecce* and the *homo* of this text, is itself at bottom a duality, something divided from itself.[38]

And if this is true of oneself, there is no reason to believe that it is not also true of one's texts. However this is something that can only be recognized if our understanding of style is finally divorced from intentionalist conceptions of meaning. Until this happens, the new approach to Nietzsche will remain barely distinguishable from the old.

Chapter 2

Nietzsche's Theory of Language and Rhetoric

> *Tropes, the nonliteral significations, are considered to be the most artistic means of rhetoric. But with respect to their meanings all words are, in themselves and from the very beginning, tropes.*
>
> *—Nietzsche, "Description of Ancient Rhetoric"*

> *I believe I know him . . . he always lies and he never lies. His mendacity is his genuineness—it sounds complicated, but it is utterly simple. He believes everything and he believes nothing. He is an actor.*
>
> *—Klaus Mann,* Mephisto

THE UNPUBLISHED WRITINGS OF THE EARLY 1870s

Following the publication of *The Birth of Tragedy* and the storm that this book was to provoke, Nietzsche began work on a second book—most often referred to today as *Das Philosophenbuch*—which would serve as a "companion piece" to his book on tragedy (KSAB, 4/132).[1] This new book would consider many of the same questions addressed in *The Birth of Tragedy*, but it would do so in a different, more explicitly philosophical manner. Rather than using the genesis of tragedy out of the Apollinian and Dionysian artistic forces as a point of departure, the new book would focus on the figure of the philosopher, his role within the culture at large, and the relationship between philosophy and art. In one of the many outlines he prepared during this period, Nietzsche conceived of the text as having two parts, an introduction that would be devoted to a theoretical discussion of truth and lies, and a second, larger section that would trace the origin of Western philosophy from Thales to Socrates (KSA 7, 19.190–191). Although Nietzsche worked on this project intensively for over a year, at times believing it was close to completion,[2] he was never able to bring it to fruition. In April 1873, Nietzsche finished a draft of the second part of the text—the text today known as "Philosophy in the Tragic Age of the Greeks"—which he was preparing to bring with him on a visit to Bayreuth and read aloud to Richard and Cosima Wagner. However, as a letter to Gerdsdorff written shortly before his departure reveals, he was not at all happy with his work, calling it "quite far from book form" (KSAB, 4/301). Shortly after returning from Bayreuth, Nietzsche echoes this sentiment in a letter to his sister and mother. "I am," he writes, "still working on my Greek philosophers, however the book is not at all complete and a good deal of time could pass before I am able to come to an end" (KSAB, 4/ 306). A little over two months later, Nietzsche dictated the essay "On Truth and Lie in the Extra-Moral Sense," which strongly suggests that he was still trying to complete the project. However, this essay was to be the last substantive work on *Das Philosophenbuch*, and, as his notebooks demonstrate quite clearly, the project itself was given up shortly thereafter.[3]

The precise reasons why Nietzsche abandoned his plans for a book on the early Greek philosophers will most likely never be known. Neither his correspondence nor his notebooks reveal much that bears on this point. Nevertheless, Nietzsche's failure to complete this book and his decision not to publish any of the preparatory material, raise the important question of what place should be accorded to these texts within the Nietzschean corpus. The issue in this case is different somewhat from the more general and often debated question concerning the relationship of Nietzsche's notes to his published texts,[4] since both on "On Truth and Lie" and "Philosophy in the Tragic Age of the Greeks" are polished, fairly lengthy prose pieces quite unlike the sketches to be found in the notebooks. In fact, with the exception of the lectures Nietzsche gave while at Basel, there is not a single example of a text as polished and seemingly complete as these texts appear to be which remained unpublished. This is especially true of "On Truth and Lie," which is the more original and interesting of these two texts.[5] There is little doubt that the essay which we have before us could have been published, even if not in the form and context originally conceived of by Nietzsche. This is a point which has been largely overlooked in the discussion of these early texts. While it is no doubt true that "On Truth and Lie" is a fragment to the extent that it was intended to be part of a book which Nietzsche never brought to fruition,[6] Claudia Crawford surely overstates the case when she characterizes this essay as one of a group of "fragments and notes that [Nietzsche] never intended for publication."[7] Nevertheless, the fact that Nietzsche, who was never particularly coy about presenting his ideas to the public, decided not publish this text raises the possibility that his reason for not doing was that he came to realize that the philosophical position elucidated in the essay rested on questionable and possibly incoherent ideas. One idea which stands out among others as particularly vulnerable to such suspicions is the well-known claim that truth is a type of lie, and is therefore in principle indistinguishable from it. If Nietzsche did in fact come to reject this view of truth, as a number of commentators have recently suggested, this would provide a plausible explanation for his decision to keep this essay "secret."[8]

Although there is no direct evidence in support of this hypothesis—Nietzsche's only published reference to the essay is decidedly ambiguous[9]—one could reasonably draw such a conclusion from the fact that the texts published following his decision to abandon *Das Philosophenbuch*—the final three *Untimely Meditations* and the first part of *Human All-Too-Human*—contain few if any traces of the vocabulary which is the hallmark of these unpublished writings. In the published texts the concepts of metaphor and illusion which are central to "On Truth and Lie" and the notes from this period have all but disappeared from Nietzsche's vocabulary. The distance separating these texts seems hardly confined to modifications of vocabulary, for even a cursory glance appears to confirm the fact that Nietzsche has undergone a philosophical conversion which has radically altered his view of art and science, to name just two of the most important motifs common to these two sets of texts. The apparent change in Nietzsche's philosophical orientation is announced in the opening section of *Human All-Too-Human*—the first book length publication following *The Birth of Tragedy*—where he expresses his intention to practice a new type of philosophy which "can no longer be thought of apart from the natural sciences."[10]

Leaving aside the ambiguous posture towards the natural sciences expressed by Nietzsche in books such as *The Gay Science*, its seems as if one could trace a straight line from this new beginning to the writings of Nietzsche's last two active years, where, in the words Maudemarie Clark, we find "a uniform and unambiguous respect for facts, the senses and science."[11] This new found respect for the vocabulary and methods of science finds expression in a pragmatic, common sense conception of truth, which Clark sees as diametrically opposed to the "denial" of truth characteristic of "On Truth and Lie" and the other unpublished texts from the early 1870s. In Clark's view, the question of whether Nietzsche ultimately moves away from the linguistic skepticism of "On Truth and Lie" to adopt a form of pragmatic neo-empiricism is not a minor matter of academic dispute, but is of central importance for our understanding of Nietzsche's mature philosophy. According to Clark, the critique of morality which is the central subject of Nietzsche's later thought rests on the conviction that Judeo-Christianity has propagated a false and pernicious view of human life, which in turn logically assumes that one can in fact offer truthful interpretations of morality and its various historical manifestations, such as the ascetic ideal. In order to be justified in describing the Judeo-Christian worldview as a lie and in proclaiming himself to be "the first to *discover* the truth by being the first to experience lies as lies" (EH, IV.1), Nietzsche must accept that there is a non-chimerical distinction between truth and falsity, which is precisely what he sought to deny in "On Truth and Lie."[12] Otherwise, Clark argues, Nietzsche undermines the very ground of his critique. Rather than constituting something like a key to Nietzsche's philosophical praxis, the analysis of truth and language that forms the centerpiece of the unpublished writings undermines the very possibility of the revaluation of values. On this view, Nietzsche was right not to have published "On Truth and Lie" or any of the other notes and studies from the early 1870s. Consequently, these texts have little or nothing of value to tell us about Nietzsche's later thinking, and should instead be viewed as articulating a misguided philosophical position that Nietzsche rightly later rejected.

The strength of the foregoing argument seems to leave little room for reasoned opposition, a fact attested to by the prominence of those scholars who have either expressed support for Clark's interpretation of have independently reached similar conclusions.[13] The alternatives that most immediately present themselves, either to reject the assertion that the project of a revaluation of all values—broadly conceived so as to include the critique of morality—is not central to Nietzsche's thought, or to admit that Nietzsche has a self-contradictory conception of truth which, if taken at face value, undermines the very possibility of such a revaluation, are quite unappealing. Assuming that one could demonstrate that the revaluation is not central to Nietzsche's philosophy, the result would be to rob his thought of its most influential and enduring aspect. Admitting that Nietzsche's conception of truth is self-contradictory would prove even less satisfying, except to those who, like Georg Lukács, prefer to see Nietzsche as an irredeemably irrational thinker and a forerunner of contemporary nihilism.

In spite of the compelling nature of Clark's argument, there are reasons for thinking that the very dilemma that her interpretation seeks to avoid is the product of an overly narrow understanding of the concept of truth. While it may seem indisputable from a logical point of view that if Nietzsche's critique of morality is to succeed he must be able to say that the interpretation of life propagated by morality is false and that this requires a perspective of truth from which Nietzsche can make this claim, there is a third possibility that is not explored by Clark, namely, that in his later writings Nietzsche employs the concept of truth in a way that exceeds the logic of binary opposition which grounds the traditional philosophical understanding of truth. That rather than seeing an essential opposition between true and false, there is instead a sense in which truth and falsity are essentially implicated within one another in such a way that the value of what is true is constituted by the fact that it is "insidiously related to, tied to, and involved with [. . .] wicked, seemingly opposite things—maybe even one with them in essence" (BGE, 34). If this were the case, then Nietzsche's critique of morality would neither be dependent on his adoption of a common-sense conception of truth, nor would there be an essential opposition between the idea of a revaluation of values and the conception of truth Nietzsche articulates in the unpublished writings from the early 1870s.

Before considering the question at hand, namely, whether there is a scientific turn in Nietzsche's thought in the last two years of his creative life, it is necessary to consider the concept of truth he developed in the 1870s. And the most obvious place to look is in the unpublished writings on language and rhetoric, because it is here that the question of truth is taken up most explicitly. The central problematic of these texts is the relationship between language and truth, and how a radical reflection on the tropological structure of language leads to an equally radical reinterpretation of the traditional conception of truth as correspondence or adequation. If Heidegger is correct in asserting that with Aristotle the judgment became the locus of truth, then it was Nietzsche who was among the first to question the transparency of the judgment and to interrogate language as its medium.[14] Since truth for Nietzsche is essentially linguistic, the ability to make good on the promise of correspondence is inescapably dependent upon the epistemological reliability of language itself; any structural indeterminicies within language will necessarily be reflected within the structure of truth. In what follows below, we will consider in some detail the theory of language and rhetoric formulated by Nietzsche in two unpublished texts from the period of *Das Philosophenbuch*, as well as the reinterpretation of truth which was to be a necessary consequence of this theory. The remaining sections of the chapter are in large part devoted to demonstrating that there is an underlying coherence and consistency to Nietzsche's views on language and truth, stretching from the early 1870s up through his very last writings.[15] A necessary part of this task will be to show that Nietzsche never rejected the views on truth and language advanced in these early texts, and therefore never had reason to adopt a common-sense conception of truth. Moreover, I hope to demonstrate that a rigorous reading of Nietzsche's later writings assumes both a rejection of precisely the neo-empiricist view of truth which Clark and others attribute to Nietzsche and an appreciation of Nietzsche's radical reinterpretation of truth.

"ON TRUTH AND LIE" AND THE COURSE ON RHETORIC

In retracing Nietzsche's early interrogations of truth we will be principally concerned with two unpublished texts: the notes for a lecture course on rhetoric which, in all probability, Nietzsche prepared and delivered in the winter semester of 1872–1873, and the unpublished essay "On Truth and Lie in the Extra-Moral Sense," dictated by Nietzsche to his friend Carl von Gersdorff during the latter's stay in Basel during the summer of 1873. Although there is some disagreement as to the exact dating of the lecture course, and even some question whether the course was given at all, these questions are not central to the matter at hand.[16] What is of some importance, however, is the relationship between these two texts, a question which surprisingly has received very little attention. The need for a closer look at the relationship between the course on rhetoric and "On Truth and Lie" has become more urgent in light of recent research which convincingly illustrates the extent to which both texts draw extensively—sometimes word for word—on Gustav Gerber's book *Die Sprache als Kunst*, which Nietzsche borrowed from the Basel University library in the Winter of 1872–1873.[17] In the case of "On Truth and Lie," Gerber's influence is evident in the arguments Nietzsche advances to support his account of language and truth, in his choice of examples that illustrate these arguments and, finally, in the distinctive vocabulary in which Nietzsche describes the translations of nerve stimuli into sounds and sounds into words, which constitute the relationship between language and the world. This schema, which has never failed to puzzle readers of this essay, turns out to be a much abbreviated version of the schema described by Gerber in *Die Sprache als Kunst*.[18] Gerber's influence on the course on rhetoric is less evident, principally because it is concentrated into two explicitly theoretical sections of the course, whose remaining parts are mainly historical in nature. Not surprisingly, these two sections, entitled "The Relation of the Rhetorical to Language" and "The Tropical Expression," have the most in common with "On Truth an Lie," both in terms of their subject matter—the relationship of figurative and literal meaning—and their vocabulary. One can assert, without too much exaggeration, that these are parallel texts which can best be read together; a point which is confirmed, not disputed, by the enormous stylistic differences separating them. Reading these two texts in tandem should allow for a richer appreciation of each text and, most importantly, of Nietzsche's understanding of truth and language in the early 1870s.[19]

THE FABULOUS ORIGIN OF KNOWLEDGE

Like so many of Nietzsche's texts, "On Truth and Lie" narrates the history of an origin, in this case, the origin of the drive for truth. However, both this history and the origin it traces need to be understood in contrast with what one might call objective history, which seeks to identify a fixed point or pure origin which gives rise to a linear development or 'history' of an institution, a concept or a psychological drive. The history Nietzsche is interested in recounting should be thought of less as something waiting to be discovered or found, than as a chain of traces or signs which need to be retrieved, brought out of the forgetfulness into which they have fallen, and then read. In *The Birth of Tragedy* Nietzsche provides an early example of this way of thinking about history, which he will later give the name genealogy.[20] Insofar as genealogy involves both a rejection of the myth of a pure, unalloyed origin, and a commitment to retrieving and reading the traces of the past that have been handed down by tradition, then narrating the birth of Greek tragedy will be much more a matter of deciphering the figures of Apollo and Dionysus in the extant plays, than of determining the "objective" characteristics of the historical gods themselves. The philosophical underpinnings of this approach to history are thematized by Nietzsche in the opening section of *Human All-Too-Human*, where he announces a project of a "historical philosophy" which can do without the myth of a "miraculous origin [. . .] arising directly from the kernel and essence of the 'thing-in-itself,'" and seeks instead to trace "the most magnificent colors [back to] humble, even maligned material" (HH, 1).[21] The goal of such genealogical investigations is not, as is often thought, to uncover the humble origin of an institution or concept so as to be able to do away with it, as if one could choose to do away with a concept, for example that of justice, once one has demonstrated that it roots lie in injustice. Rather, Nietzsche's concern in these early texts is to use historical philosophy as a means of revaluation, in the way that tracing the origins of the Greek tragedy to an *agon* between the Apollinian and the Dionysian artistic forces, opens up the space for a new understanding of tragedy, its decline, and the Socratic culture that arises in its place. If it is correct to suggest that "On Truth and Lie" can most profitably be read as one in a series of genealogical texts Nietzsche wrote in the 1870s, then the genealogy of the drive for truth articulated in this text should be considered as a means towards a revaluation of truth, not, as is too often assumed, as a way of rejecting or denying truth. However, to get a better understanding of precisely what kind of revaluation Nietzsche was interested in effecting, let us turn to the text itself.

"On Truth and Lie" begins, as is appropriate enough for a genealogical text, with a fable of the origin of knowledge:

> In some remote corner of the universe that is poured out in countless flickering solar systems, there once was a star on which clever animals invented knowledge. That was the most arrogant and the most untruthful moment in 'world history,' yet indeed only a moment. After nature had taken a few breaths, the star froze over and the clever animals had to die.— (TL, 246/875)[22]

Although this part of Nietzsche's essay is, with rare exceptions, quickly passed over to reach the properly "philosophical" argument, we would do well to pause for a moment to consider its significance; for the remainder of the essay can in very many ways be read as an elaborate commentary and repetition of the fable recounted in this passage.[23] The fable marks the beginning or origin of the essay. As both origin and fable (or a fable of an origin) it must be separated from the rest of the essay. Nietzsche indicates this separation by one of his signature punctuation marks, the *Gedankenstrich.* In this context, the dash signifies the distinction between the figurative (the "poetic") and the literal (the "philosophical") parts of the essay, just as a border might separate an illustration from the text proper. But the dash has another function as well, namely to facilitate the movement from the fable to the essay itself. If the difference between the fable and the rest of the essay were absolute, there would be no possibility of passing from the one to the other; one would be frozen as if suddenly thrust before a wall devoid of windows and doors. Graphically and grammatically, then, the dash serves both as a marker of difference and as a bridge from the one sphere to the other. It is this ambiguous function of the dash that is so often forgotten as the reader makes the transition from the fable to the more serious portions of the text. But paying attention to this ambiguity is not a matter of "reading into" the text (unless, of course, one is reading the essay in translation, in which case the translator may have predetermined that the dash is of no importance and dutifully deleted it),[24] but of *reading* the text, attending to the way in which the relationship between the fable and the philosophical argument is inscribed into the text, rather than assuming *ante facto* that the two can be absolutely distinguished. We have only to read the paragraphs which follow to note how much is potentially misread and misunderstood when the dash is not read.

On the other side of the dash, the text continues as follows: "Someone could invent [*erfinden*] such a fable and still not have illustrated adequately how pitiful, how shadowy and fleeting, how purposeless and arbitrary the human intellect appears within nature" (TL, 246/875). Nietzsche's initial commentary on the fable mitigates the transitional force of the dash; rather than moving us away from the fable towards the text, as the horizontal line of the dash indicates, we are pulled back within the invisible borders of the fable. The repetition of the word *erfinden*, to invent, begins what will be a repetition of the fable itself within the text. Just as the clever animals invented knowledge so, Nietzsche suggests, someone could invent a fable which would describe this invention. Such a tale would be a fable of invention, an invention of invention. Like the fable, which narrates a movement from the invention of knowledge to the death of the clever animals, the text recounts a similar movement with respect to the intellect: "There were eternities when [the intellect] did not exist; and someday when it is no longer there, not much will have changed" (TL, 246/875).

It is significant that Nietzsche fails to refer to the birth of the clever animals and the intellect, noting only their death. The reason for this omission is clear enough, for birth is a concept which has a place only within the parameters of knowledge; before knowledge was invented there was neither birth nor death. The invention of knowledge is not an isolated event, but creates the possibility of other inventions, such as birth, death, and world history. Principal among these inventions is the incipient creation of a distinction between knowledge and that which is other-than-knowledge. The invention of knowledge and its other and the subsequent legislation of differences of this kind differ from other inventions in one important respect. In order to constitute themselves in contradistinction to their opposites, for example truth as opposed to lie, they have to hide the fact that they are inventions. The invention of knowledge is coextensive with a second invention, namely, the invention of the origin, a pure unalloyed source from which knowledge and all the other similar inventions arise.

The person who is most affected by the invention of knowledge is the philosopher: "the proudest man of all, the philosopher believes he sees the eyes of the universe focused telescopically from all direction upon his actions and thoughts." But as Andrzej Warminski has noted, the philosopher's pride is a deception produced by a chiasmic reversal of corner and middle.[25] The philosopher who believes that he represents the center of creation is the direct inversion of the fable's clever animals who invented knowledge "in some remote corner of the universe." This reversal is an inevitable effect of knowledge, which must obscure the true source of its creation and invent the myth of the origin: "The arrogance associated with knowledge [. . .] lays a blinding fog over man's eyes and [. . .] deceives him about the value of existence by instilling in him a most flattering estimation of this faculty of knowledge" (TL, 246/876). The repetition of the word arrogance [*Hochmut*], which appears in its adjectival form in the fable—Nietzsche describes the invention of knowledge as "the most arrogant [*hochmütigste*] and the most untruthful moment in 'world history'"—once again pulls us back to the fable. The arrogance of this moment of invention is mirrored by the arrogance instilled in human beings by knowledge; a relationship intensified by Nietzsche's description of the intellect as an aid to "the most delicate and most perishable creatures in order to preserve them for a moment [. . .]." Reading the opening paragraph of "On Truth and Lie" from this perspective, it is not difficult to see how the fable reinscribes itself in the text, blurring the distinction between fable and text. The reader of the first paragraph of "On Truth and Lie" finds herself in a position similar to the one the intuitive man finds himself in at the end of the essay, unable to learn and falling into the same hole again and again. This blurring of the distinction between figurative and literal discourse, between fable and philosophical text, which the opening section of "On Truth and Lie" describes, is paradigmatic for what is to come in the remainder of the essay. It is perhaps with this in mind that Nietzsche suggests that the intellect's "most universal effect is deception [*Täuschung*]—but even its most specific effects have something of this same deceptiveness" (TL, 246/876).

Having described the intellect as a means of preserving the individual through dissimulation—"for this is the means by which weaker, less robust individuals survive"—and consciousness as a mere surface phenomenon akin to "clinging to a tiger's back in dreams," Nietzsche begins to trace the origins of that "puzzling drive for truth." The first steps towards the acquisition of this drive are taken when a decision is reached to end the war of all against all and to live socially. This results in the invention [*erfinden*] of a "uniformly valid and binding terminology for things" and "the first laws of truth," which are enacted by "the legislation of language" (TL, 247/877). Because language and truth are both invented in order to provide a solid foundation for social existence and not to satisfy an abstract desire for knowledge, there is a tension between their pragmatic origins and the roles which they are destined to play within society, roles which the dissimulating structure of truth and language themselves determine. We have already noted how knowledge arises in conjunction with something other-than-knowledge, against which knowledge can be defined and determined, as well as with the myth of origin which dissimulates both the invention of knowledge and its need for an other. The same process of institution and dissimulation takes place with regard to the invention of language and truth. In order to perform the functions for which they were invented—to create a stable world of objects and a discourse about them, and to institute a normative standard that would govern this discourse—the social, invented origins of language and truth must be hidden from the very beginning; the very process of instituting language and truth turns back on itself by inventing an other of language and truth and then by dissimulating the process of invention and instantiation by means of the myth of origin.

In the case of language, this other is an objective world transparently named and described by language, and in the case of truth, this other is the lie.

It is precisely this process of dissimulation which Nietzsche seeks to recover when, in Socratic like fashion, he considers the provenance of the word, the concept, and finally of truth itself.[26] This part of Nietzsche's essay is the most famous as well as the most controversial. Much of the controversy can surely be traced back to the obscurity and seeming capriciousness of some of Nietzsche's arguments; elements that have led Clark to describe the essay itself as incoherent, and to accuse Nietzsche of making logical errors so simple and obvious that "no major philosopher since Descartes would accept" them (NTP, 67). The puzzlement that more often than not has left readers of this essay shaking their heads in wonder and disbelief would be mitigated to a large degree if, as I have suggested, the essay were read in conjunction with Nietzsche's notes for a course on rhetoric. These notes, which are written in a plain, didactic manner uncharacteristic of the style of Nietzsche's published texts, reveal the background for arguments that are given barely a sentence or two in "On Truth and Lie," and make explicit the theory of tropes that is only hinted at in the essay. It is in this regard that the notes on rhetoric constitute an important supplement to "On Truth and Lie."

AN IMAGE TRANSLATED INTO A SOUND

The process of recovering the forgotten origins of language and truth begins with an enquiry into the nature of the word:

> What is a word? The copy [*Abbildung*] of a nerve stimulus in sounds. But to infer from a nerve stimulus to a cause outside ourselves is already the result of a false and unjustified application of the principle of sufficient reason. What would allow us, if the truth about the origin of language were alone decisive, what would allow us to say 'The stone is hard,' as if 'hard' were known to us otherwise than as a subjective stimulation! (TL, 248/878)

The foregoing argument sounds very much like a restatement of the Kantian view (and its Schopenhauerian and Langean versions) that we can never know things-in-themselves—objects as they exist apart from being perceived—but only our impressions of things, the ways in which objects affect our sense organs. Thus we can never say that the stone is hard in itself, only that the stone appears hard to us. In spite of these affinities, Nietzsche's argument has less to do with Kantian principles of perception than with the metonymic structure of causality, as the notes on rhetoric make clear.[27] In section three of the notes, Nietzsche suggests that "with respect to their meanings, all words are tropes in themselves, and from the very beginning" (Rh, 23). The reason for this is that "things do not pass over into consciousness, but only the manner in which we stand towards them [. . .]. Instead of the thing, the sensation takes in only a sign [*Merkmal*]" (Rh, 23). In other words, perception does not provide unmediated or direct access to objects in the world, but rather is part of a symbolic order whose structure is essentially linguistic. To demonstrate this point, Nietzsche, following Gerber, considers three principal tropes, synecdoche, metaphor, and metonymy, each of which is described in some detail in both the notes on rhetoric and in "On Truth and Lie."

In the notes on rhetoric, Nietzsche considers metonymy in both sections three and seven, the sections which, as we noted earlier, bear the strongest mark of Gerber's influence. In the first of these sections, Nietzsche defines metonymy as "the substitution of cause and effect." Two of the examples he offers are quite instructive: "We say 'the drink is bitter' instead of 'it excites a particular sensation of that kind in us'; 'the stone is hard,' as if hard were something other than a judgment on our part" (Rh, 25). A sentence such as 'the stone is hard' can be described as a metonymic substitution because what we refer to as hard is actually an effect, namely hardness, which is projected back on to the object as a cause of that effect: "We attribute to the appearances as their cause that which is still only an effect" (Rh, 59).[28] What we take to be the cause is, in the words of Paul de Man, "in fact, the effect of an effect, and what has been considered an effect in turn seems to function as the cause of its own cause."[29] In section seven, Nietzsche will enlarge upon this schema and describe the formation of concepts as the result of precisely this kind of metonymic substitution. What interests us in this context are the implications of Nietzsche's analysis of sentences such as "The stone is hard," in terms of metonymy. As his choice of examples makes clear, Nietzsche does not understand metonymy as a rhetorical figure in the traditional sense of the term, an ornamental figure of speech used to supplement or embellish a more literal statement or experience, but rather as a constitutive element of experience itself. Nietzsche says this explicitly in a striking note from the year 1888, where he juxtaposes the philosopher's uncritical acceptance of the certainty of so-called inner experience with a more rhetorically aware understanding of the structure of sensation:

> We have learned that the sense impression which we naively suppose to be conditioned by the outer world is, on the contrary, conditioned by the inner world [. . .]. The fragment of outer world of which we are conscious is born [*nachgeboren*] after an effect from outside has impressed itself upon us, and is subsequently [*nachträglich*] projected as its 'cause' [. . .]. In the phenomenalism of the 'inner world' we invert the

> chronological order of cause and effect. The fundamental fact of 'inner experience' is that the cause is imagined after the effect has taken place—. (KSA13, 15.90) [30]

Experiences such as sensing the hardness of a stone or the softness of wax that has been heated, which are often used as evidence of the immediate and perspicacious certainty of sense perception and the subsidiary role of language in forming these perceptions, are understood by Nietzsche first and foremost as linguistic events whose structure is not derived from a relationship of identity or correspondence between the world and a sentient subject, but rather by the tropological structure of language.

In light of this, we can understand why Nietzsche, in "On Truth and Lie," describes the inference from a nerve stimulus to a cause outside ourselves as "already the result of a false and unjustified application of the principle of sufficient reason," for the nerve stimulus is not an effect produced by an "external" cause, but is rather the cause of that which is taken to be its cause. The inference from a nerve stimulus to a cause outside ourselves is always already false and unjustified because the structure of logical inference has been shown to be epistemologically unreliable, prone to a potential confusion between cause and effect.

Nietzsche's analysis of the word continues with the following rather obscure remark: "We arrange things by genders, we designate the tree [*der Baum*] as masculine, the plant [*die Pflanze*] as feminine: what arbitrary transferences [*Übertragungen*]! How far-flung beyond the canon of certitude!" (TL, 248/878). Taken by itself, the suggestion that designating some nouns as feminine, others as masculine or neuter undermines the epistemological reliability of language does little to advance Nietzsche's argument. Once again a comparison with the notes on rhetoric provides us with a richer understanding of Nietzsche's text. Reading "On Truth and Lie" in light of the notes, we can see that in this essay Nietzsche attempts to make good on his claim that all words are tropes by analyzing the provenance of the word in terms of the three tropes, metonymy, metaphor, and synecdoche, explicitly discussed in the notes. There is, however, an important difference in the way in which the two texts approach their subject matter. In the notes on rhetoric the tropes themselves are explicitly named and discussed at some length. By contrast, although Nietzsche's genealogy of the word in "On Truth and Lie" relies on precisely the sort of tropological analysis—and examples—presented in the notes, the tropes themselves are not named. We have seen this already in Nietzsche's use of the sentence 'The stone hard' in "On Truth and Lie" to illustrate the metonymic structure of causality, without naming metonymy as such. A comparison of the two texts allows us to identify this reference, which otherwise might well have remained obscure.

The same sort of comparison illuminates Nietzsche's assertion, cited above, that the gendered status of nouns exemplifies the epistemological unreliability of language. Looking back at the notes on rhetoric, we find the following sentence: "Metaphor shows itself in the designation of gender; *genus* in the grammatical sense is a luxury of language and pure metaphor" (Rh, 23). What becomes clear from this remark is that Nietzsche is using the term metaphor in a rather specific, unconventional way, for at first glance it is not at all clear why the designation of gender as such should be understood as a metaphorical construction. A key to unlocking the meaning of this obscure remark can be found in Nietzsche's insistence that gender designations are metaphorical in a "grammatical sense." The meaning of this reference to grammar becomes clear once we consider that in the German language there is a radical disjunction between the gender of particular nouns and their meaning. For example, the gender of the word meaning young woman, *Mädchen*, is neuter, while that of the word *Katze* is feminine, irrespective of whether the cat is male or female.[31] But why metaphor? Nietzsche's use of the term metaphor in this context, a usage which itself seems arbitrary and far-flung beyond the canon of certitude, is best understood by considering the somewhat idiosyncratic way in which metaphor, for Nietzsche, functions as a designation for the tropological structure of language, for the fact that words "can be exchanged" (Rh, 67). This sense of metaphor as exchange or transfer is reflected principally in Nietzsche's use of the German term *Übertragung*—a literal translation of the Greek *metapherein*—as a designation for metaphor. The synonymy of these terms is confirmed by a comparison of "On Truth and Lie" and the notes on rhetoric, where the designations of gender are described as "arbitrary transferences" [*willkürliche Übertragungen*] and "pure metaphor" [*reine Metapher*], respectively. The sense of metaphor as an *Übertragung*, a carrying over or transference of a meaning, gender or sense from one word or sphere to another, is perhaps more clearly illustrated by the following well-known passage from "On Truth and Lie":

> A nerve stimulus first translated [*übertragen*] into an image. First metaphor! [*Metapher*] The image, in turn, is transformed [*nachgeformt*] into a sound. And each time there is a complete overleaping [*Überspringen*] of spheres, from one sphere to the center of a totally different one. (TL, 248–249/879)

Unless metaphor is understood in a technical manner as transference or carrying over, rather than as a general term for figurative language in general, the sense of this passage is lost. Nietzsche's description of the translation from a nerve stimulus to an image as the "first metaphor" underscores the fact that what is taking place is a linguistic translation, that the movement from one sphere to another is a linguistic event, just as in the case of sensory perception the linguistic structure of the experience is emphasized, rather than its specific "content."[32] The nerve stimulus and the image cannot, therefore, be understood as mimetic reflections of an originary phenomenon or experience, but are themselves metaphors, since they are always already members of a linguistic economy whose principal transaction is that of exchange. Consequently, it is a mistake to read Nietzsche's references to nerve stimuli as evidence of a naive materialism, whereby language would be reduced to so-called pre- or non-linguistic phenomenon.

The third and final moment in Nietzsche's genealogy of the word is *synecdoche*: "We speak of a *serpent*; the term applies to nothing but its winding, and so it would apply equally to the worm. What arbitrary delimitations, what one-sided preferences for one trait or another of a thing! The various languages juxtaposed show that words are never concerned with truth, never with adequate expression, otherwise there would not be so many languages" (TL, 248/879). In the notes on rhetoric, the point is expressed in similar terms: "If the rhetor says 'sail' instead of 'ship,' 'waves' instead of 'sea,' the synecdoche, an 'encompassing' [*Mitumfassen*] has taken place [. . .]. A partial perception takes the place of the entire and complete intuition" (Rh, 23). Nietzsche is not here making the naive mistake—which some commentators have accused him of making—of denying the possibility of truth because there is not an organic connection between words and the objects to which they refer. As a philologist Nietzsche was, of course, familiar with Plato's arguments against this position in the *Cratylus*, and it is quite difficult to believe that he would fall unawares into a trap such as this. Rather, I suggest that this passage should be read in light of the foregoing remarks on the tropological origins of the word. Against this background, the point of the passage would not merely be negative—to deny that words are organically connected with objects in the world—but the positive and more complicated assertion that meaning is not a simple mirroring of the referential relationships between which exist between words and "extra-linguistic" objects in the world, but is principally a product of the intra-linguistic resources of language itself. In the case of synecdoche, the exchange that takes place results in an "encompassing," the substitution of one part of feature of an object for the whole. In the same way that the German word *Schlange* privileges the snake's means of transportation, its winding, over other characteristics, so the Greek word *drakōn* foregrounds the snake's shiny appearance. Finally, it is also worthwhile noting that Nietzsche does not here deny that words can be true, but that with respect to in their multifarious origins they are not principally concerned with truth as correspondence or identity.[33] This is entirely consistent with his account of the origin of language and truth as arising out of a need for social stability, not out of a natural drive for truth.

FROM WORD TO CONCEPT

In the foregoing analysis of the word we have emphasized the genealogical nature of Nietzsche's narrative and the twofold logic of origination and forgetting that governs his account of the origin. As the most basic linguistic element, the word represents an important moment in the instantiation of one of our most deeply held beliefs about language, namely, that it is a neutral medium which mediates human beings' experiences of a world of pre-existing extra-linguistic objects. One of the aims of Nietzsche's genealogy of the word is to criticize this naively held belief by demonstrating that even those experiences that we consider most basic, tactile sensation for example, are not immediately given but are always already determined by linguistic structures such as metonymy, metaphor, and synecdoche. However, the tropological structures to which Nietzsche refers in his consideration of the word are not in any sense said to be pre-existing, as perhaps Kantian categories can be understood. Language is not an empty shell waiting to be filled in by the chaos of sensory experience, and is not therefore in any ordinary sense to be understood as a medium. Rather, Nietzsche's ruminations on the origin of the word point to the contemporaneousness—and ultimately unmasterable—origins of our notions of language, experience, and world, and the necessity of forgetting the fact of their co-origination.

The plaited logic of instantiation and forgetting which describes the event of origination forecloses the possibility that experience—understood either as subjective experience, as in Descartes or Husserl, or the experience of pre-linguistic objects, as in Locke—can ever function as a ground of language as such. The tropological structure of the word points to the fact that language, in its most basic form, resists being reduced to anything that might function as such a ground of meaning outside of the boundaries of the linguistic economy, by demonstrating that a word or expression is meaningful only insofar as it can be exchanged for another; something Nietzsche will allude to when he describes truths as coins that have lost their image and can no longer be considered as coins, as something that has exchange value, but only as metal. But if words are already once removed from something like an originary experience of subjective self-certainty, then concepts—words that refer to "more or less similar [. . .] hence absolutely dissimilar cases"—are irretrievably and absolutely removed from such experiences. In Nietzsche's vocabulary, concepts are tropes of tropes, metaphors to the second power whose reversals or turnings can never result in a return to the one, the proper, the purely literal: "It makes no sense to speak of a 'proper meaning' [*'eigentliche Bedeutung'*] which is carried over [*übertragen*] to something else only in special cases" (Rh, 25).

The concept is a word that has become intensified and abstract by means of a metonymic exchange whereby individual effects are seen to be part of a single abstract quality that is then projected back as their cause. In "On Truth and Lie" Nietzsche describes the substitution of cause and effect that gives rise to concepts in the following terms:

> Every concept arises by the equation of the dissimilar. Just as no leaf is ever exactly the same as any other, certainly the concept 'leaf' is formed by arbitrarily dropping those individual differences, by forgetting the distinguishing factors, and this gives rise to the idea that besides leaves there is in nature such a thing as the 'leaf,' i.e. an original form [*Urform*] [. . .]. We call a person 'honest.' We ask, 'Why did he act so honestly today?' Our answer usually goes: 'Because of his honesty.' Honesty! that means once more: the 'leaf' is the cause of the leaves [. . .] we formulate out of them a *qualitas occulta* with the name 'honesty.' (TL, 249/880)

In the notes on rhetoric Nietzsche is even more explicit about the metonymic structure of concepts:

> the abstract *substantiva* are qualities [. . .] which are torn away from their substrata and set forth as independent essences [. . .]. These concepts, which owe their origin only to our experiences, are presupposed *a priori* to be the inner essences of things [*das innere Wesen der Dinge*]: we attribute to the appearances as their *cause* that which still is only an effect. The *abstracta* evoke the illusion that *they* themselves are these essences which cause the qualities, whereas they receive a figurative reality only from us, because of those characteristics. The transition from the *eidē* to *ideai* by Plato is very instructive; here metonymy, the substitution of cause and effect, is complete. (Rh, 59)

Nietzsche could hardly have been clearer about the tropological structure of the concept. Like the word from which it arises, the concept receives its authority from the intra-linguistic resources of language, not from a correspondence to an extra-linguistic referent. However, what is most striking about these two passages is the manner in which Nietzsche links his analysis of the concept to the instantiation of metaphysics. The hypostatization that is an essential component of all metaphysical thinking results from a process akin to what Kant, in the second part of the *Critique of Pure Reason*, refers to as the transcendental illusion (B 350–355). Just as reason necessarily posits totalities that can never be verified by experience, so language posits abstract entities as the inner essences of things themselves; entities whose structure is not one of correspondence or adequation, but is rather tropological. Metaphysics arises, therefore, out of the very structure of language itself, which in a double movement paradigmatic of all origination, posits the concept as essence and concurrently dissimulates its tropological origin in favor of a mimetic, referential structure. This act of dissimulation produces the forgetting within which every metaphysics and language itself must recede and from whose inner recesses they can never be recalled, for the double logic of origination resists every attempt to break its hold, continually reproducing and reasserting itself. As Nietzsche will write some years later "a philosophical mythology lies hidden in *language* which reemerges every moment no matter how careful one might otherwise be" (HH II, 11). It is precisely for this reason that exposing or recollecting the tropological origins of the concept does not clear the way for an escape or overcoming of metaphysics.[34]

The forgetting that is inscribed into the very structure of the concept is not a merely passive effect, but an active, even violent force.[35] It is at the same time the condition of possibility of the concept and discursive thought, and a condition of the blindness (or, more precisely, the blinding) that is a necessary aspect of conceptual knowledge. This blindness manifests itself in two ways. First, in the fact that with respect to the concept one can only think in terms of the binary opposition of particular and universal. What can be thought is precisely that which can be subsumed under the law of the concept. This schema leaves no room for what Nietzsche, in "On Truth and Lie," refers to as the "unique, absolutely individualized originary experience" (TL, 249/879). The concept does not, in fact cannot, respect that singularity since its very logic is one of integration and subsumption, which involves a forgetting of singularity in favor of what is particular and generalizable. As we noted earlier, the concept is not an empty shell that passively waits to be filled in by the chaos of sensory experience. Rather the law of the concept in general, and the content of an individual concept in particular, actively determine what can be recognized and known by limiting the range of phenomena which comes under its purview. The figure of Oedipus is paradigmatic in this respect, as a "symbol of science" and of the blinding violence of conceptual knowledge (KSA 7, 7.22).[36]

The second way in which this blindness manifests itself is the synecdochic character of words and concepts which, like the nomological structure of the concept, violently determines the extension of a given word by focusing on a particular aspect or feature of an object, while blinding us to other aspects. In "On Truth and Lie" Nietzsche emphasizes the capriciousness of this aspect of language, citing as an example the genesis of the concept 'leaf,' which "is formed by arbitrarily dropping [. . .] individual differences, by forgetting the distinguishing factors" (TL, 249/880). In the course of our consideration of the notes on rhetoric we have had occasion to refer to a second example, namely, the German word *Schlange*, which emphasizes the winding motion of the snake rather than its propensity to bite. Unlike the arbitrary delimitations in the concept 'leaf,' naming a snake 'the winding one' rather than 'the biting one,' could have more immediately deleterious effects.[37]

WHAT IS TRUTH?

Nietzsche's search for the origins of the drive for truth lead him from the intellect to the word and the concept, and then finally to truth itself, which is described in terms more famous than understood. Partly this is due to the widespread belief that this description amounts to a denial of truth, to the negative assertion that there is no such thing as truth, merely lies. The foregoing resume of the opening sections of the essay will make it easier, I believe, to show that Nietzsche does not deny truth in the rather simplistic and polemical manner so often claimed. What is being denied—if one wishes to employ this vocabulary—is the coherence of the correspondence theory of truth, not the concept of truth itself. Although commentators have long recognized Nietzsche's critique of the correspondence theory of truth, they have failed, to a surprising degree, to recognize this as a prelude to a radical reinterpretation of the concept of truth. Before proceeding any further, let us cite Nietzsche's now-famous description of truth from "On Truth and Lie":

> What is truth? A mobile army of metaphors, metonyms, anthropomorphisms, in short, a sum of human relations which were poetically and rhetorically heightened, transferred, adorned, and which after long use seem solid, canonical and binding to a people. Truths are illusions which we have forgotten are illusions, metaphors which have been used up and drained of sensory force, coins which have lost their image [*Bild*] and are now considered as metal, no longer as coins. (TL, 250/880–881)

The first sentence of this passage, with its assertion that truth is a trope, should come as no surprise to those who have read the preceding sections of the essay with any care. There, as we have noted at some length, Nietzsche rigorously argues that words and concepts are essentially tropes, which is to say, that the meaning of words and concepts is dependent less on a structure of correspondence between these terms and "extra-linguistic" objects, than on the possibilities of exchange between such terms. It is these possibilities of exchange that produce adjectives such as "hard" and abstract nouns such as "honesty" by means of metonymy, an exchange of cause and effect. But if words and concepts are tropes, it follows that truth must also be a trope. This is for two reasons. First, and most obviously, because truth itself is an abstract noun which is produced in the same manner as abstract nouns such as "honesty," "courage," and the like. Although the concept of truth has had a privileged status within the history of Western philosophy, it does not follow from this that one can read back from this history to a pure, unalloyed origin. Quite often, in fact, Nietzsche suggests that the contrary is more likely to be true; the more highly valued something is, the more likely it is that its "beginnings were, like the beginnings of everything great on earth, soaked in blood thoroughly and for a long time" (GM, II.6). The traditional interpretation of truth as something whose origin is pure and free and unalloyed with traces of falsehood is not an argument against the possibility that quite the opposite might be true, since "the cause of the origin of a thing and its eventual utility, its actual employment and place in a system of purposes, lie worlds apart" (GM, II.12). If truth cannot be said to have a "miraculous origin," then it too must be considered to be part of the "radically open tropological system" that is language.[38] Second, if words and concepts are tropes, it follows that truth must be a trope as well, for by what means can truth be expressed other than through words and concepts? This inescapable fact rules out the possibility that the tropological structure of the word and the concept could be vitiated, controlled or harnessed in some manner, so that what was designated as "true" would be kept pure somehow, untainted by the indecency of the trope.

In keeping with the twofold logic of the origin we have described, the origination of truth produces a forgetting of its tropological roots in favor of a conception of truth as correspondence or adequation. This tale of forgetting is narrated by the passage cited above from "On Truth and Lie." Truth is here initially described as a "mobile army of metaphors, metonyms and anthropomorphisms." The mobility of truth consists in its ability to be transferred, traded, or exchanged. Truth is not fixed, either in place or value, because, like the coin with which truth is compared in this passage, its value is a species of exchange value. In both cases, value inheres not in the thing itself, be it the metal out of which the coin is minted or the literal referents of the terms used to convey a particular truth, but in the possibility of exchange, in the fact that what is represented by a particular truth or coin can be exchanged for something else of equal value. Truth can be exchanged insofar as it retains its image, which is to say, its status as a figure. But the mobility of truth, the very possibility that a particular truth could be exchanged for another without regard for its referential relations, conflicts with the utilitarian origins of truth. Let us recall that according to "On Truth and Lie," truth—in the extra-moral sense—first comes into existence with the creation of a fixed and universally binding language, created in order to establish a firm foundation for social existence. If truth and language are to serve the function of providing this foundation, they can only do so if their mobility is arrested and if they are understood as being principally referential, not tropological. Given this, truth needed to become solid and binding, something whose value was henceforth determined by the fact that it could be exchanged only in exceptional cases, as in fictional discourse, for example, where untruth could not produce harmful effects, but perhaps beauty or pleasure. The forgetting of truth's tropological origin was not, in any sense, something accidental or capricious, but rather an event whose necessity was built into its very origin.

The question remains, however, whether Nietzsche's emphasis on forgetting does not open up the possibility that recollecting the forgotten origins of truth and language provides a way of overcoming this enforced amnesia, leading to the recovery of an originary tropological language. One could perhaps point to the intuitive type referred to in the second part of the essay, who rejects the hardened edifice of concepts for the motile and changeable web of intuitions, as an example of what such a recovery might be like. However, this manner of interpreting "On Truth and Lie" misconstrues both the nature of the forgetting identified by Nietzsche and the role assigned to the intuitive type. First, the forgetting to which Nietzsche refers in this essay is not a subjective forgetting, one that could be identified with a particular people or individual, nor is it a forgetting that can be reduced to states of consciousness. On the contrary, the forgetting of which Nietzsche speaks is a forgetting within language itself that arises out of the apparently transparent referential structure of language, and that gives rise to the almost unavoidable tendency to think of words as names that are tied to objects just as a kite is tied to a string.[39] This tendency, which is doubtlessly connected to both the utilitarian origins of language and the instrumental manner in which language is often used, leads to a separation and exclusion of figurative meaning, as well as a privileging of literal over figurative discourse. Paradigmatic in this respect is philosophical discourse which, at least since Plato, has sought to enforce this separation and exclude figurative language from its parameters. In contrast, much of "On Truth and Lie" is aimed at showing that this division and separation are untenable, principally because the very structures that produce figurative and literal meaning—for which the trope is paradigmatic—are identical. If, as Nietzsche suggests, "tropes are not just occasionally added to words, but constitute their most proper nature" (Rh, 25) and "there is absolutely no unrhetorical 'naturalness' of language to which one could appeal" (Rh, 21), then the distinction between literal and figurative discourse is at best pragmatic and provisional.

This does not, however, mean that all meaning is figurative and that we should cease speaking of a literal or proper meaning, but rather that the difference between them is radically undecidable. The attempt to separate, absolutely and definitively, a literal from a proper meaning runs up against the same stumbling block as the attempt to isolate, and grant a privileged status to, the concept of truth. Since truth is an abstract concept, the tropological structures that produce abstract concepts such as "honesty" and "hard" will also be those that give rise to the concept of truth. Just as there is no way of isolating the concept of truth from these structures and securing for it a proper origin, so one cannot isolate literal from figurative meaning. The upshot of this is that there is an irreducible and radical undecidability between truth and falsity, literal and figurative meaning, which will ultimately disrupt any attempt to enforce an absolute division where there cannot be one. Language is thus both necessarily referential and disruptive of the literal meaning to which it gives rise. If de Man is right to assert that "the notion of a language entirely freed from referential constraints is properly inconceivable," then the converse must also be admitted, namely, that the notion of a language entirely dependent on referential constraints is equally inconceivable.[40] It follows from this that the intuitive type cannot be considered to symbolize a mode of interpretation which would seek to recover an originary figurative language. On the contrary, for the second part of the essay does not, as is often claimed, privilege the intuitive over the rational type. Rather, the conclusion of the essay must be regarded as ironic, with both the rational and the intuitive types understood as caricatures of those who, on the one hand, focus on the referential properties of language to the exclusion of the figurative (rational), and those who, on the other hand, emphasize the figurative properties of language to the exclusion of the referential (intuitive). Warminski captures the irony of the second part of the essay when he writes that "with his convulsed expressions and his inconsolable cries, the unreasonable intuitive man is just the comic counterpart of the rational man: the one under a cloud, the other in a hole."[41]

Nietzsche's reflections on language in "On Truth and Lie" and the notes on rhetoric do not, as has often been suggested, result in a rejection of literal language in favor of a figurative, non-referential *poiēsis*.[42] In spite of Heidegger's well-known assertions to the contrary, Nietzsche's thought rarely takes the form of an "either/or" decision between two poles or positions.[43] Nietzsche was keenly aware of the trap that such an oppositional thinking—rejecting the literal in favor the figurative, the philosophical in favor of the artistic—too easily falls into, as his reference to the possibility of an "artistic Socrates" and his characterization of the ascetic priest as "among the greatest *conserving* and yes creating forces of life" rather aptly illustrate.[44] Rather than reversing poles or choosing one position at the expense of the other, Nietzsche explores the ambiguities within each position, thereby often eliminating the very possibility of a decision for or against one or the other. This is clearly the case with the unpublished writings on language that have often—and incorrectly—been described as simply an impassioned plea on behalf of figurative discourse. Rather than succumbing to the temptation of this type of oppositional thinking, these writings insist on a radical undecidability between literal and figurative discourse, which in turn leads Nietzsche to reject the traditional conception of truth as correspondence or adequation in favor of a conception of shining truth.

SHINING TRUTH

If the difference between literal and figurative discourse is, literally speaking, undecidable, then any discourse of truth that privileges one of the two poles at the expense of the other will be inherently violent.[45] In the case of a discourse that privileges a purely figurative conception of truth, the resulting violence might have consequences no more severe than falling into the same pit over and over again, though one could not rule out the possibility that the reptile identified as "the winding one" will turn out to be "the biting one," with unpleasant, if not fatal results. At the same time, the violence of a discourse putatively free from the taint of figuration with a literal or referential conception of truth is of a different order, and produces two related sets of consequences. First, the correspondence theory of truth carries with it a conviction in the teleological structure of truth, that is to say, a belief that the essential nature of the world can, albeit incrementally, ultimately be fathomed. This conviction, Nietzsche suggests, "first saw the light of the world in the person of Socrates: the unshakable faith that thought, using the thread of causality, can penetrate the deepest abysses of being, and that thought is capable not only of knowing being but even of *correcting it*" (BT, 15). The teleological structure of truth, the belief in truth's infinite potentiality, turns back on itself and transforms truth into a normative value. Truth is no longer understood as the correspondence of a judgment with a state of affairs in the world, but becomes a standard for judging what the world should be, for correcting the world.[46] In "On Truth and Lie," the normative power of thought is considered with regard to the concept, which by rigidly determining the range and type of phenomena that can appear under its umbrella, establishes a "regulatory and imperative world" [*das Regulierende und Imperativische*] for human beings. The normative structure of the concept violently excludes those aspects of phenomena which cannot be subsumed within the parameters established for them, thus enforcing a stable and homogeneous view of a world which is essentially chaotic, mobile, and irreducibly heterogeneous.

The critique of the correspondence theory of truth in "On Truth and Lie" should be read as a critique of both the ideal of correspondence and the integrative violence of the concept. However, it does not follow from this that Nietzsche rejects the language of truth, or that he deems it possible to do away with the conceptual structure of language altogether. The ironic denouement of the essay with the intuitive one in a hole and the rational one wrapped in his raincoat under a storm cloud, should be a sufficient caveat against either of these two romantic possibilities. Putting aside the suggestion that Nietzsche's critique of the correspondence theory of truth is tantamount to a rejection of truth per se, a second, more interesting possibility presents itself, namely, that Nietzsche's critique opens up the space for a radical reinterpretation of the concept of truth.[47]

There is, of course, one obvious way in which "On Truth and Lie" can be read as an attempt at a reinterpretation of truth. Insofar as Nietzsche describes truth as an "illusion," a lie made "according to established convention" (TL, 250/881), he emphasizes that the origin of the drive for truth is to be found within morality, not in any putatively natural desire for truth. There are however clear indications that the type of reinterpretation Nietzsche seeks in "On Truth and Lie" is more radical and far reaching than the assertion that truth is an illusion fostered by society, a position which would be close to the kind of oppositional thinking emphasized by Heidegger in his reading of Nietzsche. The most direct evidence against such a reading is to be found in the second part of the essay, where Nietzsche explicitly contrasts scientific truth, which is essentially conceptual, with what he refers to as truths "of a completely different sort." The existence of these other truths threatens the scientist and the conceptual edifice in whose shadow he seeks protection, for there are "terrible powers" that "constantly press upon him, and [. . .] oppose scientific truth with 'truths' of a completely different sort [*ganz anders geartete 'Wahrheiten'*] bearing the most divers coats of arms" (TL, 254/886). Here, as elsewhere in the essay, Nietzsche refrains from explicitly naming this other species truth, but he provides ample clues as to how it should be understood.

One such clue is to be found in the terrible powers which produce these truths, namely, the drive to form metaphors and the pleasure in the fictional or unreal, or what Nietzsche here refers to as "the invincible tendency to let oneself be deceived." The first of these powers, the drive to form metaphors, should be quite familiar to us by now. Let us recall that in the first instance, the term *metaphor* names one of the three tropes, along with metonymy and synecdoche, which Nietzsche singles out in his genealogical analysis of the word, the concept, and truth in "On Truth and Lie" and the notes on rhetoric. This more technical meaning of metaphor yields to a more general, one might say figurative, use of the term to denote those tropological processes—principally of exchange, transference, and translation—which are constitutive of linguistic production itself. Metaphor in this sense does not refer to one part or function of language, against which one might place the literal, the proper and the true, but stands as a figure for those processes which produce the figurative and literal alike, the common root out of which they arise. In keeping with this more general meaning of metaphor, Nietzsche uses the term and its modern synonyms—transference and translation—to describe the processes of perception and understanding.

We have already noted how Nietzsche analyses our discourse of cause and effect in terms of a metonymic displacement or exchange that posits as an effect what is really a cause of its own cause. Even the simplest statements such as "The stone is hard" cannot properly be said to refer back to an originary and proper experience that would be immune from the excesses of this tropological economy. From this most basic of experiences Nietzsche generalizes that the relationship between the subjective and objective spheres cannot be conceived otherwise than on the basis of a metaphorical model, where perception and understanding are conceived of not as replication, the mirroring of the external world in the perceptions and representations of the mind, but as processes of production. In one of the more memorable passages of the essay, Nietzsche contrasts the ideal of the correspondence theory, "a contradictory absurdity," with this model of metaphorical production:

> between two absolutely different spheres such as subject and object, there can be no causality, no correctness [*Richtigkeit*] , no expression [*Ausdruck*], but at most an *aesthetic* stance, I mean a suggestive transference, a stammering translation into a completely foreign language [*eine andeutende Übertragung, eine nachstammelnde Übersetzung in eine ganz fremde Sprache*]. This requires, in any case, a freely poeticizing and freely inventing middle sphere and mediating force. (TL, 252/884)

In the years to follow Nietzsche will make frequent use of this model of understanding. In a well-known passage from *The Gay Science*, Nietzsche describes the philosophical conception of knowledge as "nothing more than this: Something strange is to be reduced to something familiar" (GS, 355). Most familiar, of course, are the inner facts of consciousness, perceptions such as "The stone is hard": "Even the most cautious among [the philosophers] suppose that what is familiar is at least *more easily knowable* than what is strange, and that, for example, sound method demands that we start from the 'inner world,' from 'facts of consciousness' because this world is *more familiar to us*" (ibid.). But sensation is more familiar only because we forget that it, too, is produced by a process of metaphorical transference or translation: "'inner experience' enters our consciousness only after it has found a language the individual *understands*—that is to say, a translation of a condition into conditions more familiar to him; 'to understand' means merely: to be able to express something new in the language of something old and familiar" (KSA 13, 15.90). The drive to form metaphors is not an ornamental or supplementary drive, but is constitutive of what it is to be a human being: "That drive to form metaphors, that fundamental drive of men, cannot be discounted for one moment, because that would amount to ignoring man himself" (TL, 254/887).

The second of the two terrible powers that press on the scientific type and produce unscientific truth is the "invincible tendency to let oneself be deceived" [*unbesiegbaren Hang sich täuschen zu lassen*]. When Nietzsche writes of the inclination of human beings to let themselves be deceived, he is, in the first instance, referring to the pleasure we take from fictional stories and tales of all kinds: "He is as if enchanted with happiness when the rhapsodist tells him epic legends as true or the actor in the drama plays the king more regally than any real monarch does" (TL, 255/888). Deception in this case is not destructive, but produces a genuine pleasure akin to that we feel when in the midst of play. It should not surprise us that deception of this kind should be pleasurable, since it is merely an extension of the intellect itself, whose "most general effect is deception" (TL, 246/876). We might recall that the deception that the intellect here engages in bears some relation to the deception involved in fiction, for just as the actor is able to play the king more regally than the monarch himself, thus making the imaginary appear more real that reality itself, so the intellect is able to appear as if "the whole world hinged upon it." This spectacle, which is played before all, has the greatest effect on but a few, those who have perhaps the greatest interest in letting themselves be deceived in this manner, namely, the philosophers. "Just as every porter [*Lastträger*] wants to have his admirer, so, too, the proudest man, the philosopher, believes that he sees from all sides the eyes of the universe telescopically focused on his actions and thoughts" (TL, 246/875–876).

By believing that the eyes of the universe are focused on him, the philosopher produces a deception akin to that of the actor, who appears more majestic than the king himself. As we noted above, the deception effected by the philosopher takes the form of a reversal between the "remote corner of the universe" where Nietzsche's text begins, to the center of universe occupied by the philosopher. The philosopher achieves the *Täuschung* of making himself the center of the universe by means of a *Vertauschung*, a chiasmic reversal, of center and corner. The philosopher's complicity in this scheme of deception is also suggested by the comparison Nietzsche draws between the philosopher and the porter. As the word *Lastträger* tells us, the porter is one who carries a burden, but the similarity between the root verb *tragen* and *Übertragung*, one of the synonyms Nietzsche uses for metaphor, is hardly incidental.[48] The burden carried by the philosopher is always *über-tragen*, carried over or transferred to someone else's shoulders. But in this case the philosopher is no better than the liar, who practices a similar breed of deception: "The liar uses the valid terms [. . .] to make the unreal appear real [. . .]. He misuses established conventions by arbitrary substitutions and even *reversals of names*" (TL, 248/877–878; emphasis added).

The actor and the philosopher are both deceivers; each makes the unreal appear real by performing a metaphorical reversal, a creative transformation that is brought about through the means of exchange, transference, and translation. What, then, remains to distinguish these two masters of dissimulation, or are we to believe that their deceptions are equal in kind and value? An important difference between the philosopher and the actor are their distinct attitudes to truth, or perhaps more precisely, the different type of truth each believes in. The philosopher believes in the absolute value of truth and understands his task to be "to find something in things, under them or behind them" (GS, 355). The terms Nietzsche uses in this description are revealing because they illustrate rather well the philosopher's belief that truth is to be discovered—not invented—beyond or behind all surface appearance and shadow in the realm of true being, which is to say, beyond that which is apparent, variable, heterogeneous, and temporal. This Manichaen view of the world produces a hatred of appearance, becoming and the senses, in short, a hatred of all that which separates the philosopher from the truth. The philosophers

> all believe, desperately even, in what has being. But since they never grasp it, they seek for reasons why it is kept from them. 'There must be mere appearance, there must be some deception which prevents us from perceiving that which has being: where is the deceiver?' 'We have found him,' they cry ecstatically, 'it is the senses [. . .].' (TI, III.1)

The structure of philosophical truth has clear affinities with the rhetoric of truth that has developed within the Western tradition, together with its hierarchical binary logic. One of the most prominent examples of this is the privileging of light over dark, a practice which in philosophical writing can be traced back at least as far as Parmenides' description of the distinct paths of night and day, but which is also pointedly expressed by Plato in the allegory of the cave, where that which has true being is represented by means of an analogy with sunlight, while what is false or merely apparent is depicted in shadow. The echoes of this identification of the sun, and light in general, with knowledge are still to be found in our modern epistemological vocabulary. Thus one speaks of an example as 'illuminating' or 'shedding light on' a question. We are also accustomed to speaking about truth in spatial terms. A particular analysis is described as 'penetrating,' which is to say that it goes beneath the surface and mere appearance to the 'core of the matter.' An example that combines both spatial and visual elements is the adjective 'insightful,' namely, that which allows one to 'look into' something.

Whereas the philosopher digs earnestly for truth beneath the surface of things, in the world of being, the actor takes pleasure in that which is superficial and mere appearance, seeking truth not behind appearance, but in the form of appearance itself. For the actor, the structure of truth cannot be described as a contrast between identity and difference, light and dark, depth and surface, but rather in the shining forth of appearance. The actor's truth does not subsist in its correspondence or identity with an external referent, but rather in the way in which this truth exposes itself as appearance or *shine*.[49] In a passage that unites three figures of great importance for Nietzsche, the actor, woman, and the Jew,[50] he describes the actor in the following terms:

> Falseness with a good conscience; the delight in dissimulation [. . .] the inner craving for a role and mask, for shine; an excess of the capacity for all kind of adaptations that can no longer be satisfied in the service of the most immediate and narrowest utility [. . .]. (GS, 361)

This description of the actor echoes in important respects Nietzsche's account of the liberated intellect in "On Truth and Lie":

> That enormous structure of beams and boards of the concepts [. . .] is for the liberated intellect just a scaffolding and plaything for his boldest works of art. And when he smashes it apart, scattering it, and then ironically puts it together again [. . .] he reveals that [. . .] he is guided not by concepts, but by intuitions [*Intuitionen*]. From these intuitions no regular road leads to the land of ghostly schemata or abstractions. The word is not made for these intuitions. (TL, 255–256/888–889)[51]

Like the actor who craves a mask, the liberated intellect takes pleasure in mere appearance or *shine*. A prime example of this is the attitude the liberated intellect adopts towards the concept, which it no longer views as solely an instrument of knowledge, a normative standard which rigidly determines the useful and the true, but as a plaything of sorts whose value does not subsist solely in its power of subsumption, but also in what lies on its surface, in the material character of the concept, its qualities as a signifier. It is precisely this material aspect of the concept that philosophy has consistently denied by, on the one hand, privileging the signified, the abstract entity or form which the signifier represents, and on the other hand, by privileging the "full presence" of speech over the dull and lifeless materiality of writing.[52] To be sure, philosophy's denial of the materiality of language is part of a more general privileging of the spiritual over the material which, Nietzsche suggests, began with Parmenides' "fully erroneous separation of 'spirit' and 'body' [. . .] which, particularly since Plato, lies upon philosophy like a curse" (PTA, 843). But in the case of language we can identify a more particular motive, namely, that the material aspects of language, those elements which belong to what we might call its appearance or *shine* are excluded by the subsumptive logic of the concept and, consequently, must remain outside of the instrumental calculus that is constitutive of conceptual discourse.

But it is precisely the *shine* of language which will play an increasingly important role in Nietzsche's understanding of truth and, consequently, in his philosophical praxis. Because he no longer understands language in solely referential terms, Nietzsche emphasizes the philosophically productive role played by the materiality of language in an effort to rethink the structure of truth. In an unusually spirited essay, Clayton Koelb describes the consequences which follow from this renewed attention to the material aspects of language:

> If there is no distinction to be made between the figurative nature of even the most ordinary language and truth, then one way to think about 'truth' in fresh ways would be to 'let language do some thinking for us' by interrogating the figures themselves. [This would] mean accepting both the literal and figurative meanings as belonging to the same order—both, of course, figurative [. . .] [and assuming] that all available meanings are equally useful. From this assumption comes a strategy for writing that derives from reading [. . .]. The discovery that all truth is nothing but figuration ceases to be an alarming or paralyzing problem for the philosopher; on the contrary, it opens up a new space for investigation.[53]

In the unpublished writings on language and rhetoric from the 1870s Nietzsche rejects the traditional understanding of language as a transparent medium or instrument of knowledge and instead emphasizes the material aspects of language. This movement away from an instrumental view of language is accompanied by a corresponding shift in Nietzsche's understanding of the structure of truth. The realization that language can no longer be regarded as a transparent medium of communication whose epistemological reliability is beyond question necessarily leads Nietzsche to reject the traditional conception of truth as correspondence or adequation and embrace a concept of truth whose essential structure is identical with that of appearance itself. The figure Nietzsche will adopt for this newly constituted conception of truth is that of woman, or more precisely, the veiling daemon of truth.[54]

Clear evidence of Nietzsche's reinterpretation of truth is to be found already in *The Birth of Tragedy*, where he explicitly contrasts the traditional approach to truth taken by philosophers, here represented by the image of "the theoretical man," with that of the artist. While the theoretical man desires to behold the "naked goddess" who is revealed when the veil is torn away and considers this alone to be true, the artist is enraptured by the veil itself, even after the 'the truth' has been dis-covered: "Whenever truth is uncovered [*Enthüllung der Wahrheit*], the artist will always cling with rapt gaze at what still remains covering [*Hülle*], even after such uncovering; but the theoretical man enjoys and finds satisfaction in the discarded covering and finds the highest object of his pleasure in the process of an ever happy uncovering" (BT, 15). In two prefaces he wrote in the years 1885–1886, Nietzsche explicitly returns to this image of truth as a veiled woman. In the first of the two prefaces, Nietzsche describes the philosophers' search for truth as a kind of elaborate, albeit unsuccessful, courting ritual:

> Supposing truth is a woman—what then? Are there not grounds for the suspicion that all philosophers, insofar as they were dogmatists, have been very inexpert about woman? That the gruesome seriousness, the clumsy obtrusiveness with which they have usually approached truth so far have been awkward and very improper methods for winning a woman's heart? What is certain is that she has not allowed herself to be won. (BGE, P)

A close reading of this passage shows that Nietzsche is not here interested in denying truth, but rather in the more difficult project of reinterpreting the traditional concept of truth. That this is Nietzsche's motive is borne out by the suggestion that methods with which philosophers have approached truth have been "awkward and very improper" and by the conclusion Nietzsche draws at the end of the passage, namely, that truth has "not allowed herself to be won." The terms of this passage suggest that the reason why philosophers have been so inexpert about truth, why they have thus far failed to win truth, is that they have misunderstood the nature of truth itself. However, if philosophers have failed to understand truth, it is not because they have failed to think of truth as a woman, but because they have misunderstood both woman and the figure of truth.[55]

An example which is perhaps paradigmatic of the way in which philosophers have understood woman as truth—hence misunderstanding both woman and truth—is Parmenides' allegorical description of the journey from darkness into light in the first of the surviving fragments. The fragment begins as follows:

> The car that bears me carried me as far as ever my heart desired, when it had brought me and set me on the renowned way of the goddess, which leads the man who knows through all the towns. On that way was I borne along; for on it did the wise steeds carry me, drawing my car and

> maidens showed the way. And the axle, glowing in the socket—for it was urged round by the whirling wheels at each end—gave forth a sound as of a pipe, when the daughters of the Sun, hasting to convey me into the light, threw back their veils from off their faces and left the abode of night.[56]

What interests us in this context is Parmenides' account of revelation, his description of the journey from the darkness of ignorance into the light of truth. The crucial moment in the narrative is the transition from darkness into light, which occurs as the daughters of the sun "threw back their veils from off their faces." The account of truth suggested by this description differs markedly from that indicated by the passage cited above from the Preface to *Beyond Good and Evil*. To begin with, the maidens' gesture of unveiling that marks the entrance into light signifies that truth has indeed been won. Her face is without any covering, hence there is nothing about her that remains hidden from the possessive gaze of the philosopher. To win truth means to unveil her, to entice her to reveal that which lies hidden behind the veil. Here the veil acts as a barrier and a lure, hiding woman and, perhaps because she is hidden, enticing the philosopher to pursue her. The structure of truth indicated by this image is one of surface and depth, absence and presence. In order to know truth, one must get beyond the surface; one must convince truth to unveil, to reveal her being as presence, as nakedness. The philosopher's lack of expertise regarding truth (and woman) is expressed in this desire to remove the veil and in the belief that the truth of truth lies hidden therein.[57]

In contrast with this image, Nietzsche provides us with another way of conceiving of truth, not as an unveiled goddess, but as a *veiling* daemon. Unlike the naked goddess who gives herself openly and whose presence as nakedness constitutes a pure positivity, Nietzsche's truth cannot be won; on the contrary, her giving is concurrently a holding back and a concealing, her presence a stubborn absence. Nietzsche's truth, so it would seem, is modesty itself. But this modesty should not be misunderstood as a contrived coquettishness, for if Nietzsche's truth refuses to let herself be unveiled, it is because to win her in this way would amount to nothing more than to lose her completely. This is made explicit in the second of the two prefaces referred to above:

> As for our future, one will hardly find us again on the paths of those Egyptian youths who [. . .] want by all means to unveil, uncover, and put into bright light whatever is kept concealed for good reasons [. . .]. We no longer believe that truth remains truth when the veils are withdrawn; we have lived too much to believe in this. Today we consider it

> a matter of decency not to wish to see everything naked, or to be present at everything, or to understand and 'know' everything [. . .]. One should have more respect for the bashfulness with which nature has hidden behind riddles and iridescent uncertainties. Perhaps truth is a woman who has reason for not letting us see her reasons. Perhaps her name is, to speak Greek, *Baubo*? (GS, P.4)

To speak the name *Baubo* is to speak a language of truth other than the one philosophers have spoken for over two millennia. It is to depart from the logic of truth as correspondence, as the light which shines from above, as the value of values. In contrast with Parmenides' veiled goddess of truth who waits for the philosopher to win and disrobe her, Nietzsche's goddess *Baubo* is a primitive and obscene female daemon, one who, in keeping with her origin as a personification of the female genitals, is nothing more than a veil or integument.[58] Whereas Parmenides' goddess needs to be unveiled in order to be a goddess of truth, *Baubo*, as the veil itself, eludes such attempts to disrobe her. If one were to remove her veil, one would not find the truth but at best a second veil, or perhaps nothing at all. In the following two passages Nietzsche emphasizes that truth no longer be understood as a relationship of identity or correspondence between language and the world, but rather as the unfolding of appearance itself, a process of shining forth:

> It is no more than a moral prejudice that truth is worth more than *shine*; it is even the worst proved assumption there is in the world. Let at least this much be admitted: there would be no life at all if not on the basis of perspectival judgments [*Schätzungen*] and appearances [*Scheinbarkeiten*]; and if, with the virtuous enthusiasm and clumsiness of some philosophers, one wanted to abolish the 'apparent world' [*die 'scheinbare Welt'*] altogether, well supposing *you* could do that—at least there would be nothing left of your 'truth' either! Indeed, what compels us to suppose that there is an essential opposition of 'true' and 'false' at all? Is it not sufficient to assume degrees of appearance [*Scheinbarkeit*], and, as it were, lighter and darker shadows and shades of *shine* [. . .]?(BGE, 34)

> Oh those Greeks! They knew how to *live*. What is required for that is to stop courageously at the surface, the fold, the skin, to adore *shine*, to believe in forms, tones, words, in the whole Olympus of *shine*. Those Greeks were superficial—*out of profundity*. And is not this precisely what we are coming back to [. . .] are we not, precisely in this respect, Greeks? Adorers of forms, of tones, of words? And therefore—Artists? (GS, P.4)[59]

NIETZSCHE'S *KEHRE*?

In the opening section of this chapter we raised the question of what status should be accorded to Nietzsche's unpublished writings on rhetoric and language. The crux of the matter is whether Nietzsche's decision not to publish these texts and the absence of a rhetorical vocabulary in his subsequent writings do not suggest that these writings, like the lectures "On the Future of Our Educational Institutions" with which they are contemporaneous, should be considered a minor part of the Nietzschean corpus and of little interest to those interested in understanding Nietzsche's later philosophy. In the intervening sections of this chapter we have argued that there are grounds for believing that there is an underlying continuity in Nietzsche's thinking about truth and language from the early 1870s, when he composed "On Truth and Lie" and the notes on rhetoric, to the late 1880s, when his last texts were completed. If this argument is correct, it suggests that that the early writings on language and rhetoric might contain important clues as to how the later writings should be read, and that rather than being an "eccentric and minor part" of the Nietzschean corpus, the early theory of language and rhetoric could be a "possible main road to central problems in the interpretation of Nietzsche" (RT, 103–104).

As we noted earlier, this view of the unpublished writings has encountered strong resistance from some quarters. One opponent to this approach to Nietzsche is Maudemarie Clark, whose views were considered briefly in the opening section of this chapter. Clark's position with respect to Nietzsche's unpublished writings on language and rhetoric can be summarized as follows: while it might be true that there is some continuity in Nietzsche's thinking about truth and language from the early 1870s until the mid-1880s, in the writings of his last two active years Nietzsche came to repudiate these views and adopted instead a common sense conception of truth along with a newfound respect and appreciation for the senses, science, and scientific matters in general. Hence reading Nietzsche's later writings in light of the theory of rhetoric and language he formulated in the early 1870s ignores an important development in his thinking and makes the mistake of attributing to Nietzsche's later writings a theory of language he came to reject in place of the less fashionable, but more sober and philosophically interesting views of these texts. Given the degree to which these objections, if substantiated, would undermine the reading of Nietzsche pursued here, it would be apposite to briefly consider Clark's claim that the writings of Nietzsche's last two active years mark a substantial shift in his thinking about truth and represent an unambiguous repudiation of the views outlined in the unpublished writings on language.

We can evaluate Clark's interpretation most directly by considering her exegesis of a chapter of *Twilight of the Idols* entitled "'Reason' in Philosophy." Clark considers this chapter to be one of two possible counterexamples to the otherwise overwhelming evidence that Nietzsche's understanding of truth underwent a radical change after he completed the fifth book of *The Gay Science*. In the books that follow, Clark writes, "there is no evidence of Nietzsche's earlier denial of truth: no claim that the human world is a falsification, no claim that science, logic, or mathematics falsify reality . . . it becomes difficult to avoid the conclusion that his view of truth has changed radically" (NTP, 103).

The chapter "'Reason' in Philosophy" begins, in a way reminiscent of the first chapter of *Beyond Good and Evil*, with a consideration of the idiosyncrasies of philosophers, their veneration for being and their hatred for becoming. The valuation of being over becoming leads to distrust and disdain for the senses, which deceive us concerning the true world, the world of being, by showing nothing but change, passing away and the like. Nietzsche makes a point of excepting Heraclitus from this "philosophic folk." He does so, however, not because Heraclitus correctly interprets the testimony of the senses, but because he rejects their testimony for the right reason, namely, because he believes that the senses show things as if they have permanence and unity, rather than showing multiplicity and change. But

> Heraclitus too did the senses an injustice. They lie neither in the way the Eleatics believed, nor as he believed—they do not lie at all. What we *make* of their testimony, that alone introduces lies; for example the lie of thinghood, of substance, of permanence. 'Reason' is the cause of our falsification of the testimony of the senses. Insofar as the senses show becoming, passing away, and change, they do not lie. (TI.III. 2)

According to Clark, the falsification to which Nietzsche refers is not, as in "On Truth and Lie," an inevitable falsification, one necessarily involved in our perception and understanding of the empirical world, but rather a falsification that results from a philosophical interpretation of this world as a distorted copy or echo of the one true world, the world of being and permanence. "Because he places it in quotation marks, Nietzsche evidently does not use "reason" to refer to a faculty he believes human beings possess. He evidently refers instead to the interpretation of our faculty for reasoning . . . as a non-natural faculty . . . capable of knowledge of reality uncontaminated by connection to the senses" (NTP, 106). This interpretation would seem to gain support from Nietzsche's claim, in the following section, that "today we possess science precisely to the extent to which we have decided to *accept* the testimony of the senses—to the extent to which we sharpen them further, arm them, and have learned to think them through." Not only does this chapter of *Twilight* not contradict the interpretation of Nietzsche as a common-sense realist, it also appears to provide one of the strongest pieces of evidence in favor of Clark's interpretation and call for a reconsideration of the whole Nietzschean corpus. Indeed, in the last chapters of her book, which consider Nietzsche's conceptions of the will to power and the eternal recurrence of the same, Clark indicates the direction such a rethinking of Nietzsche should take.

Before too hastily accepting the need for such a radical reassessment of Nietzsche's thinking, let us take a second look at "'Reason' in Philosophy." As we have noted, the first three sections of this text read like a characteristically Nietzschean history of philosophical error. The error in this case is the devaluation of the senses and the empirical world for the sake of a true world of being and permanence. The conclusion of the argument, stated in section 3, that we possess science to the extent that we have decided to accept the testimony of the senses, along with the assertion in the previous section that the senses do not lie at all, seem to unequivocally support Clark's interpretation. However, a close reading of section 5 reveals that the issue is not as simple as Clark suggests. For, after considering that other philosophical idiosyncrasy, the insistence on believing that the highest values must be *causa sui*, Nietzsche returns to the problem of error and appearance and reconsiders the source of the erroneous belief in a world of being and permanence. Section 5 begins by repeating the observation that alteration, change, and becoming have traditionally been understood as signs of deception. As before, Nietzsche juxtaposes the philosophical interpretation of the testimony of the senses with what he takes to be the real cause of error, namely, the prejudice of reason:

> Today, conversely, precisely insofar as the prejudice of reason forces us to posit unity, identity, permanence, substance, cause, thinghood, being, we see ourselves *as it were caught in error, compelled into error.* So certain are we [. . .] that this is where the error lies. (emphasis added)

On Clark's interpretation this passage would merely restate what Nietzsche has already written in section 2, namely, that the senses do not lie and that error or lie is introduced by philosophical reason. But why would Nietzsche feel compelled to restate barely one page later what was already quite clearly expressed in section 2? The conclusion of the argument, stated in section 3, would seem to make this repetition even more gratuitous. But is this a repetition? Does Nietzsche merely restate in the opening paragraph of section 5 what he has already asserted in section 2? Let us recall Nietzsche's words: "What we *make* of their testimony, that alone introduces lies [. . .]. 'Reason' is the cause of our falsification of the testimony of the senses. Insofar as the senses show becoming, passing away, and change, they do not lie." Nietzsche emphasizes the word "make" [*machen*] in this passage. What is it exactly that we make? We might say, with Clark, that what we make is a second, true world behind the one given to us by the senses by means of the concepts of pure reason, being, thinghood, substance, and the like. But who are "we"? If the falsification of the empirical world is not an inevitable falsification, but, as Clark would have it, the result of a philosophical interpretation of this world, one would have to say that "we" refers to the community of philosophers. But then how is it with the rest of us? Do the senses give us a world free of philosophical falsification? This would seem to be implied in Nietzsche's assertion that the senses "do not lie at all." Yet Nietzsche does not say that the senses thereby tell the truth. In fact, Nietzsche qualifies this statement near the end of the passage when he says that the senses do not lie insofar as they "show becoming, passing away, and change."

The opening paragraph of section 5 gives a better indication of how to answer this question. Let us recall that here, Nietzsche once again identifies reason—this time without quotation marks—as the source of error, but with an important difference. Whereas in section two Nietzsche says it is what we make of the testimony of the senses that creates error, thus implying that we could choose to "make" something else of their testimony—truth, for example—the emphasis in section 5 is very different. We do not produce error, but are forced into it by reason. Nietzsche says exactly this: "precisely insofar as the prejudice of reason forces us [*zwingt uns*] to posit unity, identity [. . .] we see ourselves as it were caught in error, *compelled* into error" [*uns gewissermaassen verstrickt in den Irrthum*, necessitirt *zum Irrthum*].[60] Once again it is a question of "we," and let us not forget that at the beginning of section 5, Nietzsche draws attention to and emphasizes the word "we," emphasis which, as is the case with the word "compelled," is lost in the English translation.[61] But how is it that we are compelled into error? Nietzsche tells us: "It is no different in this case than with the movement of the sun: there our eye is the constant advocate of error, here it is our *language*." Language, reason's advocate, compels us into error. Nietzsche provides the following explanation for this compulsion:

> In its origin language belongs in the age of the most rudimentary form of psychology. We enter a realm of crude fetishism when we bring to light the basic presuppositions of the metaphysics of language, in plain talk, the presuppositions of reason. Everywhere *this fetishism* sees a doer and doing; it believes in will as *the* cause; it believes in the 'ego' [*Ich*], in the ego as being, in the ego as substance, and it *projects* this faith in the ego-substance to all things—only thereby does it first *create* the concept of 'thing.' Everywhere being is projected by thought, *pushed underneath*, as the cause; the concept of 'being' follows, and is a derivative of the concept of 'ego' [. . .]. Indeed, nothing has yet possessed a more naive power of persuasion than the error concerning

> being, as it has been formulated by the Eleatics, for example. After all, every word we say and every sentence speak in its favor! [. . .] I am afraid that we are not rid of God because we still have faith in grammar. (TI, III.5)[62]

Clark, in accordance with her interpretation of section 2, takes this passage to be a description of the philosophers' error of believing that the structure of the world is reflected in the structure of grammar. The philosopher posits categories on the basis of grammatical structures and concludes that these categories cannot be of empirical origin, because everything empirical contradicts them. This is perhaps clearest in the case of the category of substance and the subject-predicate structure of Indo-European languages. Rejecting faith in grammar would thus allow us to "make" something other than metaphysics from the testimony of the senses. But is the text not somewhat more complicated than this? Looking more closely, we find that the text does not say that the philosopher produces error by misinterpreting language, but rather that the philosophers' error is merely an error added to a previous, more original error produced by language itself. The philosophers seek to prove that the categories have a purely rational or divine cause, but according to the text, these categories themselves are already the result of an error whose source is the "basic presuppositions of the metaphysics of language," which Nietzsche describes as a "crude fetishism." Whereas in section 2, "reason" is said to be the "cause of our falsification of the senses," Nietzsche here locates reason itself within language, which is recognized in this passage as the root cause of our falsification. This is most explicit when Nietzsche describes "the presuppositions of reason" as a vulgar expression of the "basic presuppositions of the metaphysics of language" [*die Grundvoraussetzungen der Sprach-Metaphysik, auf deutsch, der Vernunft*]. What Nietzsche is in fact describing here is the linguistic or rhetorical structure of reason itself.[63]

That the philosophers' error is dependent on errors inherent in language is also implied in the temporal structure of Nietzsche's narrative that begins with the origin of language as a crude fetishism and proceeds to a time "very much later" when philosophers "concluded that these categories could not be derived from anything empirical." The same error concerning being, Nietzsche tells us, was made in India and in Greece. But this is no wonder, since "every word and every sentence we use supports it!"[64] This explains why Nietzsche claims that we are compelled into error, rather than merely deceived into believing something false. Although the senses do not lie insofar as they show becoming, change and alteration, we are forced into error as soon as we begin to refer to a world of stable objects existing in space and time, as for example, when we describe a single object, the sun, moving through the sky: "It is no different in this case than with the movements of the sun: there *our eye is the constant advocate of error*, here it is our language" (TI, III.5; emphasis added).

Just as the philosopher who posits a "true" world is unable to escape from error, but merely adds one error to another, so the artist finds herself in the same position. In the final section of "'Reason' in Philosophy," Nietzsche condenses his insights concerning the problem of error and appearance into four theses. The final thesis asserts that the distinction between a "true" and an "apparent" world as it has been thought by metaphysics "is only a suggestion of decadence, a symptom of *declining* life." The artist, who esteems appearance higher than reality, does not, however, provide an objection to this proposition because "'appearance' in this case means reality *once more*, only by way of selection, intensification, and correction." The artist does not seek a 'true' world, but rejoices in appearance as appearance, and in this sense is more profound than the scientist who seeks to uncover appearance at all cost. The artist is also more truthful than the scientist, for she "stops courageously at the surface, the fold, the skin [. . .] forms, tones, words" and recognizes that truth no longer remains "truth when the veils are withdrawn" (GS, P.4).

This conclusion throws into question Clark's claim that Nietzsche's history of how the 'true' world became a fable "indicates that he gives up ascribing reality to any other world than the empirical world (stage 5), *and* that he recognizes that this requires him to relinquish his claim that the empirical world is illusory" (NTP, 114). Having abandoned the idea of a 'true' world, Nietzsche loses all grounds for describing the empirical world as illusory, the result of error. But, as we have seen, neither the philosopher nor the artist is able to escape error. The tragic artist, who Nietzsche describes as saying yes to everything questionable, even to the terrible, creates an appearance that is reality once again. This means, however, that reality cannot be identified as empirical reality nor as "the common sense picture of the world of relatively enduring middle-sized objects or the scientific world view" (NTP, 108), as Clark would have it. Nietzsche's description of the artist's world of appearance as reality "once again" undermines the very oppositions of reality/appearance, literal/figural, upon which Clark's interpretation depends. The abolition of the apparent world in stage six of Nietzsche's history of an error does not leave us with the "empirical world," but rather with an apparent world once more. This is the conclusion Nietzsche draws at the end of section 2 of "'Reason' in Philosophy: "The 'apparent' world is the only one: the "true world" is merely *added by a lie*." The ostensible contradiction between this conclusion and the conclusion of section six of Nietzsche's history of an error disappears when we attempt to think of "appearance" as it is used in this sentence not in opposition to "reality," but as a name for the other of this metaphysical opposition. Nietzsche has, after all, reminded us often enough that the faith in opposite values is the metaphysicians' most fundamental faith, one produced by the inability of language to "get over its awkwardness" and cease talking "of opposites where there are only degrees and many subtleties of gradation" (BGE, 24).

Rather than representing a movement away from Nietzsche's writings on rhetoric and language, these texts and others from the same period (*Ecce Homo*, e.g.) invite comparison with the texts of the early 1870s. In fact, a comparative reading of these texts reveals that what Nietzsche describes in "'Reason' in Philosophy" as the projection of being by thought is nothing other than the tropological structure he described as metonymy in the lectures on rhetoric. Let us recall that in the notes on rhetoric, Nietzsche defines metonymy as

> the placement of one noun for another [. . .] the abstract nouns are properties within and outside us, which are torn away from their supports and set forth as autonomous entities. These concepts are posited as if they were the inner essence of the things: we attribute to appearances a cause which is in truth only an effect. (Rh, 59)

The text locates the origin of abstract terms in a tropological system of exchange whereby sensations that we locate as either inside or around us are projected onto an abstract quality or concept that is then believed to be the cause of the quality itself. Abstract nouns posited as causes are in fact revealed to be merely effects of effects. This argument, which lies at the heart of the theory of tropes formulated by Nietzsche in the unpublished writings on language and rhetoric, is the very same argument used by Nietzsche in "'Reason' in Philosophy" to describe how language is the constant advocate of error: "it believes in the ego, in the ego as being, in the ego as substance [. . .]. Everywhere "being" is projected by thought, pushed underneath, as the cause." A characteristic of consciousness, the apparent unity of the ego, is projected as the cause of that unity in the form of the concept of being. The concept of being is thus found to be aberrant, an effect of an effect, and not a cause at all. The philosophical interpretation of this error, of being as a rational concept or *causa sui*, is thus the error of an error. But it would be a mistake to conclude from this that disclosing of the philosophical error would set things right. For according to this text, our understanding of the empirical world, insofar as it rests on the oppositions such as cause and effect, is already the result of an error. The recognition that what we call "causality" is in fact a linguistic, tropological structure disturbs the entire system of binary oppositions that grounds classical metaphysics. It does not take much to recognize that what Nietzsche describes as projection in this text puts into question our understanding of the oppositions cause/effect, before/after, and inside/outside. What initially seemed to be a "closed and coherent system" reveals itself to be "arbitrary, open system in which the attributes of causality, [of temporality] and of location can be deceptively exchanged, substituted for each other at will" (RT, 107–108).

The recognition that the same rhetorical structure described by Nietzsche as giving rise to the Platonic *ideai* in the lectures on rhetoric is used to account for the production of the concept being in "'Reason' in Philosophy," one of the texts described by Clark as evidence of Nietzsche's 'conversion' to common-sense realism, undermines Clark's claim that Nietzsche's understanding of truth changed radically in the writings of his last two years.[65] This does not, of course, explain why Nietzsche never published any of the other texts on language and rhetoric from this period. It does, however, provide compelling reasons for reconsidering the place of these texts within the Nietzschean corpus and, consequently, the importance of language in Nietzsche's philosophy as a whole.

Chapter 3

Language and Rhetoric in *The Birth of Tragedy*

The domain of metaphysics and the province of 'absolute' truth have unquestioningly been placed on a par with poetry and religion [. . .]. Metaphysics [. . .] is essentially construction; on the other hand, it is art, namely, the art of a conceptual poetry [Begriffsdichtung]. *What is clear, however, is that metaphysics, neither as religion nor as art, has anything to do with the so-called 'truths or things-in-themselves.'*
—Nietzsche to Deussen, May, 1868

Your [friend] Ribbeck[1] *has given me particular pleasure with his request for testimony and proof. How then should the testimony run approximately? One struggles to get to the origin of the most puzzling things and now the esteemed reader demands that the entire problem should be solved through testimony, probably out of the mouth of Apollo himself, or would a word from Athena be just as good? For some people this would be even better.*
—Nietzsche to Rohde, August 4, 1871

OUT OF THE SPIRIT OF MUSIC

The Birth of Tragedy seems an unlikely place to look for Nietzsche's theory of language and rhetoric, or at least for traces of a theory worth looking for. From almost every perspective the text seems to bespeak nothing less than a denigration of language and its signifying power in favor of music, which in virtue of its unique relationship to the will opens up the possibility of an intuitive, pre-linguistic understanding of being. Language, an insignificant and pale medium, "is repeatedly denigrated for its inability to 'approach' . . . the essence of music and its 'world symbolizing function,'" which it can only poorly copy.[2] This view of *The Birth of Tragedy* and its theory of language is almost universally held among readers of Nietzsche and has been partly responsible for the peculiar incomprehension with which the book is often received; one might even be tempted to say that the low estimation of the book among many of Nietzsche's auditors is inversely proportionate to the incredulity with which they react to reading Nietzsche endorse views he will soon decisively reject. The apparent contrast between the unabashed metaphysics of *The Birth of Tragedy* and the schooled suspicion of the later writings provide almost irrefutable evidence of a development in Nietzsche's thinking. Even those who, quite justifiably, might shy away from the trappings of overly schematized genetic interpretations would be hard pressed to deny that there is a development from the metaphysical philosophy of *The Birth of Tragedy* to the linguistic aestheticism of Nietzsche's unpublished essay "On Truth and Lie in the Extra-Moral Sense," written less than two years later.[3] This brief essay is usually, and perhaps correctly, seen as the initial step away from Nietzsche's first book and its Schopenhauerian metaphysics.[4] It is not difficult to see why. In contrast with the earlier text, "On Truth and Lie" contains no references to music and to the possibility of an intuitive, pre-linguistic understanding of being. The absence of any discussion of music, itself quite striking, becomes most marked when we consider the critique of the concept essayed by Nietzsche in this text. Expecting an elaboration of his earlier view that language reaches the height of its expressive power only when accompanied by music, we find instead an immanent critique of the concept which takes its cue from a recognition of the tropological structure of language. It comes as no surprise, therefore, when we read that the origin of art is no longer to be found in nature's own artistic drives, the Apollinian and the Dionysian, but rather within language itself. "The drive to form metaphors, that fundamental desire in human beings," writes Nietzsche,

> is in truth not overcome [. . .] by the fact that out of its diminished products, the concepts, a regular and rigid new world is built up for it as a prison fortress. It seeks a new province for its activities and a different riverbed and finds it in myth and generally in art. (TL, 254)

Philippe Lacoue-Labarthe, who was perhaps the first to explore the relationship between these texts, expresses what has become a commonly held view when he describes rhetoric as a "discovery" of Nietzsche's which, "once introduced, begins to destroy everything. . . ."[5] One of those things destroyed is the theory of language articulated by Nietzsche in *The Birth of Tragedy*, "which falls apart when rhetoric enters the scene" (D, 26).

The change in Nietzsche's view of language seems to parallel another, closely related, movement in Nietzsche's thought, namely, the turn away from Schopenhauer and Wagner. Most readers of *The Birth of Tragedy* unquestioningly assume that the book is most profitably read as the product of Nietzsche's early obsession with Wagner and Schopenhauer. Again, it is not difficult to see why. Nietzsche's glowing dedication to Wagner, his correspondence, which contains unbridled praise for both Schopenhauer and Wagner,[6] and the many references to his two mentors in the text itself all point to a profound and direct influence. Considered from a philosophical perspective, Nietzsche's views on the dependency of language on music and the latter's unique relationship to the will, are clear signs that Nietzsche wrote *The Birth of Tragedy* "as a disciple of Schopenhauer."[7] The view of *The Birth of Tragedy* as an undisguised homage to Schopenhauer and Wagner and the assertion that Nietzsche's views on language changed following his discovery of rhetoric are, of course, connected. The discovery of rhetoric can, in retrospect, be seen as the lever Nietzsche needed in order to free himself from the suffocating influence of his two mentors. It seems reasonable to conclude that once Nietzsche had gained his independence, he could afford to discard rhetoric and take up more important matters, which he was able to do shortly thereafter. *The Birth of Tragedy* thus seems doubly unsuited to serve as a starting point for an investigation into Nietzsche's theory of language: not only is the theory elucidated in that book not worthy of serious attention *as* a theory of language, but Nietzsche was to give up this theory shortly after the book's publication.

Given the obviousness of this point it seems that only a critical pedantry of the most extreme sort would inspire one to look to Nietzsche's first book for his theory of language. There are, however, compelling reasons why one might want to pursue this line of thought, however unpromising it may appear. One such reason is the great internal tension to be found in this book, a tension which makes it, in Nietzsche's own words "an impossible book," one which, according to John Sallis, "remains at variance with itself, remains divided from itself, lacking identity."[8] Clearly one reason for this, as Sallis points out, is the book's suspension between tragedy and philosophy, a tension revealed, though not resolved, by Nietzsche's posing the question of whether "the birth of an 'artistic Socrates' is altogether a contradiction in terms" (BT, 14). Nietzsche was well aware of this tension. In early 1870 he confesses to his friend Erwin Rohde that "scholarship, art and philosophy are now growing inside me so much that in any case I'll give birth to centaurs one day" (KSAB, 3/58). A second reason for this tension, not entirely unrelated to the first, involves a different kind of division than that between tragedy and philosophy, one which could tentatively be described as a conflict between the book's explicit statements concerning language and its subordinate status and the theory of signification implicitly at work in this text (a theory which will ultimately make it impossible to distinguish between implicit and explicit meaning). To put this thought in the form of a question, we can ask whether there is in fact a genuine development in Nietzsche's understanding of language in the early 1870s, or, despite all appearances to the contrary, whether the same tropological view of language expounded by Nietzsche in "On Truth and Lie" is not perhaps already operative in *The Birth of Tragedy*?

ON MUSIC AND IMAGE

The Birth of Tragedy is often taken to be Nietzsche's most unified and metaphysical work. "It might be," writes Lacoue-Labarthe, "ultimately Nietzsche's only 'Book'" (D, 17, note 10). This description, although somewhat ironic given the almost haphazard manner in which the text was composed,[9] certainly seems justified on both a rhetorical and thematic level. The quasi-dialectical relationship of Apollo and Dionysus and Nietzsche's frequent references to primordial unity and reconciliation with nature reinforce the totalizing power of the book's ontological vocabulary.[10]

As is well known, the most immediate source of this ontology are the writings of Schopenhauer, which Nietzsche had come across by chance in a bookstore some years earlier. Following Schopenhauer, Nietzsche posits a tripartite division of being.[11] The first and most central element in this schema is the will, which is described at different junctures in the text as the "thing-in-itself" (BT, 16) and "the truly existent and primordial unity, the eternally suffering and contradictory" (BT, 4).[12] The will constitutes the essence of the world as such, and it is from this source that the all other beings come into existence. The second element in Nietzsche's schema is the empirical world. In accordance with his understanding of the will as the thing-in-itself, empirical reality is said not to exist independently, but is continuously produced by the will as its "representation" [*Vorstellung*] or "appearance" [*Erscheinung*]. Although it objectifies itself in appearances, the will as such does not appear in the world, for this would violate the distinction between "the concept of essence [*Wesen*] and that of appearance," according to which the will is "the unaesthetic-in-itself" [*das an sich Unaesthetische*] (BT, 6). The third and final element in the division of being is representational art and language, which are mere copies of the representations and appearances produced by the will.

Although the proximal source of this ontological schema is Schopenhauer, its origins can be traced back as far as Plato and the division between idea, appearance, and representation as three distinct modes of being.[13] Two important affinities between Nietzsche and Plato deserve to be noted. First, like Plato, Nietzsche claims that imagistic art and language, being representational in nature, cannot depict true being but are destined to be mere copies of appearance. In a formula that echoes Plato's description of painting as "imitation of a phantom" [*mimēsis phantasmatos*],[14] Nietzsche refers to the naïve or Apollinian work of art—of which Raphael's *Transfiguration* is an example—as the "semblance of appearance" (BT, 4).[15] Second, Nietzsche shares with Plato the conviction that "the primal one" can be known. For Plato, the path to the idea of the Good is dialectics, argument without the use of the senses. Nietzsche, on the other hand, eschews this possibility and instead looks to art as a means of knowing the will. However, since imagistic art, together with language, can only produce copies of appearance and hence could never provide access to the will, the source of all appearance, there must be an art form that is not merely representational, but that is able to depict true reality. That is to say, a type of imitation or *mimēsis* must exist that does not merely depict what is given, but which constitutes a genuine doubling or repetition such that the copy maintains an essential relationship with the original. The copy would constitute, in the strictest sense of the word, a re-*presentation* of the original. The art form that performs this function is, of course, music.

Music, Nietzsche tells us, is different in "character and origin" [*Charakter und Ursprung*] from images and concepts which are essentially representational and whose origins lie within the individuated world outside of true being. In contrast with these, "the origin of music lies beyond all individuation," a fact which allows music to be essentially non-representational.[16] The advantage of this is that music is thus the one art form which is not merely a "copy of appearance [*Abbild der Erscheinung*] but an immediate copy [*unmittelbar Abbild*] of the will itself, and which therefore represents to everything physical in the world, the metaphysical, to all appearance, the thing in itself" (BT, 16). As the immediate copy of the will, music is able, paradoxically, to represent the essence of the world without itself being representational. Unindividuated and non-representational, music occupies a unique place between that essence and its appearance as empirical reality.

An important consequence of music's unique status is that it is completely—and necessarily—independent of both images and concepts; since what is in truth can never be dependent upon that which is individuated and hence mere imitation. Nietzsche makes this quite plain following his description of the lyric poet in section 6:

> Our whole discussion insists that lyric poetry is dependent on the spirit of music just as music in its absolute sovereignty does not need the image [*Bild*] and the concept [*Begriff*], but merely endures them as accompaniments. The poems of the lyricist can express nothing that did not already lie in the vast universality and absoluteness in [. . .] music. (BT, 6)

In an important fragment written in the Spring of 1871 and included in a fifty-nine-page manuscript that constituted an early version of *The Birth of Tragedy*,[17] Nietzsche puts the point in slightly different terms:

> There can, therefore, be no question of a necessary relationship between poetry [*Lied*] and music; for the two worlds of tone [*Ton*] and image, which are here employed together, stand too far from one another to be able to enter into more than an external relationship [*äußerliche Verbindung*]; the poem is only a symbol [*das Lied is eben nur Symbol*] [. . .]. In respect to the highest god who actually reveals himself, the symbol no longer has any meaning; it appears now as something offensively superficial [*eine beleidigende Äußerlichkeit*]. (1871, 366)

Leaving aside the remarkable neo-Platonic tone of this last sentence, these two citations state quite plainly that with respect to music images are merely arbitrary signs or "hieroglyphs" that have nothing more than an external relationship to that universal medium. Lying outside of truth and being, images are improper and insignificant. The distinction between music and image can rightly be said to be the linchpin of Nietzsche's theory of tragedy, which is grounded in a belief in the ontological and semiological superiority of music over images, and what is decisive for this theory, in the possibility of a translation of music into images.

The translation from music into images is not extraneous to tragedy, but rather constitutes its very essence: "The essence of tragedy [. . .] can only be interpreted as a manifestation and representation in images of Dionysian states, as the visible symbolization of music, as the dream-world of a Dionysian rapture [*Rausch*]" (BT, 14).[18] Nietzsche employs an explicitly linguistic vocabulary when, two sections later, he describes "the metaphysical joy in the tragic" as "a translation [*Übersetzung*] of instinctive unconscious Dionysian wisdom into the language of images" (BT, 16). Since tragedy depends on the possibility of a translation of music into images, that is to say, of the Dionysian into the Apollinian, it follows that what holds true of the relationship between music and image must also hold true of the relationship between Apollo and Dionysus. Nietzsche says precisely this when he tells us, in the middle of section 16, that the question of the relationship between music and image is a simplified form of the question of the relationship between Apollo and Dionysus:

> Perhaps we may touch on that fundamental problem [of the essence of Greek tragedy] by asking: what aesthetic effect results when the essentially separate [*an sich getrennten*] art-forces, the Apollinian and the Dionysian, enter into simultaneous activity? Or more briefly: how is music related to image and concept? (BT, 16)

In what follows we will need to examine Nietzsche's explanation of just how it is that this translation between the Apollinian and the Dionysian, two "fully separate spheres of expression," is possible. However, before penetrating further into the complications of Nietzsche's argument, we would do well to first turn our attention to one of the key terms that figure in this translation, namely, image or *Bild*.

THE FIGURATIVE IMAGE

At first glance, the word *Bild* seems to have a clear and unambiguous meaning: image, with a specific connotation of visual image. This is consistent with the manner in which *Bild* is usually translated (into English) and understood. Thus Walter Kaufmann, in the passage cited above, renders the German sentence "*Wie verhält sich die Musik zu Bild und Begriff?*" as "How is music related to image and concept?" Or again, in a passage from section 8, Kaufmann translates the term "*Bilderwelt*'" as "world of images." This tendency is also confirmed by Silk and Stern, who render Nietzsche's reference to Apollo, in section 1, as the "*Götterbild des principii individuationis*" as the "divine image of the *principium individuationis*" (NoT, 170). This manner of translating *Bild* is consistent with Nietzsche's description of the "image world of dreams" [*Bilderwelt des Traumes*] in which the natural Apollinian artistic drive satisfies itself, which draws heavily on the visual connotations of *Bild*:

> It is not only the agreeable and friendly images [*Bilder*] that he experiences as something universally intelligible [. . .] the whole divine comedy of life, including the inferno, also pass before him, not like mere shadows on the wall—for he lives and suffers with these scenes—and yet not without that fleeting sensation of illusion. (BT, 1)

The same is also true of this passage from section 8:

> For a genuine poet, metaphor is not a rhetorical figure, but a vicarious image [*stellvertretendes Bild*] that he actually beholds in place of a concept. (BT, 8)

There seems to be little reason to doubt that *Bild* deserves be translated as image and understood, primarily, as visual image.

Probing the text more deeply, we find traces of another, more complex and nuanced sense of *Bild* that could prove to have an important bearing on our attempt to elucidate Nietzsche's claim that the essence of tragedy is a translation of music into images. In this case, *Bild* is be understood both as visual image—which the passages cited above clearly indicate is appropriate—and as 'figure' in both senses of this word, namely, as something possessing form and as a rhetorical figure. The latter sense is present in the passage Nietzsche cites from Christian Gellert in section 14, where truth is said "*durch ein Bild*" [by means of a figure].[19] This broader interpretation of *Bild* is consonant with the meaning of the word in colloquial German, which, in addition to visual image, can be used to mean metaphor and simile, as is the case in the expression "*in Bildern reden*" which means to speak figuratively,[20] as well as something possessing form, a meaning reflected in the verb *bilden*—to form, fashion, shape or to be formed, hence *Bildung*—and "*bildende Künste*"; the latter principally refers to sculpture and the plastic arts, but can also be used in reference to painting and the other visual arts. Choosing to hear all of these different senses in the word *Bild* would place it on a par with the word *Schein*, which John Sallis has recently argued "needs to be read in its full range of senses: shine, look, appearance, semblance, illusion . . . since clearly it is not here a matter of simply [*sic*] polysemy" (CRS, 25).[21] As Sallis' remark suggests, it is not simply a question of choosing among the various meanings of a word, of finding the most appropriate meaning for a given context, but rather of allowing the multiple meanings of a term such as *Bild* to be heard along side one another.

Choosing to hear image and figure—in both of its senses—in the word *Bild* does not require a leap of the imagination, as it were, but rather what Nietzsche in another context refers to as the ability to "read what is hidden between the lines,"[22] for the various meanings of *Bild* are inscribed in Nietzsche's text from the very beginning. In the opening section of *The Birth of Tragedy*, we read that the figures of Apollo and Dionysus reveal that

> in der griechischen Welt ein ungeheurer Gegensatz, nach Ursprung und Zielen, zwischen der Kunst des Bildners, der apollinischen, und der unbildlichen Kunst der Musik, als der des Dionysus, besteht.
>
> in the Greek world there is a monstrous opposition, in origin and end, between the art of the plastic artist, the Apollinian, and the non-imagistic art of music, that of the Dionysian.

Since this is the first description of the distinction between Apollinian and Dionysian art, it would seem rather important to attend to what Nietzsche has written. The focal point of the passage is the distinction between what Nietzsche calls "*die Kunst des Bildners*" and "*die unbildlichen Kunst der Musik,*" expressions that are most frequently rendered as "the art of sculpture" and "the non-imagistic art of music."[23] Although there are good grounds for translating *Bildner* as sculpture—for example, Nietzsche's references to Apollinian music as "Doric architecture in tones" (BT, 2) and the "artistic structure of Apollinian culture" (BT, 3)—something is surely lost in such a translation. This should be clear from the fact that (i) Nietzsche never explicitly discusses sculpture in *The Birth of Tragedy*—the two examples of Apollinian art he considers are the Homeric epic and Raphael's *Transfiguration*—and (ii) the contrast Nietzsche wants to draw in this passage depends on the fact that music is described as non-imagistic, which is obscured, rather than captured by translating "*die Kunst des Bildners*" as sculpture, rather than, for example, as "the art of the plastic artist." By contrasting "*die Kunst des Bildners*" and "*die unbildlichen Kunst der Musik*," Nietzsche wants us to understand the plastic artist as a "form-giver" in the quite literal sense that it is under the influence of the Apollinian dream inspiration that the non-imagistic Dionysian music takes form, that is to say, is translated into an image. This understanding of the Apollinian is consistent with Apollo's role as the god of the *principium individuationis* who "exacts measure [*Maass*] from his disciples," which is to say, "adherence to the boundaries of the individual" (BT, 4). This requirement of remaining within oneself—the very opposite of Dionysian *ecstasis*, which is precisely a being-outside-oneself—is implicit within the very conception of *Bild*.[24] The imagistic character of our dream experience produces a sensation of its unreality, which protects the dreamer from any pathological or excessive reactions:

> But even when this dream reality is most intense, we still have the sensation of its shine glimmering through [. . .]. We must include in our image of Apollo that delicate boundary which the dream image [*Traumbild*] must not overstep lest it have a pathological effect [. . .] we must keep in mind that measured restraint [*maassvolle Begrenzung*], that freedom from wilder emotions, that calm of the god of the plastic arts [*des Bildnergottes*]. (BT, 1)[25]

And in section 5:

> Thus, by this mirror of shine, [the plastic artist][26] is protected from becoming one and fused with his figures.

That *Bildner* should be understood principally as plastic artist, the form-giver, is confirmed by reading two further passages from section 1 in which the word appears. The first is to be found in the second paragraph of section 1 (in both the German and English texts), where Nietzsche recounts Lucretius' belief that it was in dreams that "the glorious divine figures first appeared to the souls of men; in dreams the great plastic artist [*der grosse Bildner*] beheld the splendid bodies [*entzückenden Gliederbau*] of superhuman beings." Here, as in our previous example, the primary sense of *Bildner* is that of the form-giver. The great plastic artist beholds the bodies of the gods in a dream and gives form to them in sculptures, bas reliefs and mosaics. This is reflected in Kaufmann's rendering of *Bildner* not as sculptor, as before, but rather as "shaper," which perhaps comes closer to the sense of form-giver than plastic artist, but at the cost of some stylistic elegance. The second passage comes from the following page where we find Apollo described as the god of "all plastic powers" [*bildnerischen Kräfte*]; a description that Kaufmann and Sallis render as "all plastic energies," and "all plastic powers," respectively. In this context, "*bildnerisch*" can only mean plastic powers or something quite similar, not, as Silk and Stern would have it, "energies embodied in the visual arts" (NoT, 170). The tension between these two extremes—between *Bild* as visual image one the one hand, and *Bildner* as sculptor on the other—is resolved if we read *Bild* as both visual image and figure, where figure is understood both as that which possesses form and as a rhetorical figure.

So understood, *Bild* and *Bildner*—in their nominal and adjectival forms—would come to have overlapping meanings; something which is implied by the German, where *Bildner* clearly contains *Bild* as its root, but lost when the words are translated into English as 'image' and 'sculptor.'[27] That the closeness of the relationship between the two German words is retained by the readings I have suggested is confirmed by the etymology of the word plastic, which comes from the Greek *plastikos,* which in turn derives from the verb *plassein*, meaning to mold or form. The plastic artist, then, is literally the form-giver, and the image or figure, that which is formed.

What then is the relationship between image and dream? One clue to how we should understand this relationship—beyond the obvious sense that both images and dreams are visually perceived—is given to us in the continuation of one of the passages cited above: "Apollo, as the god of all plastic powers, is at the same time the soothsaying god." This description is repeated by Nietzsche in section 2, where he refers to Apollo as "the Delphic god." These references to Apollo's role as the god of the Delphic oracle seem obscure, not to say superfluous, and do not appear to contribute in any substantive way to Nietzsche's argument; perhaps one reason there are almost no references to the Delphic oracle in the literature on *The Birth of Tragedy*. However, Nietzsche's references to Apollo's role as the soothsaying god become clearer when we understand image in the manner suggested above, namely, as visual image and figure. (Here the emphasis is to be placed on the sense of figure contained in the expression 'figurative language.') For it is precisely in the sense of image as figure that the relationship between the various components of Apollo's description become clear, namely, as the god of plastic arts and the Delphic god. What the plastic arts and the sayings of the Delphic oracle have in common is that they are both constituted by figures which, in turn, need to be read. Understanding image in this way also sheds light on Nietzsche's insistence that we first think of the Apollinian drive as the world of dreams. Dreams, like images, need to be interpreted. This is precisely what Hans Sachs describes as the poet's true task:

> Mein Freud, das grad' ist Dichters Werk,
> dass er sein Träumen deut' und merk.'
> Glaubt mir, des Menschen wahrster Wahn
> wird ihm im Traume aufgethan:
> all' Dichkunst und Poëterei
> ist nichts als Wahrtraum-Deuterei.
>
> The poet's task is this, my friend,
> to read his dreams and comprehend.
> Believe me, the truest human fancy seems
> to be revealed to us in dreams:
> all poems and versification
> are but true dreams' interpretation.

A more explicit connection between dream interpretation and soothsaying is drawn by Orestes in *The Libation Bearers*, who, by interpreting Clytamnestra's dream, also assumes the role of seer:

> I'll play the seer—
> it all fits together, watch!
> If the serpent came from the same place as I . . .
> As she bred this sign, this violent prodigy
> so she dies by violence. I turn serpent,
> I kill her. So the vision says.

The leader of the chorus responds:

> You are the seer for me, I like your reading.
> Let it come! But now rehearse your friends.
> Say do this, or don't do that—[28]

As the god of the Delphic oracle and of all plastic powers, Apollo is also the god of figuration. This is not a minor point, for as we shall see, it is Apollo who effects a translation of Dionysian music into allegorical dream images [*gleichnissartige Traumbilde*], and it is precisely this figuration, this *form*ation of music into image, which makes tragedy possible.

READING APOLLO AND DIONYSUS

The interpretation of Apollo offered above is supported by a number of Greek sources. Perhaps the most famous of these sources is Heraclitus' saying that "The lord whose oracle is in Delphi neither declares not conceals, but gives a sign [*semainei*]."[29] What Heraclitus refers to as a sign in this fragment is precisely what Nietzsche names as image: a figure that signifies by referring to another figure outside itself; a figure, therefore, that stands in the place of another and that must be read in order to be understood. This sense of a figure as a place holder is evocatively illustrated by a passage from the *Iliad* in which Apollo rescues his charge Aineias by replacing him on the battlefield with a figure, a spitting image:

> Apollo . . . caught Aineias now away from the onslaught, and set him
> in the sacred keep of Pergamos where was built his own temple. . . .
> he of the silver bow, Apollo, fashioned an image
> in the likeness of Aineias himself and in armor like him,
> and all about this image brilliant Acaians and Trojans
> hewed at each other. . . .[30]

The brilliant Acaians and Trojans do not, however, understand Apollo's image. They are deceived by the image of Aineias because they are unable to read it, just as Oedipus fails to correctly read the prophecy he receives at Delphi and, by fleeing from Corinth, runs directly into the face of the terrible fate which awaits him.

Understanding Apollo as the god of figuration also offers an important clue as to how *The Birth of Tragedy* itself is to be read. Let us recall that in section 1 Nietzsche refers to Apollo as the "divine image of the *principium individuationis*." Apollo is not merely the god of figuration, he is a figure himself, which, like the very figures he creates, must be read to be understood. In the opening sentences of his book Nietzsche tells us that not just Apollo, but Dionysus too is a figure: together these figures [*Gestalten*] hold the key to understanding the "profound mysteries" of the ancient Greeks' view of art:

> The names [the Apollinian and the Dionysian] we borrow from the Greeks, who disclose the profound mysteries of their view of art to those who are insightful, not, to be sure, in concepts, but in the intensely clear figures of their gods. (BT, 1)

The figures of Apollo and Dionysus are penetratingly clear, but only, so it seems, to those who are insightful, that is to say, to those who are able to read these figures. This is no small task, because as Nietzsche makes abundantly clear in the rest of his book, these figures have never been correctly read. But is this not then a paradox? The appearance of a paradox is diminished if we read the foregoing remark from section 1 as a reference to the great difficulties involved in a genuinely historical and philosophical understanding of Greek tragedy that arise out of the tremendous distance separating the moderns from the ancients. Nietzsche explicitly alludes to this problem in the preparatory studies to *The Birth of Tragedy*. In the first of two lectures on tragedy he was to give at Basel in January 1870, "The Greek Music Drama," Nietzsche declares that "the Aeschylus and Sophocles known to us are only known as textbook poets, as librettists, that is to say, they are unknown to us" (KSA 1, 517). Near the end of the essay, after repeating this statement, Nietzsche gives the following explanation as to why the Greek poets are unknown to us: "We are incompetent [*incompetent*] concerning Greek tragedy because its central effect derives for the most part from an element which is lost to us [*das uns verloren gegangen ist*]" (KSA 1, 528). The distance separating us from the ancients rules out the possibility of a direct encounter with their artistic doctrines, one which could be equated with the vain historicist attempt to relive what the Greeks experienced, or which could be reduced to a mere conceptual analysis of manuscripts. Rather we can only approach the Greeks indirectly, by reading the signs which have been passed down by the tradition. These signs, Nietzsche tells us, are the "intensely clear figures of their gods."[31]

Seen in this light, the project of *The Birth of Tragedy* is comparable with that of *On The Genealogy of Morals*; in fact, one could very well say that Nietzsche's first book represents his initial attempt at genealogy. In both cases, historical understanding is understood as a type of reading—something Nietzsche reminds us in the Preface to the *Genealogy* that "has been unlearned most thoroughly nowadays"—a reading of figures, to be precise, which have been misunderstood heretofore because they betray their secrets only to those who have mastered the art of reading well. Nietzsche's description of genealogy in the Preface to that book reads, with some allowances for the differences in subject matter, like an elucidation of the first paragraph of *The Birth of Tragedy*:

> For it must be obvious which color is a hundred times more vital for a genealogist of morals than blue: namely *gray*, that is, what is documented, what can actually be ascertained and has actually existed, in short, the entire long hieroglyphic script, so hard to decipher, of the moral past of mankind. (GM, P.7)[32]

The figures of Apollo and Dionysus are two such hieroglyphs. Accordingly, it would be wrong, as has often been done, to reproach Nietzsche for employing a strategy which would take "the Greek Apollo and Dionysus, extend their significance, raise it onto a symbolic plane, and then use his symbols as quasi-historical verities like the 'real' gods themselves" (NoT, 170). For by denying that we can ever have direct access to the Greek experience of art, Nietzsche has problematized precisely that which Silk and Stern refer to as "the 'real' gods themselves." Moreover, if one understands Dionysus and Apollo figuratively, the question then becomes one of reading, not of 'historical fact.'[33]

SYMBOL AND ALLEGORY

This is precisely what is at issue when we consider the distinction between music and image, to which we can now return. The relationship between music and images and their respective modes of signification is illuminated by attending to a parallel distinction Nietzsche makes between symbolic [*symbolisch*] and allegorical [*gleichnissartig*] modes of signification.[34] The importance of this distinction has, to the best of my knowledge, not been adequately remarked upon in the literature on Nietzsche and *The Birth of Tragedy*; a fact due no doubt in part to philosophers' general reluctance or inability to recognize so-called literary distinctions, and partly to the ambiguity of the word *Gleichnis*, which "has the general sense of *resemblance* or *image* . . . but . . . can designate *comparison* and, consequently, *symbol*, *allegory*, *parable*, etc." (D, 28).[35] In the case of American and British Nietzsche scholarship, the situation has not been helped by the fact that in his translation of *The Birth of Tragedy*, Walter Kaufmann systematically obscures the difference between *Symbol* and *Gleichnis* by translating both words with the English word 'symbol.' The one exception to this practice is an instance where the use of 'symbol' would have resulted in an obviously awkward translation.[36] However, the most significant reason why this distinction has all but been ignored would seem to be the fact that Nietzsche fails to draw a distinction between *Symbol* and *Gleichnis*; a state of affairs which has lead Lacoue-Labarthe to remark that "Nietzsche uses these two terms interchangeably [*indifféremment*]" (D, 28).[37] Although Lacoue-Labarthe is a very careful reader of Nietzsche, this judgment is almost certainly premature. For if we look closely at the text of *The Birth of Tragedy*, there are clear indications that not only does Nietzsche not use *Symbol* and *Gleichnis* interchangeably, but that, on the contrary, at least in the case of *Gleichnis* he is quite careful, one might even say particular, about how and when the word is used. A more attentive reading of the text reveals that Nietzsche uses *Gleichnis* almost exclusively when he is considering the relationship between music and image, and more tellingly, only to describe the image and its mode of signification. That is to say, although Nietzsche uses both *Symbol* and *Gleichnis* in reference to image, or its equivalent, word—as for example when, in section 2, he writes of the "symbolism of the word" and "allegorical dream images"—*Gleichnis* is never used in connection with music, either to describe music and its mode of signification, or to describes music's relationship to the will. Music is always *symbolisch*, never *gleichnissartig*. The significance of this fact should not escape us, for it points to the distinct possibility that the distinction between *Symbol* and *Gleichnis* concerns the disparate ways in which music and image signify. As we have noted, music and image are not merely two distinct artistic media which can be distinguished solely on the basis of *what*, not *how* they signify, rather what distinguishes music and image is precisely the fact that they signify in radically different ways: music, non-individuated and non-representative, is able to reveal the truth of being, while image, whose origin is to be found within the world of individuation, can only depict the appearance of that which is already appearance, and thus already removed from being. Music, in virtue of its connection with the will is in truth and being, while image is twice removed from the same.

Given this state of affairs, we might reasonable expect that Nietzsche would use two different terms to describe the radical differences which exist between music and images and their respective modes of signification; differences, which we have noted previously, are central to the theory of tragedy Nietzsche puts forward in *The Birth of Tragedy*. Why then the apparent equivocation between *Symbol* and *Gleichnis*, an equivocation which threatens to obscure the distinction itself? One reason can be traced back to a fundamental ambiguity in the usage of rhetorical terms such as symbol, metaphor, and allegory, which, in the first instance, are used to refer to figurative language in general. When we speak of an author's metaphorical style or use of symbolism, we are using these terms synonymously to refer to one feature of an author's writing; in this case metaphor and symbol are genuinely interchangeable. Yet rhetorical terms also have more narrow and technical meanings which, as any handbook of rhetoric will illustrate, allow us to distinguish between the logic of symbolic, metaphoric, and allegorical figures. For example, we refer to the cross as a symbol of the relationship between God and man, and not as a metaphor for this relationship. The cross is a symbol because its significance exceeds that of the concrete object, the physical cross—in this sense it is figurative—yet the relationship between the physical cross and its meaning is non-arbitrary, for the cross is concretely connected to the relationship it figures. As a symbol the cross signifies the unity of concrete and abstract meaning. By contrast, metaphor signifies a correspondence between two objects that is based on resemblance or similarity.

These distinctions, which might as first seem merely scholastic and of interest only to rhetoricians or students of literature, become philosophically important when they can be shown to play a constitutive role in the argument of a given text. This is especially true of a text like *The Birth of Tragedy*, whose central concern is the various modes of representation—musical, imagistic, and linguistic—and their relationship to one another, and for an author like Nietzsche, whose relationship to the German romantics, for whom the distinction between symbol and allegory was of great importance, remains largely unexplored.

There is evidence, I would like to suggest, of both senses—the general and the technical—in Nietzsche's use of *Symbol*, and it is due to a failure to attend to this polysemy that has made it appear as if the two terms are used synonymously. Recognizing this ambiguity within Nietzsche's text is the first step towards grasping the distinction between *Symbol* and *Gleichnis*.

The general meaning of *Symbol* is evident from the following passage from section 2:

> In the Dionysian dithyramb man is incited to the greatest exaltation of all his symbolic [*symbolisch*] faculties [. . .] the entire symbolism [*Symbolik*] of the body is called into play, not the mere symbolism of the lips, face and speech, but the whole pantomime of dancing, forcing every member into rhythmic movement.

In contrast, the word carries a different weight and meaning in the following passage from section 6:

> The world symbolism [*Weltsymbolik*] of music can never completely be approached [*erschöpfend beizukommen*] by language, because music stands in symbolic relation [*sie sich . . . symbolisch bezieht*] to the primordial contradiction and primordial pain in the heart of the primal unity, and therefore symbolizes [*symbolisirt*] a sphere which is beyond and prior to all appearance.

In the second passage, the term *Symbol*—which is here used in its nominal, adjectival and verbal forms—has a narrower and more technical sense than in the first passage. This is evident from the fact that language, which was described as a type of symbolism in the first passage, is distinguished from music by the fact that it does not stand in a symbolic relationship with the primal unity. The world symbolism of music is of a higher order than the symbolism of speech because, in contrast with language, music has a truly symbolic relationship with the primal unity. In other words, music is part of and belongs to the primal unity, while language does not.

The recognition that Nietzsche uses *Symbol* in both a general and a technical sense in *The Birth of Tragedy* should come as no surprise to those familiar with the notes, essays, and fragments Nietzsche wrote in the two years prior to the publication of this text. In these writings we find numerous examples of both usages of *Symbol* but, more important, little trace of the word *Gleichnis*, which is almost completely absent from these notebooks. In fact, in almost four-hundred pages of notes and fragments Nietzsche wrote prior to January 1872, the word *Gleichnis* appears in a total of four texts, the most significant of these being the important 1871 fragment. As its posthumous title suggests, this fragment is principally concerned with the relationship between music and words, and it is certainly a place where one would expect to find evidence of a distinction between *Symbol* and *Gleichnis* similar to what we find in the published text, an expectation which is in fact borne out by a close reading of the text. By contrast, the term *Gleichnis* is absent from the longer essays and the lectures from this period, which were composed prior to the 1871 fragment. This suggests that the appearance of the term *Gleichnis* in *The Birth of Tragedy*, where it appears quite frequently and is used in pointed fashion—three times with italics—represents a marked change from the vocabulary of all but the last preparatory material. I believe we can infer from this without too much speculation that Nietzsche introduced the term *Gleichnis* in order to sharpen the crucial distinction between music and image. This conclusion is supported by the fact that the 1871 fragment was originally conceived to be part of the text of *The Birth of Tragedy* and that several passages from the 1871 fragment in which the term *Gleichnis* appears have direct parallels, in sections 5 and 6, in the published text.[38] The fact that Nietzsche introduced the term *Gleichnis* as a technical term while still retaining the both the general and technical uses of *Symbol* would go some way towards explaining the ambiguity we find in the rhetorical vocabulary of *The Birth of Tragedy*, and why it first appears that Nietzsche uses *Symbol* and *Gleichnis* interchangeably.[39]

That Nietzsche does in fact sharply distinguish between these terms is evident from the following passage, which we shall now quote in full:

> The world symbolism of music can never completely be approached by language, because music stands in symbolic relation to the primordial contradiction and primordial pain in the heart of the primal unity, and therefore symbolizes a sphere which is beyond and prior to all appearance. Rather, every appearance compared with it is merely an allegory [*Gleichnis*]: hence language as the organ and symbol [*Symbol*] of appearance can never by any means disclose the innermost heart [*tiefste Innere*] of music [. . .]. (BT, 6)

Music, Nietzsche suggests, differs from language in that it signifies symbolically. This description captures both the how of music, how it is that music signifies; and the what of music, what, considered from an ontological point of view, music can be said to be. These questions are, as we have seen, inseparable in the case of music and image. Music is able to symbolize the primal unity—a sphere beyond and prior to all experience—because it has a symbolic relationship to this primal unity. Nietzsche says this explicitly: "Music stands in symbolic relation to [. . .] the primal unity, and therefore symbolizes a sphere which is beyond and prior to all appearance." This standing-in-symbolic-relation is not an arbitrary relationship between music and the primal unity, but signifies the fact that music belongs to, and is part of, the will, like the ancient token of identity, the *symbolon*, which was verified by comparing it with its other half.

Nietzsche does not, therefore, contradict himself when he writes at the end of this passage that language is the symbol and organ of appearance. For it is evident that *Symbol* is here being used in a general sense to describe what Nietzsche at one point in his notes refers to as a "purely conventional symbolism in which convention has exhausted all natural force" (KSA 7, 7.127). This is a form of symbolism in which the relationship between the symbol and that which is symbolized is an arbitrary, external relationship determined by mores, not nature. This interpretation becomes unavoidable when we consider the following sentence, which has to be regarded as the central claim of this passage: "Rather, in comparison with [music], every appearance is merely an allegory [*Gleichnis*]." The contrast between music and appearance testifies to the unique status assigned to music in this text, which allows it to represent the will without itself being representative, to be something other than will and yet its immediate copy; characteristics which are summed up and described by the word symbol. As the symbol of the will, music is a proper language, a language of truth and being which reveals the world as it is in itself. In contrast with music, all appearance and its representations, which is to say its images and concepts, are mere allegories, an improper game of signs and shadows. Appearance and language are always already improper, always already outside of truth. Nietzsche emphasizes this by contrasting language with music, not as we might expect, with the will: "language as the organ and symbol of appearance can never by any means disclose the innermost heart of music." Music, not the will, becomes the point of reference, the standard against which all appearance and language are to be compared, and (necessarily) found wanting.[40]

MUSIC AND IMAGE AS FORMS OF *MIMĒSIS*

The distinction Nietzsche draws between *Symbol* and *Gleichnis* and the manner in which this distinction is articulated in *The Birth of Tragedy* suggests that music and image signify in fundamentally different ways. We are now in a position to describe the differences separating their disparate modes of signification more precisely. As we noted earlier, Dionysian and Apollinian art arise by imitating the natural artistic states of rapture and dreams. This imitation cannot however be understood as an imitation of these states themselves, but rather as an imitation that is modeled upon them. This is the sense in which Nietzsche refers to the artistic drives of dreams and rapture as "*Urbilde*" or archetypes for Apollinian and Dionysian art (BT, 2). Music, therefore, does not imitate Dionysian rapture, but rather the will itself. However, the structure of this imitation—by means of which music becomes the immediate copy of the will—is determined by the excessive structure of rapture. Rapture, as an ecstatic being-outside-oneself, structures music, which in so far as it is formless and unindividuated, constitutes a mirror image of rapture. A parallel structure is at work in Apollinian art, which is inspired not by rapture, but by our experience of dreams. The object of Apollinian art is appearance, which is perfected in the production of Apollinian images. However, just as the experience of *shine* in the dream state—an experience of image qua image—protects the dreamer from mistaking her dreams for reality, so the Apollinian artist is protected from becoming one with his images. The experience of the Apollinian artist, just like that of the dreamer, represents a confirmation of the boundaries of individuation.[41]

The differences the ways in which music and image signify can be seen to depend on two factors: (1) differences in the mimetic processes that give rise to music and image and the archetypes on which these processes are predicated, namely, dreams and rapture; and (2) differences in the entities that constitute the objects of these mimetic processes, namely, the will and appearance. Music can be the language and truth and being because its object is the will, the thing-in-itself, and because the ecstatic structure of Dionysian rapture allows music to imitate the will's formlessness. We might say, then, that Dionysian art is truth preserving, in that it allows music to reveal the truth of being by making it possible for music to be isomorphic with the will. Again, this structure is echoed in Apollinian art. In this case, however, what is preserved is not truth, but lie, appearance. Like the dream experience, Apollinian art is "*der Schein des Scheins*," a repetition of the apparent structure of empirical reality:

> If we, for a moment, look away from our own 'reality,' if we conceive of our empirical existence, and that of the world in general as a continuously manifested representation of the primal unity, we shall then have to look upon the dream as the *shine of shine*, hence as a still higher appeasement of the primordial desire for shine. And that is why the innermost heart of nature feels that ineffable joy in the naïve artist and the naïve work of art, which is likewise only the 'shine of shine.' (BT, 4)

The isomorphism of the image and appearance is reflected in Nietzsche's description of both these forms as allegorical. In a passage cited above we recall that Nietzsche refers to appearance as a *Gleichnis* or allegory. In section 2 we read that in tragedy Dionysian wisdom is revealed "*in an allegorical dream image*" [in einem gleichnissartigen Traumbilde]; a statement that is repeated three times in the text.[42] The allegorical structure of image and appearance is revealed in the fact that they are dependent on an anterior element with which they can never be united, but to which, in a movement that resembles dissimulation, they necessarily refer. In the case of image, this anteriority is the world of appearance; in the case of appearance, it is the will itself. The significance of appearance and image therefore lies outside of themselves, and it is in this sense that allegory, as defined by Nietzsche in the lectures on ancient rhetoric, is presenting one thing, and meaning another (Rh, 63).[43] As allegories, image, and appearance are to be understood as *actio in distans*, as a type of dissimulation whose fundamental form is a repetition of the distance separating the medium of representation from its object, without the possibility that this gap will ever be bridged. Precisely the opposite is true with regard to music, which, as a symbol of the will, is necessarily united with it. The fissure separating the medium of representation from its object, which is characteristic of allegory, is completely absent in symbolic representation. Music reveals the truth of the world, is truth preserving, precisely to the degree that it is one with the will. Whereas Apollinian art preserves the structure of appearance while, like its divine namesake, working from a distance.[44]

In contrast with Lacoue-Labarthe's judgment that Nietzsche uses the terms *Symbol* and *Gleichnis* interchangeably, we have seen that Nietzsche sharply distinguishes between symbolic and allegorical modes of signification and that this distinction is not only consonant with the distinction between music and image, but considerably sharpens this opposition. Insofar as this opposition is the cornerstone of Nietzsche's theory of tragedy—and inseparable from the opposition between Apollinian and Dionysian art—one can fairly say that the distinction between symbol and allegory plays a significant role in this text.

The contrast between symbol and allegory sharpens the distinction Nietzsche makes between music and image by drawing attention to the fact that music, as a symbol of the primordial unity, is organically connected with the will; that is to say, music has a synecdochic connection with the will: it is part of what is in essence an organic totality and meaning. In an essay devoted to Goethe's *Elective Affinities*, Walter Benjamin describes the symbolic as "that within which the indissoluble and necessary connection of a truth to an object appears."[45] Allegory, however, emphasizes the unbridgeable distance of a sign from its origin. Whereas in symbolic language the relationship between the sign and the totality of which it is a part is primarily spatial, allegory consists of a relationship between signs that, according to Paul de Man, "contains a constitutive temporal element; it remains necessary, if there is to be allegory, that the allegorical sign must refer to another sign that precedes it. The meaning constituted by the allegorical sign can then consist only in the *repetition* . . . of a previous sign with which it can never coincide, since it is of the essence of the previous sign to be pure anteriority."[46] This is precisely how Nietzsche describes the predicament of language, which as the dialogue of tragic drama is "the Apollinian manifestation [*Versinnlichung*] of Dionysian insights and effects," and hence is a repetition of the Dionysian, but one which remains "completely separate" from it (BT, 8). Nietzsche emphasizes the unbridgeable distance between these two spheres when he writes that the language of lyric poetry must forever remain only "in superficial contact with music; while all the eloquence of lyric poetry cannot bring the deepest significance of the latter one step nearer to us" (BT, 6). Music, as the symbol of the primal unity, is this pure anteriority in respect to which both appearance and the realm of images and concepts must remain arbitrary, external and improper.[47]

TRAGEDY: A STUTTERING TRANSLATION

In spite of appearances to the contrary, Nietzsche's theory of tragedy is not a theory of music alone, but a theory which purports to explain how music and image, that is to say, how the Dionysian and the Apollinian, come together to produce Attic tragedy, an art form Nietzsche tells us, which owes as much to Apollo as to Dionysus. We recall that Nietzsche describes this meeting of Apollo and Dionysus as a translation, a carrying over between two completely separate spheres, which can properly be said to constitute the essence of tragedy. Let us cite this passage a second time:

> The essence of tragedy [. . .] can only be interpreted as a manifestation and representation in images of Dionysian states, as the visible symbolization of music, as the dream-world of a Dionysian rapture. (BT, 14)

On reflection it is not at all surprising that Nietzsche describes the translation from music to image as the essence of tragedy, for the question of the relationship between music and image permeates the text with an almost mechanical regularity. The most important points of reference in the text are the consideration of lyric poetry in section 5, the elucidation of the chorus and its place in tragedy in section 8, and the extended discussion of music and image, supported by a lengthy citation from Schopenhauer, in section 16. The recurrence of this theme is understandable when we recall that in section 16 Nietzsche explicitly equates the question of the relationship between music and image to the question of the relationship between Apollo and Dionysus; the former question is merely a shortened form of the latter. It is, therefore, a matter of the greatest importance that the relationship between music and image be precisely delimited and that the question, how a translation of music into image is effected, be given a definite answer. One could say, without exaggeration, that the success of Nietzsche's book, as an analysis and theory of tragedy, hangs in the balance.

However, before considering the translation itself, it might be apposite to first address the question why a translation between music and image is necessary at all. For at first glance it is not at all obvious why, after he has gone to great pains to assert the ontological and artistic superiority of music over image, Nietzsche should claim that words and images are essential components of tragedy. Or to ask this question in a slightly different way: Why is tragedy and not music itself the highest art form? In comparison with music, which symbolizes the essence of the world, tragedy seems to be a mixed mode, a centaur of sorts. The answer to this question is well known: music reveals the essence of the world as eternal contradiction and pain while the image, which is mere appearance and illusion, acts as a healing agent [*Heilmittel*], comforting and restoring the spectator who has, in virtue of music, shared in Silenus' dark wisdom. Images, not music, enable one to live on in the face of the knowledge that life is truly abysmal. Images are thus both a prophylactic and a stimulus to life, a necessary antidote to Dionysian music, which if experienced in their absence would cause one literally to expire (BT, 21). "Tragedy," writes Nietzsche in a note from late 1869 or early 1870, "is the natural healing power against the Dionysian [. . .] the pure Dionysian is impossible" (KSA 7, 3.33). At this point, Nietzsche's reflections on the relationship and importance of music and image seem aporetic. Images, we are told, are lifeless and arbitrary signs when compared with music, which is in no way dependent on images for its significance, but bears them as a soul might bear a body. Images, however, are necessary to life; one might even go so far as to say that they are more necessary than music since the latter can be nothing less than fatal to the unfortunate listener, while images convince us that life is worth living and inspire us accordingly.

Tragedy's uniqueness lies in the fact that it combines both music and images, separate and opposed artistic modes, in a single work of art; an achievement so astonishing that Nietzsche says it arises by means of a "miracle of the Hellenic 'will'" (BT, 1). How is this miracle brought about? The first account of the translation from music to image is to be found in section 5, where Nietzsche describes the genesis of lyric poetry. In contrast to the epic poet—typified by Homer—whose absorption in images confirms the limits of subjectivity by being self-consciously an experience *of* images, the lyricist, being a Dionysian artist, surrenders his subjectivity in the artistic process. This point is of some importance because it marks a clear departure from an aesthetics based on, or reducible to, a division between subject and object. The phenomenon of the lyricist cannot be understood in terms of such an aesthetic because

> as a Dionysian artist, he has first of all fully become one with the primordial unity, its pain and contradiction and produces the copy of this primordial unity as music [. . .] this music becomes visible to him again as in an *allegorical dream image*, under the Apollinian dream inspiration [*diese Musik wird ihm wieder wie in einem* gliechnissartigem Traumbilde, *unter der apollinischen Traumwirkung sichtbar*]. (BT, 5)

A first exegesis of this passage might proceed along the following lines: The lyricist, under the influence of Dionysian rapture, surrenders his subjectivity and becomes one with the primordial unity. This fusion with the primordial unity and the concurrent abdication of subjectivity, enables the lyricist to produce music, an art form which is neither representative nor individuated. This music, which is in itself imageless [*bildlos*], becomes visible to him as an allegorical dream image, produced by the Apollinian dream inspiration. Lyric poetry, a nascent form of tragedy, thus accomplishes precisely that which tragedy itself, though on a grander scale, will accomplish, namely, a translation from music to image. Here, as in tragedy, Dionysian music and Apollinian dream image meet and become one.

A closer reading of this passage reveals that the situation is somewhat more complex than Nietzsche might lead us to at first believe.[48] The reason for this is Nietzsche's use of the word "*wie*"—like or as—before the expression "allegorical dream image," which calls attention to the fact that the translation between music and image cannot literally be made; a fact obscured by Kaufmann's translation of this passage.[49] The passage says something quite different when we *read* it, thereby paying attention to Nietzsche's use of "*wie*," than when we merely pass over this word, interpreting the sentences in question in a manner consistent with what, applying the principle of charity,[50] we expect them to say. What we expect is that they will tell us how this translation *is* possible, but when we take the time to read this passage what we find is that the very opposite is the case. To say that music appears to the lyricist *as* in an allegorical dream image is, of course, to assert that the relationship between music and image is a figurative relationship, and hence that the "translation" between them is not a translation in the usual sense at all, but rather a transformation. Or, to use an expression from "On Truth and Lie," it is a "stuttering translation in a completely foreign sphere." Andrzej Warminski describes this predicament as follows:

> If Dionysus is opposed to Apollo [. . .] it is only in the sense that music is 'opposed' to and the 'negation' of images, that is, only in a figurative sense. . . . And because this opposition is *only* figurative, because it is not an opposition at all but two radically different spheres, its bridging can only take place in figure, only in impossible metaphors. (xliii)

While commenting on Kaufmann's translation of this passage, Warminski adds the following remark:

> The German text *does not* make the passage, *does not* close the gap, between music and images . . . but rather bridges them by an impossible figure that at the same time insists on the impossibility of the bridge. (xliv)

Although one might be tempted to object that Nietzsche's use of the word "*wie*" is an isolated remark, a slip or error which, for the sake of Nietzsche's argument, should be ignored or left to one side, we find this pattern repeated at least twice more in the text. The second instance occurs at the very end of the paragraph in which the above cited remark appears, in the middle of section 5. In an allusion to Euripides' *Bacchae*, Nietzsche describes how the drunken reveler Archilochus, asleep in an alpine pasture, is touched by the Apollinian dream inspiration:

> And now Apollo approaches and touches him with the laurel. The Dionysian-musical transformation of the sleeper now emits, as it were [*gleichsam*], image sparks, lyrical poems, which in their highest development are called tragedies and dramatic dithyrambs.

Once again we see that the translation from music to image is interrupted and forestalled, this time by the insertion of the word "*gleichsam*." Music becomes image, "as it were," which is to say, that music does not become image at all, but is figured by image; a figurative movement which we have seen can itself only be described by a figure.[51]

The realization that the translation between music and image can only be understood as a figurative transformation should come as no surprise. For Nietzsche tells us more than once that Dionysian music does not merely become—or is translated into—an Apollinian dream image, but rather, that music becomes an allegorical dream image, a trope. This is, of course, in keeping with our insistence that Apollo should be understood as the god of figuration, this word being understood in the widest sense. For as the god of image, Apollo is also the god of form, the form-giver. He gives form to that which is formless, as when music becomes an image, and maintains that which already has form, as when he demands moderation and measure from his disciples. But as the form-giver, he is also the one who *transforms*. When music is given form, as when it is translated into an image, it no longer remains music but is transformed into something other, into its other, from which it is separated by a tremendous gulf. This implies, however, that music can only figuratively become an image. Nietzsche emphasizes this quite clearly when he describes the final product of this translation, the Apollinian dream image, not once, but twice under italics, as an allegorical dream image (in sections 2 and 5). This much should have already been clear to us from Nietzsche's descriptions of the Dionysian and the Apollinian. Let us recall that while the essence of the Apollinian is measure and restraint, the Dionysian is essentially ecstatic, which is to say, that the Dionysian *exceeds* every measure and standard. Given this, how could one have expected that when the Dionysian becomes image, when it is stamped with a form, domesticated, as it were, that something would not be lost? For how could the Dionysian, which resists form and every attempt at control, not remain outside, as remainder and excess, as that other to Apollinian law?[52]

This is what Nietzsche could not admit, could not openly say, but which is, and had to be, inscribed in his text. Was Nietzsche aware of these difficulties? This question must be left open. One might, however, not be far wrong in suggesting that it was an inkling of these tensions that led Nietzsche to describe tragedy as a *miracle* of the Hellenic will.

MUSIC: OUT OF THE SPIRIT OF IMAGE

If the translation from music to image cannot, literally speaking, be made, what consequences does this have for Nietzsche's analysis of tragedy? Should we conclude, perhaps with a trace of disappointment, that there is a fatal flaw in the heart of Nietzsche's theory of tragedy, that the most commonly heard opinions about the book and its immaturity are correct after all? Perhaps not. Might there not be an alternate strategy at work in this text, another manner of understanding the relationship between music and image, which instead of redeeming the notion of a literal translation between music and image, would allow us to understand the failure of this translation in a deeper and more interesting manner?

To begin with, let us return to the passage from section 5 with which our analysis commenced:

> As a Dionysian artist, [the lyricist] has first of all, fully become one with the primordial unity, its pain and contradiction and produces the copy of this primordial unity as music [. . .] this music becomes visible to him again as in an *allegorical dream image*, under the Apollinian dream inspiration.

We noted above that Nietzsche's account of the genesis of lyric poetry is meant to provide an alternative to subjectivist aesthetics, including, it should be said, Schopenhauer's, who Nietzsche explicitly criticizes in this section. "The whole opposition," writes Nietzsche, "between the subjective and objective, which Schopenhauer still uses as a measure of value in classifying the arts, is altogether irrelevant in aesthetics [. . .] the subject [. . .] can be conceived of only as the antagonist, not as the origin of art" (BT, 5). If the origin of art cannot be traced back to the subject, one expects to find another account of its origin, one that escapes those difficulties Nietzsche sees in modern aesthetics. The passage cited above seems to provide the beginnings of such an alternative, for we read here that music becomes visible to the lyricist in an image "under the Apollinian dream inspiration." This would seem to imply that the translation between music and image is effected by the Apollinian drive itself, which in some manner is able to transform music into an image, perhaps as the sculptor is able to transform a formless mass of bronze into a work of art. This role of the Apollinian drive is apparently confirmed by Nietzsche's description of the sleeping Archilochus, who, after being touched by Apollo, magically gives rise to lyric poems. On this view, the translation between music and image is effected by a cooperative effort on the part of the Apollinian and the Dionysian drives: the artist, under the influence of the Dionysian drive, produces music, which is then transformed into image by means of the Apollinian drive. Although Nietzsche writes that the Dionysian artist produces music, he is able to do this only after he has become one with the primordial unity; the artist produces music not as a subject, but rather as a medium, so to speak, of the Dionysian drive.[53]

However plausible this explanation appears, it cannot be right. Rather than affirming the Apollinian drive as the one which effects the translation between music and image, Nietzsche quite explicitly identifies the Dionysian drive as bearing the responsibility for the translation, or to be more precise, it is not the Dionysian drive but rather music itself which "acts" as the translator. After telling us that music becomes visible to the lyricist in an allegorical image, Nietzsche writes: "That imageless and conceptless reflection of the primordial pain in music, with its redemption in shine, now produces a second mirroring, as an individual allegory or example." This second mirroring is, of course, the allegorical dream image. The suggestion that music effects its own transformation into image is explicitly affirmed by Nietzsche in a passage from section 16 which refers back to the elucidation of lyric poetry in section 5. "In the phenomenon of the lyricist," writes Nietzsche,

> I have represented how music strives to express its essence [*Wesen*] in Apollinian images. If now we reflect that music at its highest stage must also seek to attain to its highest manifestation in images [*höchesten Ver-*

> *bildlichung*], we must deem it possible that it also knows how to find the symbolic expression for its unique Dionysian wisdom [. . .]. (BT, 16)

The first sentence of this citation comes as a surprise. Music, which differs radically from image in its essence and mode of signification, now seeks to express its essence in images; images, we might add, which Nietzsche has told us music does not need, but merely bears. Having said that, Nietzsche takes this thought further in the following sentence in which we read that at it highest point music must also seek to attain its highest representation in images. (There is no English equivalent of the noun *Verbildlichung*, which I have rendered as "manifestation in images." The German term, however, is stronger than this, implying literally "a becoming image," as is the case with a related word *Verkörperung*, meaning personification or embodiment.) In other words, at its highest point music must transform itself into its opposite, an arbitrary lifeless image, the exterior to its interior, with which it can have no necessary relation. Although Nietzsche does not employ a reflective verb in this sentence, the next sentence tells us that the reflective construction is implied. For if music must seek to become image, it must also know how.

In the 1871 fragment Nietzsche gives a more precise description of just how it is that music comes to express itself in images:

> When therefore the musician composes a lyric poem, he is, as a musician, stimulated neither through the images, nor through the emotional language of this text. Rather, a musical impulse coming from a completely other sphere itself chooses that poetic text as an allegorical expression of itself [*sondern eine aus ganz anderen Sphaeren kommende Musikerregung wählt sich jenen Liedertext als einen gleichnißartigen Ausdruck ihrer selbst*]. (1871, 366)

As in the previous passage, Nietzsche here describes how music chooses to transform itself into image. Nietzsche's use of a reflexive construction emphasizes the fact that the poem's text arises out of music; music, not the lyric poet, chooses the text as an allegorical expression of itself. In contrast with our earlier assumption that the Apollinian drive imposes a form on Dionysian music, Nietzsche suggests that, on the contrary, music is the "agent" of its own transformation into image. But if music is able to impose a form upon itself, is able to figure itself, does it not follow that music cannot be formless after all, that music, like image, is a figure? Music can only be figured by image because it has always already contained image within itself, and conversely, image can only be a figure of music because it always already belonged to music. This is reflected in the fact that there is no clear separation or temporal priority between the representing medium, image, and the represented, music. What began as an attempt to demonstrate the ontological priority and independence of music over image has instead revealed the impossibility of conceiving these two media as binary opposites. Rather than being understood as two completely separate artistic modes, the expressions of artistic drives differing in origin and goals, music and image must be regarded as figures whose difference can no longer be considered to be ontological, but rhetorical.

Once again, there is ample evidence in Nietzsche's text—in spite of the explicit statements to the contrary—to counter any objections of arbitrariness that might be raised against the foregoing interpretation. One important source of this evidence is Nietzsche's analysis of the chorus in section 8. As in section 5, Nietzsche here describes the necessary growth of image out of music. The subject of this description is not however lyric poetry, but tragedy itself, and the manner in which the chorus gives rise to the drama proper. "Greek tragedy," Nietzsche writes, "must be understood as the Dionysian chorus, which ever anew discharges [*entladet*] itself in an Apollinian world of images" (BT, 8). As the word *entladen* tells us, the expression of the chorus, of music, in Apollinian images, arises from within the chorus. Or, to put the matter more precisely, it arises out of the chorus:

> the scene together with the action was at bottom and originally only thought of as a vision [*Vision*] [. . .] the only 'reality' is precisely the chorus, which produces the vision out of itself [*der die Vision aus sich erzeugt*]. (BT, 8)

Nietzsche's description of just how the chorus produces the vision, the drama proper, out of itself is for our purposes quite telling. For it turns out that the vision of the drama is merely a reflection of the vision of the Dionysian artist, who under the influence of the Dionysian spell, surrenders his subjectivity and sees himself transformed. The *ecstasis* of the Dionysian reveler, this excessive transgression (and transformation) of the bounds of subjectivity is bound up with vision, in this case, the vision of oneself as another. Nietzsche says precisely this:

> In light of this insight we may call the chorus, in its primitive form in the proto-tragedy [*Urtragödie*], a self-reflection of the Dionysian man [*eine Selbstspiegelung des dionysischen Menschen*]. This phenomenon is best clarified through the process of the actor, who, being truly talented, sees the image of the role he is to play quite palpably before his eyes. The satyr chorus is foremost a vision of the Dionysian mass of spectators, as moreover, the world of the stage is a vision of the satyr chorus. (BT, 8)

According to this description, tragedy can be understood as the vision of a vision: the chorus arises by means of a transformation of a group of spectators ("this phenomenon is encountered epidemically, a whole throng feels itself transformed in this way") which then produces, out of itself, the drama proper. But on this conception, the vision that the chorus produces cannot be something external to it, since the chorus is itself the product of a vision. The dramatic world produced by the chorus must then be understood as a reflection of the images produced by the self-transformation, which is a necessary condition of the production of the chorus.

More curiously, Nietzsche describes this process of self-projection as the "primordial artistic phenomenon" [*künstlerische Urerscheinung*]. In order to illustrate this claim, which is presented in the form of a critical commentary on modern aesthetics, Nietzsche provides three examples: the true poet, the painter, and the dramatist. All three embody this basic artistic phenomenon by practicing their respective crafts in a manner that involves the process of self-projection described above. Nietzsche's description of the "genuine poet" is quite instructive:

> while nothing can be more certain than that the poet is only a poet insofar as he sees himself surrounded by figures [*Gestalten*] who live and act before him and into whose innermost essence he sees [. . .]. The character is for him not a whole composed out of particular traits picked up here and there, but an obtrusively alive person before his eyes, distinguished from the identical vision of the painter only by the fact that it continues to live and act.

It follows from this comparison that the processes by means of which the visual artist and the genuine poet—among which we must count the lyricist—create are essentially the same. On this account, both types of artist create in a manner that involves seeing an image before one's eyes, and which is, therefore, essentially imagistic. This conclusion allows us to deduce a second reason why the translation from music to image that constitutes the essence of tragedy is necessary: not only does image act as a prophylactic against the dangers of the Silenic wisdom communicated by music, but it is also an essential part of the creative process. This revelation reaffirms the conclusion we reached above, namely, that music and image must be conceived of exchangeable tropes, not binary opposites.

The relationship between music and image is aptly described by a concept introduced by Derrida in his reading of Rousseau, namely, that of supplementarity. Broadly stated, Derrida describes the logic of the supplement as a double logic, being both a surplus, something added to that which in itself is already a plenitude, and something which supplements, which fills a lack or gap. Derrida continues:

> This second signification of the supplement cannot be separated from the first. . .their common function is shown in this: whether it adds or substitutes itself, the supplement is *exterior*, outside of the positivity to which it is super-added, alien to that which, in order to be replaced by it, must be other than it.[54]

This double-edged logic is precisely what we find in Nietzsche's description of the relationship between music and image. Image is, on the one hand, condemned as being something absolutely exterior to music, which is separated from it by an absolute and unbridgeable distance. On the other hand, as we have seen, music already contains image. Image supplements music in exactly the sense described by Derrida: it is both surplus and substitute, exterior and yet essential.

The relation of supplementarity that obtains between music and image is expressed by Nietzsche in his attempt, in the 1871 fragment, to give an account of the origin of music. This attempt involves difficulties that are quite acute, since as we have noted, music has a unique status among the arts in that it is able to represent the will, the *Ding-an-sich*, without itself being representative. Given these difficulties, it comes as no surprise then that Nietzsche ends up saying the very opposite of what, in accordance with the theory's ontology, he should have said. Nietzsche's argument reaches its climax in the following passage:

> What concerns the origin of music, on the other hand, I have already explained that it can by no means lie in the 'will,' but rather rests in the womb of that power, which under a form of the 'will' produces a world of vision out of itself [*vielmehr im Schooße jener Kraft ruht, die unter der Form des 'Willens' eine Visionswelt aus sich erzeugt*]: The origin of music lies beyond all individuation, a sentence which according to our explanation of the Dionysian proves itself. (1871, 365)

Nietzsche's denial that the will can ever constitute the origin of music creates the following difficulty. In order for music to be the immediate copy of the will and not its imitation, music, in origin and essence, must be beyond all representation and individuation. But since the will itself can never appear, the origin of music cannot lie in the will. For this would require that the will, the "unaesthetic-in-itself," could be said to aesthetically manifest itself in the world, which according to its essence it cannot do. If the origin of music cannot lie in the will, it cannot, given the role assigned to music, lie in the world of individuation and representation either. Hence the dilemma. Nietzsche solves this difficulty in a manner which for our purposes is quite revealing. After asserting for the second time in as many pages that the origin of music can in no manner lie in the will, he locates its origin in an unnamed power that operates not as will, but under the form of the will. Although this power is not explicitly named, it seems safe to say it is the Dionysian that contains the origin of music within itself. More to the point is Nietzsche's mention of a second, one might be tempted to say prior, function this power performs. Returning to our citation we read that the origin of music lies "in the womb of that power, which under a form of the 'will' produces a world of vision out of itself." This is tantamount to an admission that music, in origin and essence, is inseparable from the world of representation and individuation. In fact the passage goes even further. Not content with the assertion that music and the visual world share a common origin, the passage reveals a complete reversal of the priority of music and image. The origin of music, we are told, lies in the power that produces the visual world out of itself, which implies that the production of music is a secondary function, both in importance and in temporal terms. Assuming that we have correctly identified this third power as the Dionysian, this passage contains the startling assertion that rather than being distinguished from the Apollinian in "origin and goals," the Dionysian is inseparable from its brother in arms. Hence the relationship between the Apollinian and the Dionysian is not a relationship of binary opposites, but a relationship between figures: the names Apollo and Dionysus are substitutable tropes whose relationship to one another is that of an undecidable difference. Nietzsche's insistence on the self-evidence of the proposition that the origin of music must lie beyond individuation can now be seen as a rhetorical response to the admission, made in the previous sentence, that the precise opposite is in fact true.

NIETZSCHE'S RHETORIC OF PERSUASION

If this interpretation of *The Birth of Tragedy* seems overly scholastic, its basic outlines were sketched by Nietzsche in two notes written in 1871 and published one page apart in the Colli-Montinari edition. In the first note, Nietzsche distinguishes between two uses of the symbol in the following manner:

> The symbol—in the initial period as the *language* for the *universal*, in the subsequent period as means of remembering the *concept*. Music [is] rightly the proper language of the universal. In opera it was used as a symbolism of concepts [. . .]. Here is the danger, that everything depends upon the *content of the concept* and the *musical form* itself perishes. The *concept* is the *death* of *art* insofar as it reduces art to a symbol. (KSA 7, 9.88)

The passage narrates what for us should now be a familiar story, namely, the degeneration of music from a non-representative Dionysian art form, semiotically superior to language, to a representative medium whose sole raison d'être is to imitate and be a mnemonic aid for that which is essentially conceptual in nature. However, the note takes on a different coloring when read in conjunction with a note that follows shortly thereafter. In the middle of this note we find the following remark:

> The lack of symbols in our modern world. Understanding the world in 'symbols' is the presupposition of a great art. For us music has become myth, a world of symbols. *We relate to music*, as the *Greek related to his symbolic myths.* (KSA 7, 9.92)

On a first reading this passage completes the story begun above by narrating the re-birth of a tragic worldview out of music. Music, which had degenerated and lost its symbolic meaning, now experiences a renaissance, and once again becomes "a world of symbols." A closer look at this passage reveals an interesting asymmetry between this narrative and the one familiar to us from *The Birth of Tragedy*, for in the second of these passages Nietzsche asserts that for us music "has become myth." However, in *The Birth of Tragedy* music is not identified with myth but is said to give birth to myth, much in the same manner as music produces lyric poetry and the tragic drama. Myth, far from being identified with music or the Dionysian, is said to be "a sublime allegory" [*ein erhabenes Gleichniss*] which, like Apollinian images, "protects us against the music" (BT, 21). Why then would Nietzsche describe the re-birth of music as music's becoming myth? The answer lies in the next sentence, where Nietzsche tells us that "we relate to music, as the Greek related to his symbolic myths." This implies that music has not literally become myth, but that for us music plays the same role as myth played for the ancient Greeks. If we recall that myth functions as an Apollinian art form, then it becomes clear that what Nietzsche describes in this passage is a historical reversal between the Apollinian, which the Greeks understood and which was the "presupposition" of their art, and the Dionysian, which we understand and which is, as Nietzsche tells us in the same note, the basis for a new art or our own: "There are now men who understand the world as music, that is to say, symbolically. The musical intuition of things is a new possibility for art."[55]

The reversal between image and music is made explicit by Nietzsche towards the end of the second of our two notes:

> The ancient fable symbolized the Dionysian (in images). Now the Dionysian symbolizes the image. The Dionysian was explained by

> means of the image. Now the image is explained by means of the Dionysian. Therefore a fully reversed relationship [. . .]. The ancients understood the world of images as something given, for us it is the Dionysian. (KSA 7, 9.92)

Taken together, these two notes point to the fact that the ontological structure of *The Birth of Tragedy* rests on pragmatic considerations rather than substantial truths. The privileging of music over image arises not out of a consideration of their respective proximity to the will and a comparison of their modes of signification, but out of a practical need to speak to one's audience in a language it will understand. In the words of Paul de Man, "Nietzsche's auditors have to be spoken to in Dionysian terms because, unlike the Greeks, they are unable to understand the Apollinian language of figure and appearance."[56] It follows from this that music, rather than being understood solely as the immediate echo of the will, should also be read as a trope for the symbolic status of image, which, as a consequence of the development of conceptual language, we have ceased being able to understand. Nietzsche's historical analysis of the degeneration of the symbol is thus linked to the rise of the concept and the gradual conceptualization of language, which in its origins was nothing less than a universal symbolism. Contrary to what many readers of *The Birth of Tragedy* take as a given, the unique status occupied by music in this text is less the result of a blind obedience to Schopenhauerian or Wagnerian dogma as it is the expression of Nietzsche's desire for a new symbolic view of the world. Because images have become nothing more than a vicarious concept, the means to this new world symbolism is music. Nietzsche says this quite explicitly when he writes in this same note that

> a people which only sees the world abstractly, not in symbols, is incapable of art. We have the idea in place of the symbols [. . .]. There are now human beings who understand the world as music, therefore symbolically. The musical intuition of things is a new possibility for art. (KSA 7, 7.92)[57]

THE BIRTH OF TRAGEDY: TOWARDS A REVALUATION

Nietzsche's effort to secure a new symbolic view of the world does not result, as has often been claimed, in the inscription of a new phonocentric metaphysics. The deconstruction of the opposition between Apollo and Dionysus, image and music, erases this possibility, for Nietzsche has shown that image and music are always already inscribed in one another; nor would it be correct to conclude that Nietzsche presents us with a new opposition between symbol and concept to replace the displaced opposition between music and image. For Nietzsche's critical reflections on this opposition quickly lead to a consideration of the logic of the concept and its mode of signification. The result of these reflections on the concept, contained in the notes for the never completed *Philosophenbuch* and the essay "On Truth and Lie," are well known. Less familiar to many readers of Nietzsche is the fact that this essay's definition of the concept as an "equation of the dissimilar" produced "by forgetting the distinguishing factors," can be traced back to the last half of 1870, when Nietzsche made the following notebook entry:

> Language, the word, nothing but a symbol. Thinking, i.e., conscious representation [*Vorstellen*], is nothing but the representation [*Vergegenwärtigung*] of a combination of linguistic symbols [. . .] thinking is the recollection of symbols. Just as when the eyes are closed the play of the visual organs reproduces experienced reality [*erlebten Wirklichkeit*] in a colorful and indiscriminate flux, so thinking relates to experienced reality: it is a partial repetition [*stückweises Wiederkäuen*]. (KSA 7, 5.80)

Having initially described thinking as the representation of combinations of linguistic symbols, Nietzsche adds that thinking is a recollection of these symbols, a "*Symbolerinnerung*." Conscious thought is therefore a kind of memory, a bringing to presence or "*Vergegenwärtigung*" of the past. What interests us in this context is the subsequent characterization of thought's relationship to experienced reality as a partial repetition or "*stückweises Wiederkäuen*." If conscious thought is representation by means of linguistic symbols whose cumulative effect is a partial repetition of reality, then the recollection involved in thought is not a true recollection at all, a representation of a past presence, but is necessarily constituted by a partial forgetting of the past: a forgetting of the individual characteristics of a thing and equation of the dissimilar with the similar as the condition of the possibility of all language and thought. What we have in this passage is nothing other than the description of the concept as a metaphorical construction which Nietzsche will, less than two years later, include in his essay "On Truth and Lie."[58]

This realization, together with the recognition that the tropological conception of language described by Nietzsche in "On Truth and Lie" is already operative in *The Birth of Tragedy*, should convince us of the need for a reconsideration of these two texts and their place within the Nietzschean corpus. Such a reconsideration must begin with a revaluation of the status of language in *The Birth of Tragedy*. Although the present chapter is but a small contribution to this task, it should finally put to rest the view that in this text language is "repeatedly denigrated" (NoT, 349). A rhetorically aware reading of *The Birth of Tragedy* brings us to the conclusion that rather than being a denigration of language, this text is a profound meditation on signification and its musical, imagistic and linguistic modes which, in view of our reading, must no longer be understood as separate and opposed spheres, but rather as parts of the same open tropological system. An example of this is to be found in the relationship between music and image, which can be read as a trope for linguistic signification in which the intervals, rhythms, and spacing of music figure the grammatical or syntagmatic axis of language, while the image figures the semantic or paradigmatic axis. Music and image—and by extension, syntax and semantics—are presented as exchangeable tropes, and neither pole in these apparent oppositions can be said to have have priority over, or be completely separable from, the other.[59]

Read in this manner, *The Birth of Tragedy* becomes a book whose significance is greater and more profound than is usually understood, and whose importance—within the Nietzschean corpus and the history of nineteenth-century philosophy—is not exhausted by suggestions that Nietzsche wrote his first book as an admirer of Wagner and a disciple of Schopenhauer. Nor could one rest with the assertion, taken today as gospel truth, that the theoretical underpinnings of this text derive from Nietzsche's "uncritical reliance on" Schopenhauer (NoT, 365). On the contrary. As I have attempted to demonstrate, Nietzsche's explicit statements on language, music, and their relationship to the will are effectively undone by the theory of language and signification at work in this text. Following our analysis of the relationship between music and image, the former can no longer be regarded as the immediate copy of the will, but rather as its figurative refraction. Moreover, the will itself, as the truly existent, effectively disappears from the horizon of the text. Like the translation of music into image, the objectification of the will in appearance can only be expressed in figures that turn against the text and preclude the possibility of the very actions they describe:

> just as tragedy, with its metaphysical comfort, points to the eternal life of this core of existence which abides through the perpetual destruction of appearances, the symbolism of the satyr chorus already expresses, in an allegory [*in einem Gleichnis*], that primordial relationship between thing-in-itself and appearance [. . .]. (BT, 8)

The figurative nature of the "primordial relationship" between essence and appearance is affirmed later in the text, when Nietzsche describes the will as existing "as it were [*gleichsam*] behind the *principio individuationis*" (BT, 16). This admission that the will does not, as Schopenhauer claims, literally exist beyond all appearance, but belongs to the very order of appearances of which it is said to be the cause, merely reiterates what Nietzsche had written one year earlier in the 1871 fragment:

> and we might well say that even Schopenhauer's 'will' is nothing more than the most general form of appearance of something that is otherwise completely undecipherable to us. (1871, 361)[60]

Consequently, rather than being a book devoid of irony and rhetoric, as Silk and Stern would have it, *The Birth of Tragedy* is in the first instance an ironic work.[61] As John Sallis has convincingly documented, there is a wealth of evidence, in the published text and the notes contemporary with it, as well as in a ten page fragment "On Schopenhauer" written in 1867, which shows that Nietzsche had broken with Schopenhauer's philosophy long before the publication of *The Birth of Tragedy*.[62] Consequently, the quotations from Schopenhauer included in the final version of the text, particularly the extensive citation from *The World as Will and Representation*, which we find in section 16 (along with Wagner's doctrinal seal of approval, affixed by Nietzsche),[63] need to be read as rhetorical veils covering the profoundly anti-Schopenhauerian and anti-Wagnerian thrust of Nietzsche's book.[64] Nietzsche's "discovery" of rhetoric did not, therefore, make it impossible for him to hold onto the language of his first book and indirectly lead to his "break" with Schopenhauer and Wagner, as Lacoue-Labarthe has so eloquently sought to demonstrate, because Nietzsche had already broken with this language, and with his two mentors, when he wrote *The Birth of Tragedy*.

Of course, Nietzsche did depart from the vocabulary of his first book when, in the following years he was to write a series of much underread texts, texts such as the lectures on rhetoric, the pre-Socratics and the future of modern educational institutions, "On Truth and Lie," and the four "untimely ones." But this does not prove that Nietzsche broke with this vocabulary or with Wagner and Schopenhauer when he came across the books by Gerber and Volkmann, for Nietzsche will, in the seventeen years that follow the publication of his first book, continuously alter his style and his vocabulary, in precisely the same way he was to do in the years 1872–1875. Rather, Nietzsche's unceasing experimentation with changing styles and vocabularies provides an eloquent illustration of his belief, first expressed in *The Birth of Tragedy*, of the impossibility of ever breaking free from the illusions by means of which we are able to live. As Nietzsche was to write in late 1870 or early 1871:

> Most people occasionally sense that they live in a net of illusions. But few recognize, how far these illusions reach. It is infinitely naive [*ein unendlich naiver Glaube*] to believe that one can avoid being ruled by illusions. (KSA 7, 5.33)

This is the starting point for the texts Nietzsche will write in the two years following the publication of his first book. Almost without exception and to an extreme degree, these texts will analyze the concept of illusion and its roots in a language that is in principle epistemologically unreliable. But in so doing, these texts only make explicit and sharpen what, as we have seen, was already there to be read in *The Birth of Tragedy*.

LOGIC AND ILLUSION

Maudemarie Clark has recently raised the question of whether Nietzsche's use of the term illusion in *The Birth of Tragedy* does not make the book incoherent.[65] The offending passage comes in section 18, where Nietzsche distinguishes three "stages of illusion" [*Illusionsstufen*] which compel the more noble ones to live on. Since Nietzsche clearly intends one of these stages to be the Dionysian, Clark argues that this results in a contradiction which undermines the text's central assertion, namely, that the Dionysian provides a means to know the world as it is in itself. If the Dionysian does reveal the essence of the world, it cannot at the same time be an illusion. This contradiction is so striking that it is puzzling how Nietzsche could have failed "to see that the classification of Dionysian experience as illusory undercuts his whole argument" (LD, 80). The conclusion Clark draws from this observation is scarcely salutary:

> The straightforward or analytical response to such contradictions at the heart of *The Birth of Tragedy* is that they reveal the book's incoherence and explain why Nietzsche spent so much of his later work rejecting it. (LD, 80–81)

Leaving aside the complex question of whether Nietzsche does in fact reject this book—he did, after all, oversee publication of a second (1878) and third (1886) edition—let us turn to the passage commented on by Clark and the question of whether it makes Nietzsche's book incoherent.

The passage in question runs as follows:

> It is an eternal phenomenon: the insatiable will always finds a way to detain its creatures in life and compel them to live on, by means of an illusion spread over things. One is chained by the Socratic life of knowledge and the delusion of being able thereby to heal the eternal wound of existence; another is ensnared by art's seductive veil of beauty fluttering before his eyes; still another by the metaphysical comfort that beneath the whirl of appearance eternal life flows on indestructibly—to say nothing of the more vulgar and almost more powerful illusions which the will always has at hand. These three stages of illusion are

> only for the more noble formed natures, who actually feel profoundly the weight and burden of existence, and must be deluded by exquisite stimulants into forgetfulness of their displeasure. All that we call culture is made up of these stimulants; and according to their proportion, we have either a dominantly *Socratic* or *artistic* or *tragic* culture; or, if, historical exemplifications are permitted, there is either an Alexandrian or a Hellenic or a Buddhistic culture. (BT, 18)

The first thing to note about this passage is that although Nietzsche lists three stages of illusion along with the three types of culture to which they give rise, the only one he explicitly names is the Socratic. Clark, following in the footsteps of others before her, concludes that the third stage of illusion in this list must be the Dionysian. While there are good reasons for so doing—the mention of metaphysical comfort is surely a reference to the Dionysian[66]—the fact that Nietzsche does not name the last two stages of illusion should puzzle us. More puzzling still is his description of the three types of culture and their historical exemplifications. Here we find the Socratic paired with the Alexandrian, the artistic paired with the Hellenic and the tragic paired with the Buddhistic. The most obvious question raised by these groupings is Why does Nietzsche distinguish artistic from tragic culture and link the Hellenic not with tragic culture, as we expect, but with artistic culture? For is not tragedy the art form of art forms, and is it not above all a *Hellenic* art form? As it stands, not only does this passage seem to contradict Nietzsche's account of the Dionysian, it makes nonsense of the entire book. I suggest, then, that this passage requires an alternative reading.

One approach that might be fruitful under the present circumstances is to ask whether the Dionysian provides us with access to a kind of metaphysical truth, as Clark maintains. In order for Dionysian truth to be metaphysical, referring to a supersensuous essence, the relationship of the Dionysian to this essence must be direct and unmediated. On Clark's interpretation, this condition is fulfilled by Nietzsche's identification of the will with the thing-in-itself and his description of music as "an immediate copy of the will" (BT, 16). However, our reading of the will and of the relationship between essence and appearance precludes the possibility of such a literal interpretation of truth. For if the will is merely a figure of essence and cannot thereby be identified with the thing-in-itself as such, then any truth that arises out of an experience of the will must be figurative, not literal.

The figurative status of the will is overlooked by most readers of *The Birth of Tragedy*. The principal reason for this is doubtless the fact that Schopenhauer's influence on Nietzsche remains an article of faith among these readers, which prevents them from adopting a critical perspective on the text's Schopenhauerian vocabulary. A case in point is Walter Kaufmann's translation which, as we have noted, seriously distorts Nietzsche's own vocabulary and thus obscures the text's more radical elements. The same uncritical acceptance of this vocabulary colors Clark's reading of a passage which she cites as proof of the Dionysian's access to metaphysical truth:

> We are really for a brief moment primordial being itself, feeling its raging desire for existence [. . .] the struggle, the pain [. . .]. We are pierced by the maddening sting of these pains just when we have become, as it were [*gleichsam*], one with the infinite primordial joy in existence [. . .]. (BT, 17)

Although overlooked by Clark, Nietzsche's use of the qualifying expression "as it were" disrupts the literality of this description and indicates that the experience of oneness that accompanies Dionysian ecstasy is not a literal unification of man and nature, but a figurative or metaphorical oneness. This passage cannot bridge the gap between man and nature, because the transition cannot, literally speaking, be made. Nietzsche's text does not here offer an example of metaphysical truth, as Clark claims, but rather a figure of transcendence of the self and the empirical world. But this figure of transcendence remains a figure, a phantasm that induces a transformation of the self by means of an illusory self-forgetting. This is reflected in the contrast Nietzsche draws between the satyr chorus and the man of culture in section 8. The former, Nietzsche claims, "represents existence more truthfully, really, and completely than the man of culture [. . .] who ordinarily considers himself as the only reality" (BT, 8). But the greater truthfulness of the satyr chorus is predicated on an explicitly figurative construction of self-transformation, which emphasizes the figurative nature of the truth in question. "The Dionysian Greek," writes Nietzsche, "wants truth and nature in their most forceful form—he sees himself transformed, as by magic, into a satyr [*—er sieht sich zum Satyr verzaubert*]."

If the truth revealed in Dionysian experience is merely a figurative truth, does it not follow that the metaphysical comfort which we derive from this truth is an illusion? In an important passage from section 7, Nietzsche illuminates the nature of this comfort by means of an analogy with the satyr chorus:

> The metaphysical comfort [. . .] appears in incarnate clarity as the satyr chorus, a chorus of natural beings who live ineradicably, as it were, behind all civilization and remain eternally the same, despite the changes of generations and of the history of nations. (BT, 7)

These so-called natural beings who, like the essence of the world, remain eternally the same, are not natural at all, but are mere figures of natural beings:

"for this chorus the Greek built up the scaffolding of a fictitious natural state and on it placed fictitious natural beings. On this foundation tragedy developed" (BT, 7). Nietzsche could hardly be clearer: the unity with nature produced by tragedy is a truth built on a lie, and, I would suggest, that redemption from this truth is achieved not when we take it literally, but when we accept it for what it is, namely, lie, illusion, and phantasm.

The metaphysical comfort that accompanies tragedy is not, therefore, produced by sensing the immutable essence of the world—which, literally speaking, would be impossible—but rather by experiencing the figure of this essence produced by the artistic play of the Apollinian and the Dionysian. This play is not a dialectical movement resulting in a synthesis—since the Apollinian and the Dionysian are not binary opposites, the possibility of a synthesis between them is precluded—but an expression of the relationship of supplementarity that exists between these two artistic forces. There can be, Nietzsche tells us unequivocally, no pure Dionysian. The Dionysian needs to express itself as the Apollinian, to be at play with the Apollinian. At every stage, be it in lyric poetry, in the satyr chorus or in tragedy itself, the Dionysian is represented as suffering from a need or lack which can only be filled or, more clearly said, supplemented, when music expresses itself in its other, in image. This is why, in section 7, Nietzsche distinguishes between two modes of the Dionysian: a solitary mode, which is marked by a disgust with life and an "ascetic will-negating mood," and an artistic, playful mode which is fundamentally redemptive (BT, 7). If we have correctly understood the relationship between the Apollinian and the Dionysian as a one of supplementarity, then the solitary mode of the Dionysian involves a turning against and rejection of the Apollinian, which is properly construed as a turning of the Dionysian against itself. In other words, the solitary mode of the Dionysian is ascetic in precisely the way Nietzsche defines asceticism in the *Genealogy*: it is a will to life that turns against itself in self-denial. It is Buddhistic.

Turning back to the long passage from section 18 cited above, we find a parallel distinction between what I have called the solitary and the playful Dionysian. The solitary Dionysian experiences the illusion of the loss of subjectivity and identification with the primal unity, but in so doing fails to experience it as illusion, as lie. This results in tragic resignation and an ascetic denial of the will. The playful Dionysian, on the other hand, experiences this loss of subjectivity as lie: he projects himself as other and understands this experience conditionally. The result of this movement is not tragic resignation, but artistic affirmation. The playful Dionysian embraces the Apollinian and the images of the self as other which result from this process. This stage of illusion represents the Apollinian and the Dionysian at play, and is therefore the highest affirmation of art, the truly Hellenic. Hence the conventional understanding of the "seductive veil of beauty" described by Nietzsche in this passage as a reference to the Apollinian alone is in error. For, as Nietzsche stresses in the notes to *The Birth of Tragedy*, "there is no beautiful surface without a terrible depth" (KSA 7, 7.91).[67] Beauty arises out of the play between the Apollinian and the Dionysian. This play is, as Nietzsche insists in section 9, the very essence of "Greek cheerfulness."

What then of the tragic? It seems quite clear that Nietzsche's identification of the tragic with the Buddhistic is neither a slip, nor a mistake, but a reflection on what results when the Dionysian identification with the primal one is understood literally. The imposition of a literal meaning on an essentially figurative structure results in a violent rejection of the Apollinian and, thus, of the artistic moment which redeems the disgust produced by the Dionysian. He who misreads the Dionysian and fails to make the leap into art falls prey to tragic resignation.[68] Nietzsche's description of the tragic as Buddhistic in section 18 is thus a repetition of what he had already asserted in section 7, where he distinguishes between the ascetic Dionysian and its artistic counterpart. This means, however, that the essence of the tragic cannot be understood as something tragic, but rather as something that is essentially artistic, as play.

I suggest, then, that the conceptions of metaphysical comfort, the tragic and the rebirth of tragedy, all need to be read in a manner fundamentally different from the way in which they have hitherto been interpreted. The importance of these ideas, which are linked by Nietzsche to the themes which surface in the latter sections of the book, devoted in large part to a consideration of Wagner, Schopenhauer, and the destiny of the German spirit, lies in their irony. Nietzsche sets out the three stages of illusion in such a way that given the rhetoric describing the rebirth of tragedy in Germany one can only conclude that the German spirit is passing, in a strictly historical manner, from one stage to another. If the tragic stage were the highest, the goal of the genetic-historical process, then the result would be a Buddhistic culture. This interpretation seems to be the only possible one if we are persuaded by Nietzsche's pseudo-historical rhetoric. A close reading of the following description of tragic culture reveals that this cannot be the culture on which he has pinned his hopes:

> With this insight [that the phenomenal world is illusory and distinguishable from its essence] a culture is inaugurated that I venture to call a tragic culture. Its most important characteristic is that wisdom takes the place of science as the highest end—wisdom, that [. . .] turns with unmoved eyes to a comprehensive view of the world, and seeks to grasp, with sympathetic feelings of love, the eternal suffering as its own. (BT, 18)

But seeking to grasp the eternal sufferings of the world as its own cannot be a description of an affirmative culture, but rather of a culture which embraces metaphysical comfort; that is to say, a description of a culture that denies the artistic play between the Apollinian and the Dionysian. Such a denial is the explicit result of Schopenhauer's reflections on art, which lead not to an affirmation of life through illusion, but rather to tragic resignation in the quietism of the will.

Seen in this light, the genetic movement described by Nietzsche from an Alexandrian to a tragic culture must be seen as a rhetorical ruse of sorts—reflected in the equivocal manner Nietzsche describes this process[69]—whose function is to hide the fact that the equation of the tragic and the Buddhistic ironically undermines the call for a rebirth of tragedy. Nietzsche's text does what he himself was prevented from doing, namely, laugh at "all the hasty hopes and faulty applications to the present" expressed in this book.[70] Does this make *The Birth of Tragedy* contradictory and incoherent as Clark claims? Surely not. Such a reading can only proceed by imposing on the text oppositions and assumptions which it explicitly puts into question, most notably, the opposition between the literal and figural.[71] Rather, the foregoing attests to the enormous complexity and difficulty of the issues—theoretical, cultural, psychological—with which Nietzsche's book concerns itself. I would suggest that the way to confront these difficulties is not, following Clark, to dismiss the book as incoherent, but to read its many rhetorical-philosophical strategies as best one can. In so doing we follow the example of Nietzsche, who, far from rejecting his first book, returns to its labyrinths again and again.[72]

Chapter 4

Reading Nietzsche's Naturalism

> *To translate man back into nature; to become master over the many vain and overly enthusiastic interpretations and connotations that have so far been scrawled and painted over that eternal basic text of* homo natura *[. . .] that may be a strange and insane task, but it is a* task—*who would deny that!*
>
> —*Nietzsche,* Beyond Good and Evil

> *'The story won't tell,' said Douglas; 'not in any literal vulgar way.' 'More's the pity then. That's the only way I ever understand.'*
>
> —*Henry James,* The Turn of the Screw

THE PROBLEM OF NATURALISM

Although it is commonly accepted that the two hallmarks of Nietzsche's later writings are a deeply rooted skepticism towards traditional conceptions of truth and a critique of Judeo-Christian morality, relatively little attention has been paid to the relationship between these two strands of Nietzsche's thought. One reason for this might be the fact that Nietzsche's critique of truth and morality are commonly taken to be two complementary aspects of a single endeavor, namely, a critique of the concepts and values of Western metaphysics. Eugen Fink expresses the view of many when he characterizes Nietzsche's philosophy as a reaction against "everything that has heretofore been regarded as 'holy' and 'true' and 'good.'"[1] While the origins of Nietzsche's critique of truth and morality can be traced back to different stages in his development—the former is first voiced in the essay "On Truth and Lie in the Extra-Moral Sense" dictated in June, 1873, while the latter has its origin in the

Dawn, published in 1881—there is ample textual evidence to support the view that, in the later writings, the two tasks are consonant aspects of a single critical project. In the third essay of *On the Genealogy of Morals*, written in 1887, Nietzsche explicitly links these two tasks:

> All great things bring about their own destruction through an act of self-overcoming [. . .]. In this way Christianity *as a dogma* was destroyed by its own morality; in the same way Christianity *as morality* must now perish, too,—we stand on the threshold of *this* event. After Christian truthfulness has drawn one inference after another, it must end by drawing its *most striking inference*, its inference *against* itself: this will happen, however, when it poses the question 'what is the meaning of *all will to truth*?' (GM, III.27)

For Nietzsche, Christian morality and the metaphysical concept of truth suffer from a similar structural flaw, namely, that they are interpretations which, because of their very content, are forced to deny and dissemble their status as interpretations. Although Christian morality is merely one interpretation of the world among many, it promotes itself as a code of behavior which, grounded in divine revelation, embodies the ultimate truth of existence. This dependence on revelation and the corresponding claim to ultimacy forces morality to deny its conditionality as interpretation and, consequently, to exclude the possibility of other, competing interpretations. The demonization of the Jews in the New Testament and much of the subsequent history of European anti-Semitism can be explained by the fact that the truth of Christianity's interpretation of existence was, in the eyes of many Christians, threatened by the the continued existence of the Jews and their unwillingness to accept Christ as the son of God.[2]

The logic of the metaphysical concept of truth functions in a similar manner. The claim to truth is a claim for exclusivity and universality. The binary logic of truth expressed in the principle of non-contradiction demands that if A is true, then not-A must be false. Competing interpretations which imply not-A must be weighed against the available evidence and either rejected or, if the evidence so warrants, be accepted at the expense of A. The exclusivity of truth is a function of its universality. To say that every effect has a cause is not to assert something contingent about the world, dependent on the subjective constitution of my sense organs and my experience, but rather to state something that must, on pain of irrationality, be adopted by all other persons. If a statement is true, it represents the coalescence of all potential perspectives into a single, overarching perspective, which, because it is universal and excludes other competing points of view, can no longer be called a perspective at all but a fact, an objective statement of how the world is.

Nietzsche's critique of morality and of the metaphysical concept of truth begins by calling attention to their dependence on a process of dissimulation whereby their status as interpretations is hidden and replaced by a universal claim to validity. Such a procedure, Nietzsche claims, can only be carried out by "standing truth on her head and denying *perspective* itself, the fundamental condition of all life" (BGE, P). To claim that all knowing is perspectival is not to deny the possibility of truth as such, but to undermine the plausibility of the metaphysical concept of truth, whose logic leaves no room for the possibility of competing, equally veridical perspectives and interpretations: "There is *only* a perspective seeing, *only* a perspective 'knowing'; and the *more* affects we allow to speak about one thing, the *more* eyes, different eyes, we can use to observe one thing, the more complete will be our 'concept' of this thing, our 'objectivity'" (GM, III.12). It follows from this that the concept of truth can no longer be understood as both universal and exclusive. Rather, the wedding of truth and perspective means that the concept of truth needs to be thought as a species of interpretation that is essentially particular—inseparable from the perspective that gives rise to it—and multiple, the assertion of a single truth does not rule out the possibility of other competing interpretations: "There are many eyes [. . .]. Consequently there are many 'truths,' hence there is no truth" (KSA 11, 34.230). As these two passages suggest, the richness of our understanding of a thing is proportional to the number of perspectives and the variety of truths that can be brought to bear on it. The open-ended nature of this process stands in contrast to the drive for truth in the traditional sense, whose parameters are both closed and determinate.

While there is nothing in what we have said so far that would suggest there is an essential conflict between these two aspects of Nietzsche's thought, if we move beyond the merely structural level and consider the substance of Nietzsche's critique of morality in more detail, this relationship becomes rather more complicated. For it soon becomes clear that Nietzsche's main objection to morality is not its claim to be a universal interpretation of existence, but rather what he takes to be its open hostility to life. Consider a passage from the second essay of the *Genealogy*:

> To speak of just and unjust *in itself* is quite senseless; *in itself*, of course no injury, assault, exploitation, destruction can be 'unjust,' since life operates *essentially* [essentiell], that is in its basic functions, through injury, assault, exploitation, destruction and simply cannot be thought of at all without this character. One must indeed grant something even more unpalatable: that from the highest biological standpoint, legal conditions can never be other than exceptional conditions, since they constitute a partial restriction of the will to life, which is bent upon power, and are subordinate to its total goal as a single means: namely as a

> means of creating greater units of power. A legal order thought of as sovereign and universal, not as a means in the struggles between power-complexes but as a means of *preventing* all struggle in general [. . .] would be a principle *hostile to life*, an agent of the dissolution and destruction of man. (GM, II.11)

What is striking about this passage is the fact that Nietzsche's critique of justice seems to depend on an essentialistic understanding of the concept of life. This is suggested by the assertion that the meanings of the terms just and unjust are not unconditional or in any sense absolute because certain types of actions, namely, those that fall under the categories of assault, injury, exploitation, and destruction, belong to life's basic functions, without which the concept of life cannot be thought. The italicization of the word *essentially* underscores the fact that what is being described is the essence of life, rather than a set of contingent or arbitrary characteristics. This interpretation is supported by Nietzsche's second claim, namely, that conflict belongs to the essence of what lives and that, judged from a biological standpoint, any systematic attempt to interfere with this process, such as a legal order dedicated to preventing conflict in general, undermines the aims of life.

While a seasoned reader might attribute such a passage to Nietzsche's well-known tendency for rhetorical excess and provocation and accord it little, if any, philosophical significance,[3] it proves more difficult to explain away a second passage whose vocabulary, tone, and form are remarkably similar:

> Everywhere people are now raving, even under scientific disguises, about coming conditions of society in which "the exploitative aspect" [*der ausbeuterische Charakter*] will be removed—which sounds to me as if they promised to invent a way of life that would dispense with all organic functions. 'Exploitation' does not belong to a corrupt or imperfect and primitive society, it belongs to the *essence* of what lives, as a basic organic function [*organische Grundfunktion*]; it is a consequence of the will to power, which is after all the will of life. (BGE, 259)

This passage reiterates two of the features that we found in the passage from the *Genealogy*, namely, an attempt to define and circumscribe the concept of life by reference to one or more basic functions that are then said to belong to the essence of what lives—here, too, the word essence is underscored—and the suggestion that any attempt to remove or attenuate the effects of these basic functions would be inimical to life. This last point is made quite explicitly in a section from *Twilight of the Idols* entitled "Morality as Anti-Nature" [*Moral als Widernatur*], where Nietzsche contrasts two types of morality that are characterized by their contrasting relationship to life: a natural or healthy morality that gives expression to an instinct of life is juxtaposed with an "anti-natural morality" that legislates against life's instincts (TI, V.4).

This brief sample of passages from Nietzsche's later writings displays characteristics that few would associate with Nietzschean thought. The seemingly essentialist understanding of the concepts of life and nature and the attempt to ground a view of society and morality in a crypto-biologistic concept of organic function and instinct found in these passages appear to directly violate the strictures of Nietzsche's theory of interpretation. This theory opposes the metaphysical concept of truth and its goal of an universal, objective interpretation, with a perspectivist model of interpretation that explicitly embraces the idea of interpretative multiplicity. In a particularly striking formulation of this idea Nietzsche writes of his hope that "today we are at least far from the ridiculous immodesty that would be involved in decreeing from our corner that perspectives are *permitted* only from this corner. Rather the world has become 'infinite' for us all over again, inasmuch as we cannot reject the possibility that it *includes infinite interpretations*" (GS, 374).[4] Are the passages surveyed above not immodest to the extent that they decree from their corner "that perspectives are permitted only from this corner"? How else are we to understand Nietzsche's references to the essence of life and its basic functions? Viewed in this light, these passages suggest that there is a conflict between Nietzsche's critique of the metaphysical concept of truth and his critique of morality, whose substance appears to depend on an essentialist and decidedly metaphysical understanding of the concepts of nature and life.

In what follows we will critically examine the naturalistic rhetoric that underlies Nietzsche's critique of morality and those concepts—nature, life, physiology, sickness, and health—most central to it. Our aim is to determine whether Nietzsche's naturalistic rhetoric is inconsistent with his critique of truth, whether his use of naturalistic categories as a *mochlos* against morality does not in fact resolve itself into a form of metaphysical naturalism, precisely the kind of essentialist thought ruled out by his critique of the metaphysical concept of truth.[5]

LIFE

The question of life in Nietzsche's later writings is intimately related to his conception of power. More precisely, life for Nietzsche seems to be nothing more than a will to power, a never-ending striving for greater and greater quanta of power: "What is good? Everything that heightens the feeling of power in man, the will to power, power itself" (A, 2). Accordingly, the acquisition of power becomes an end in itself and one of the main criteria for determining whether a moral code, a work of art, or a mode of social organization is life affirming—a means of increasing power—or life negating, a symptom of weakness and ever-decreasing power. This identification of life with the will to power and its application to the realm of social theory is described in detail in a passage some commentators have suggested reveal the true political colors of this self-described "last *anti-political* German." This passage, briefly cited in the previous section, will now be rendered in full:

> Refraining mutually from injury, violence, and exploitation and placing one's will on a par with that of someone else—this may become, in a certain rough sense, good manners among individuals if the appropriate conditions are present (namely, if these individuals are actually similar in strength and value standards and belong together in *one* body). But as soon as this principle [*Princip*] is extended, and possibly even accepted as the *fundamental principle of society*, it immediately proves to be what it really is—a will to the *denial* of life, a principle of disintegration and decay.
>
> Here we must be beware of superficiality and get to the bottom of the matter, resisting all sentimental weakness: life itself is *essentially* appropriation, injury, overpowering of what is alien and weaker; suppression, hardness, imposition of one's own forms, incorporation and at least, at its mildest, exploitation—but why should one use those words in which a slanderous intent has been imprinted for ages?
>
> Even the body within which individuals treat each other as equals, as suggested before—and this happens in every healthy aristocracy—if it is a living and not a dying body, it has to do to other bodies what the individuals within it refrain from doing to each other: it will have to be an incarnate will to power, it will strive to grow, spread, seize, become predominant—not from any morality or immorality but because it is *living* and because life simply *is* will to power. But there is no point on which the ordinary consciousness of Europeans resists instruction as on this: Everywhere people are now raving, even under scientific disguises, about coming conditions of society in which "the exploitative aspect" [*der ausbeuterische Charakter*] will be removed—which sounds to me as if they promised to invent a way of life that would dispense with all organic functions. "Exploitation" does not belong to a corrupt or imperfect and primitive society, it belongs to the *essence* of what lives, as a basic organic function [*organische Grundfunktion*]; it is a consequence of the will to power, which is after all the will of life.
>
> —If this should be an innovation as a theory—as a reality it is the *primordial fact* [Ur-Faktum] of all history: people ought to be honest with themselves at least this far!—(BGE, 259)

In the first part of this passage Nietzsche describes the conditions under which individuals within a given society can suspend the *bellum omnium contra omnes* and live with one another in a condition of relative peace. The principle that the members of this social body invoke in order to establish peace is only applied to a group of individuals who in certain determinate ways are already equal, individuals who, Nietzsche maintains, "are actually similar in strength and value standards and belong together in *one* body [*Körper*]." Such a social organization, observed in every healthy aristocracy, constitutes a de facto recognition of equality rather than an attempt to impose a state of social equality from the outside. Nietzsche says this directly when he writes that the state of war can be suspended "if the appropriate conditions are present (namely, if these individuals are actually similar in strength and value standards and belong together in *one* body)." If follows from this that if the appropriate conditions were to cease to exist, if some members of the social body were to become stronger and others were to become weaker, then the principle of equality which suspends the state of war could no longer be applied to this social body. It would in fact then become a principle of disintegration and decay, which would seek to enforce a state of equality upon a social body of manifest inequality. The principle of equality is therefore a descriptive rather than a normative principle, which is life affirming in those circumstances in which it is applied to existing states of equality, but which then becomes a principle hostile to life when it is applied to conditions of inequality.[6]

This is precisely what is at issue when the principle of equality is extended and recognized as the fundamental principle of society. Because societies are constituted by differing degrees of inequality, when the principle of equality is applied to society as a whole it can be nothing more than "a will to the *denial* of life, a principle of disintegration and decay." Nietzsche's insistence that the broad application of the principle of equality leads not merely to social decline but represents a denial of life, raises the question of what precisely in life is denied when the principle is applied in this way. Why does Nietzsche invoke the phenomenon of life as a standard that is violated by the generalization of the principle of equality? An initial answer to this question can to be found in the definition of life Nietzsche gives in the ensuing paragraph. Here we read that "life itself is *essentially* appropriation, injury, overpowering of what is alien and weaker; suppression, hardness, imposition of one's own forms, incorporation and at least, at its mildest, exploitation." If life is essentially agonistic and exploitative, then any attempt to enforce equality and to suspend the state of war within a given society would be tantamount to a suspension of the very conditions of life itself. And to suspend the conditions of life, those operations that belong to the very essence of life, is to deny life.

This does not, however, explain why the principle of equality does not represent a denial of life even when it is applied *ex post facto* to a social body whose members are already equal. How is it that a social body such as the one described in the first paragraph does not represent a form of life which has already begun to disintegrate and decay? Nietzsche answers this question when he reconsiders the social body within which individuals treat each other as equals. Here we find that the application of the principle of equality does not actually lead to a suspension of war—and hence a suspension of the essential conditions of life—rather, the forces that produce the state of war within an unequal society are, in an equal society, redirected outwards against other bodies. This expression of force does nor derive from any malicious or immoral intent on the part of the members of this society, but is a consequence of the operations and processes constitutive of life. For if this social body "is a living and not a dying body, it has to do to other bodies what the individuals within it refrain from doing to each other: it will have to be an incarnate will to power, it will strive to grow, spread, seize, become predominant—not from any morality or immorality but because it is *living* and because life simply *is* will to power."

Rather than extinguishing the forces essential to life, the principle of equality redirects these forces outwards when it is applied to a social body made up of individuals who, because they are similar in strength and values, belong to one body. In circumstances such as these, the principle of equality acts to conserve rather than dissipate life's agonistic forces. This act of conservation is crucial to the fate of the social body, for by expressing these forces outward, by doing to other bodies what the individual members of this social body refrain from doing to one another, it proves itself to be a *living* body. It is life itself which prescribes that the forces of appropriation, overpowering and exploitation be conserved and discharged. A cessation of this process is, Nietzsche asserts, a sign of decline and impending death. Life needs to express itself in this way because processes like exploitation belong to the essence of life and are necessary to its preservation and growth: "'Exploitation' does not belong to a corrupt or imperfect and primitive society, it belongs to the *essence* of what lives, as a basic organic function; it is a consequence of the will to power, which is after all the will of life."[7]

Drawing on this last remark, one could conclude that the concept life plays a role in Nietzsche's later writings identical to that of the concept of *arche* in Aristotle, where it comes to designate both inception and domination, a thing's beginning and its ruling principle.[8] In contrast with the logic of the principle of equality, which as we have noted is a logic of description, the concept of life performs a prescriptive or normative function in this passage. This is reflected in the way in which Nietzsche generalizes from a conception of biological life to a concept of life that serves as a standard against which different forms of social organization can be judged. Throughout the section we are considering Nietzsche extends the image of the body understood in biological terms to the social body; the forces that are at work in the former are also to be found in the latter, and more important, the same prohibitions and prescriptions that apply to the living body apply equally to the social body. Thus Nietzsche can assert that the social body must exploit the other bodies around it because exploitation "belongs to the *essence* of what lives, as a basic organic function." The social body is brought into being by imitating structures already existing in nature. What unites the two kinds of bodies, the biological and the social, in this text is the fact that both are embodiments of the will to power. Since life is nothing other than will to power, everything that is alive is subject to the same conditions and needs, principal among them, the drive for increased power.

A second affinity that this passage displays to classical metaphysics is the manner in which Nietzsche defines the concept of life. One of the most consistent themes in Nietzsche's writings is a deep-seated suspicion of any philosophy that begins with the Socratic question What is . . . ? Questions of this form unequivocally ask for a definition, an identity statement that would establish a necessary relationship between an entity and its essence. Yet the seemingly objective form of such inquiries masks their essentially axiological quality, the inescapable fact that behind the question itself stands the unspoken interest of the inquirer:

> The question 'What is that?' is an *imposition of meaning* seen from the perspective of something else. The 'essence,' 'the essential nature,' is something perspectival [. . .]. At bottom always lies 'what is that for *me*?' (for us, for everything that lives, etc.). (KSA 12, 2.149)

However, in the section under consideration Nietzsche appears to put these suspicions to one side and to define life in a manner that is striking for its essentialist tone and vocabulary. The compelling force behind this is that in order for the concept of life to function normatively, as Nietzsche's critique of morality appears to require, it is necessary to set down its parameters in a way that establishes a single standard or norm of life to the exclusion of all others.

Before examining this passage in greater detail, it would be apposite to consider a second passage from the later writings where the concept of life appears to perform a similar normative function. This second passage, part of which was cited in the previous section, is from the chapter of *Twilight of the Idols* entitled "Morality as Anti-Nature":

> —I reduce a principle to a formula. Every naturalism in morality, that is, every *healthy* morality, is dominated by an instinct of life—some commandment of life is fulfilled by a determinate canon of 'shalt' and 'shalt not'; some inhibition and hostile element on the path of life is thus

> removed. *Anti-natural* morality, that is, almost every morality which has so far been taught, revered, and preached, turns, conversely, *against* the instincts of life: it is *condemnation* of these instincts [. . .]. When it says, 'God looks at the heart,' it says No to both the lowest and the highest desires of life and posits God as the *enemy of life*. The saint in whom God delights is the ideal eunuch. Life comes to an end where the 'kingdom of God' begins. (TI, V.4)

This citation exhibits several important similarities with the passage considered above. As in the previous passage where he distinguishes between different forms of social organization on the basis of whether they are life promoting or are agents of disintegration and death, here Nietzsche differentiates between two forms of morality using similar criteria. Instead of the appellations of life and death that dominate the previous passage, Nietzsche articulates this distinction in terms of what is natural or healthy and what is anti-natural. What separates a healthy or natural morality from one that is anti-natural is the disparate ways in which they relate to the phenomenon of life. More precisely, the distinguishing factor is the manner in which each type of morality embodies—or turns against—the instincts of life.

The normative import of the concept of life is clearest in the account Nietzsche gives of the seemingly oxymoronic term *natural morality*. This account begins, in the section just cited, with the declaration that "every naturalism in morality, that is, every *healthy* morality, is dominated by an instinct of life." The description first establishes an equivalency between nature and health; the element that makes a particular morality natural also makes it healthy. This relationship between nature and health is emphasized by the repetition of the word "every" in this sentence, which precludes the possibility that there could be a natural morality that would be insalubrious. What makes a particular morality natural and healthy? Nietzsche immediately tells us: such a morality is dominated by an instinct of life. The juxtaposition here between the inclusive *every* and the reference to *an* instinct of life is of interest, since the latter is ambiguous. It could mean that every natural morality is dominated by an instinct of life, by a general interest of life, or it could mean that every natural morality is dominated by a particular instinct of life, so that the different natural moralities ("every" suggests that there is more than one) are dominated by different instincts of life. This ambiguity is not present in the sentence which immediately follows: "some commandment of life is fulfilled by a determinate canon of 'shalt' and 'shalt not'; some inhibition and hostile element on the path of life is thus removed." The phrase "some commandment of life" implies that life is capable of giving several different commandments, each of which is fulfilled by a determinate moral canon. This is consistent with Nietzsche's use of the inclusive modifier "every" to describe a natural morality. Corresponding to each commandment of life there is a particular moral canon that is an expression of life, a means of protecting and enhancing life.

Life is not a *vis inertiae*, but an active force that commands. By commanding, life speaks with the voice of nature. But how is it that life should command? What in life or in nature commands? This commanding cannot be merely an uncontrolled expression or explosion of passion or instinct. Nietzsche is careful to say that the command of life is fulfilled in a determinate canon of shalt *and* shalt not. This commanding is not a blind ordering, but a form of legislation, which incorporates prescriptive as well as proscriptive elements.[9] Life both gives and denies permission. The fulfillment of a command of life in a determinate moral canon acts to remove "some inhibition and hostile element on the path of life." The legislation of life is thus a reaction to a threat. Nietzsche does not tell us what kind of threat this is or whether it comes from inside or outside life—if one can speak of inside and outside here. What is clear, however, is that this hostile element compels life to legislate and that this legislation, this saying yes and no, requires that life turn against itself. The denial of life embodied in life's saying no is, however, qualitatively different from the negation that underlies all anti-natural moralities. Rather than conforming to the commands issued by the instincts of life, anti-natural morality turns against life's instincts and seeks to have them extirpated, removed from the general economy of life. But by condemning the instincts of life, anti-natural morality condemns nothing less than life itself: "it says No to both the lowest and the highest desires of life and posits God as the *enemy of life*."

The interpretations we have offered of these two passages lend support to the view that Nietzsche essentializes the concept of life in order to employ it normatively as a standard against which different forms of social organization and morality can be measured and judged. While some readers of Nietzsche have claimed that this conflation of ontology and politics makes Nietzsche into one of the prime forerunners of National Socialism,[10] others have argued that this confusion results from Nietzsche's own misunderstanding of the political consequences of the will to power. Mark Warren, who has passionately argued for the second of these two positions, provides the following commentary to section 259 of *Beyond Good and Evil*:

> Here is the challenge: Nietzsche *explicitly* claims that *political* exploitation can be deduced as necessary to any society from the fact that life is *essentially* will to power. . . . There is no mistaking Nietzsche's point: exploitation of one person by another is ontologically rooted in life as such. Exploitative social relations can be removed from society only at the expense of 'life.' Since 'life' is at the root of value, it follows that

> political exploitation is both natural and perhaps even desirable . . . when Nietzsche elaborates the concept of will to power, he does so metaphysically rather than critically.[11]

On Warren's account, Nietzsche violates the strictures of his own philosophy by applying the concept of will to power to the political realm in an essentializing manner. This occurs, Warren contends, because Nietzsche misunderstands the limits of the will to power. Rather than being the basis for a Machiavellian philosophy of power, the will to power provides the framework for "a philosophy of human agency that shows how individuality, responsibility, and positive freedom are possible, and . . . that could be developed consistently with the social values of reciprocity, mutual processes of individuation, and equality" (NPT, 208).[12] In support of this interpretation, Warren argues that Nietzsche's essentializing use of the will to power and its political application violates his own critique of metaphysics, and that in reading Nietzsche we should distinguish between the metaphysical-political uses of the will to power and the "critical" or non-metaphysical role this concept plays elsewhere in Nietzsche's writings.

Leaving aside the question of whether the will to power can act as a framework for a philosophy of human agency, it remains to be seen whether this strategy of saving Nietzsche from himself in the manner advocated by Warren does not do unnecessary violence to the Nietzschean text. This worry arises out of Warren's own hermeneutic method, which uncritically assumes a rigid distinction between figurative and literal meaning, and more importantly, between language and so-called extra-linguistic entities. Warren defends the second of these two distinctions in the following manner:

> Texts are appropriate as models of discursive *meaning* for Nietzsche, and are perhaps even appropriate as models of cognition. But even meanings and cognitions presuppose *nondiscursive* relations to the world: relations of sensuousness, power, limits and possibilities of the material world, and the like. These are what Nietzsche means to capture in his notion that much of life is made of multifaceted 'Dionysian' qualities. (NPT, 76)

Although Warren is generally a careful reader, this remark displays a puzzling disregard of Nietzsche's theory of interpretation, which begins by putting into question the very distinction between language and the world that Warren takes for granted. Warren denies that a concern for language and interpretation plays a significant role in Nietzsche's later writings, and accuses those "who expand Nietzsche's early emphasis on interpretation to an account of the world" of only being "able to give a thin, textual account of what institutions are" (NPT, 76–77).

But Warren is surely wrong on both counts. We have already noted (in chapter 2) the deep continuity between the views of language and interpretation Nietzsche articulates in the writings of the early 1870s and those of the later writings. Even if this were not the case, it can hardly be denied that interpretation is one of the central themes of Nietzsche's writings in the 1880s.[13] One example among many is section 22 from *Beyond Good and Evil*, which contrasts Nietzsche's own perspectivist interpretative practice with the positivistic hermeneutics of the natural sciences. Other examples could easily be culled from texts such as the fifth book of *The Gay Science* and the *Genealogy*, where, in the case of the latter, the focus is precisely on the question of "institutions."[14]

However, even taken on its own terms Warren's argument fails. Warren claims that there must be an absolute division between language and the world because even entities such as "meanings" and "cognitions" that can be understood as texts presuppose a network of non-discursive relations to the world. After providing a list of examples of such non-discursive relations such as "relations of sensuousness, power, limits and possibilities of the material world," Warren asserts that "these are what Nietzsche means to capture in his notion that much of life is made of of multifaceted 'Dionysian' qualities." In support of this interpretation he cites the final section of *The Birth of Tragedy* where Nietzsche describes the Dionysian as "the basic ground of the world" (NPT, 48).

A more considered reading of this text, something we have attempted in the previous chapter, undermines the contention that the Dionysian denotes a network of non-discursive relations which constitute, literally speaking, the basic ground of the world. Rather than repeating the essentials of this reading, it is sufficient to note that Nietzsche repeatedly emphasizes the figurative function of the Dionysian; a pattern that culminates in the description of the Dionysian as an "illusion" in section 18. The figurative import of the Dionysian is, as we have previously noted, clearly established in the opening section of the book, where Nietzsche describes the Dionysian and the Apollonian as terms "we borrow from the Greeks, who disclose to the discerning mind the profound mysteries of their view of art, not, to be sure, in concepts, but in the intensely clear figures of their gods." In this passage both the Apollonian and the Dionysian are explicitly named as figures that cannot be understood directly, which is to say inferentially, but rather only by way of analogy with the "physiological phenomena" of dreams and rapture. The purpose of the analogy is not to facilitate a reduction of Apollonian and Dionysian to a material or physiological ground, but rather to illustrate how these phenomena serve as models for the type of *mimēsis* embodied in the plastic and musical arts symbolized by the figures of the Apollonian and the Dionysian. It follows from this that if dreams and intoxication are themselves forms of artistic reproduction, then these so-called physiological phenomena are already discursively meaningful.[15] But, of course, if this were not the case it would not be possible to illuminate the Dionysian and the Apollonian through them by way of analogy. If the Dionysian does indeed function as the "basic ground of the world," it is not because it denotes a network of non-discursive relations; on the contrary, it is precisely because it symbolizes the essentially figurative nature of any discourse of ground.[16]

Warren's belief that the concept of the Dionysian precludes the use of textual models to elucidate the relationship between language and 'the material world' and his denial that Nietzsche uses such models in his later writings, encourage him to read Nietzsche in a quasi-positivistic manner. We have already seen the effect of this with regard to section 259 of *Beyond Good and Evil*, which Warren interprets in the most literal way possible, ultimately not even allowing for the possibility of interpretations other than his own: "There is no mistaking Nietzsche's point: exploitation of one person by another is ontologically rooted in life as such" (NPT, 228). Given the assumptions underlying Warren's interpretation, it is impossible not to read texts such as section 259 as gross violations of Nietzsche's critique of metaphysics, as aberrations that need to be read and, in a manner of speaking, neutralized, against the background of Nietzsche's critical philosophy as a whole.

However, if we reject Warren's assumptions and read passages such as these in their proper context and with attention to the exigencies of Nietzsche's texts, the question of their significance becomes problematic, and not something about which there is "no mistaking." One way to begin is to ask whether it would not be apposite to read section 259 of *Beyond Good and Evil* in light of section 22 of the same text. This section is a natural starting point for any discussion of section 259 because here Nietzsche considers both the status of his own art of interpretation and the concept of will to power. If the latter text is as essentializing as it appears to be, we should find some evidence of this also in section 22; if not, then maybe this section will offer some clues as to how to approach the essentializing rhetoric of section 259.

THE WILL TO POWER AS METAPHOR

The section begins with Nietzsche ironically asking for forgiveness from his addressees, modern physicists:

> Forgive me as an old philologist who cannot desist from the malice of putting his finger on bad modes of interpretation: but 'nature's conformity to law' [*Gesetzmässigkeit der Natur*], of which you physicists talk

> so proudly as though——exists only owing to your interpretation and bad 'philology'—it is no matter of fact, no 'text,' but rather only a naively humanitarian emendation and perversion of meaning [*Zurechtmachung und Sinnverdrehung*], with which you make abundant concessions to the democratic instincts of the modern soul! 'Everywhere equality before the law; nature is no different in that respect, no better off than we are'—a fine instance of ulterior motivation, in which the plebeian antagonism to everything privileged and autocratic [. . .] [is] disguised once more [. . .]. But, as said above, that is interpretation, not text; and somebody might come along who, with the opposite intention and mode of interpretation [*Interpretationskunst*], could read off of [*herauslesen*] the same nature and with regard to the same phenomena, rather the tyrannically inconsiderate and relentless enforcement of claims of power—an interpreter who could picture the unexceptional and unconditional aspects of all 'will to power' so vividly that almost every word, even the word 'tyranny' itself, would eventually seem unsuitable, or a weakening and attenuating metaphor—being too human—but he might, nevertheless, end by asserting the same about this world as you do, namely, that it has a 'necessary' and 'calculable' course, *not* because laws obtain in it, but because they are absolutely *lacking* [. . .]. Supposing that this also is only interpretation—and you will be eager enough to make this objection?—well, so much the better.—

Although this section is one of the most frequently cited by commentators writing on Nietzsche's theory of interpretation, it is also one of the most frequently unread of these passages. In part this is due to the fact that this section, like so many of Nietzsche's aphorisms, is often interpreted in isolation; as if one could read Nietzsche's books and their individual sections in any order at all without attending to the complex play between passages, the commentaries and counter-commentaries of section upon section that constitute the economy of the Nietzschean text.[17] Moreover, the complicated grammar of this section, its play of dashes and quotation marks, also makes it quite difficult to follow. A careful reading of this section and of the contrast Nietzsche draws between his art of interpretation and that of the physicists allow two main points of difference to emerge: first, the contrasting status which Nietzsche and the physicists claim for their interpretations, and second, the nature of the assumptions which underlie these interpretations. Both of these issues bear on the questions we raised in regard to section 259, to which we shall have occasion to return.

The general target of Nietzsche's criticism in section 22 is the physicists' belief in nature's conformity to law, in the essential equality of all nature before the law. However, the first objection he raises against the physicist concerns is directed less at the particulars of their belief, than at the form which it takes. After apologizing for being unable to desist from putting his finger on bad modes of interpretation, Nietzsche justifies his actions in the following manner: "But 'nature's conformity to law,' of which you physicists talk so proudly as though——exists only owing to your interpretation and bad 'philology'—it is no fact, no 'text.'" Although Nietzsche fails to finish the first part of his thought, leaving his readers guessing as to what else the physicists might believe,[18] he adamantly asserts that their belief in nature's conformity to law is only an interpretation and one which is the product of a questionable hermeneutics. What arouses Nietzsche's distrust in the first instance is not the physicists' democratic instincts, but the status that they claim for their interpretation. According to the picture Nietzsche paints of them, the physicists believe not merely in nature's conformity to law, but in the absolute veracity of this interpretation; as if one could discover this conformity in a completely objective manner that would not merely describe nature, but explain it as well. Nietzsche had already made this point eight sections earlier, where he suggests that "it is perhaps dawning in five or six minds that physics, too, is only an interpretation and exegesis of the world (in our image, if I may say so!) and *not* a world explanation" (BGE, 14). The distinction Nietzsche here draws between interpretation and explanation is consistent with his assertion that the concepts cause and effect are means of describing the world, not explaining it: "One should use 'cause' and 'effect' only as pure *concepts*, that is to say, as conventional fictions for the purpose of designation and communication—*not* for explanation" (BGE, 21).[19]

Of course what distinguishes explanation from description is that while there may be several competing descriptions of an event, each of which may be valid in its own right, there can only be one valid explanation. If the physicists' assertion that nature is lawful is to count as an explanation, then it must be either correct or incorrect, but not both. However, if this assertion as well as Nietzsche's own—that the equality before the law is actually a consequence of the will to power—are understood as descriptions, then there is no reason why one should claim an essential priority over the other. In other words, the two descriptions need not be mutually exclusive. Nietzsche says precisely this when he describes the possibility that "somebody might come along who, with the opposite intention and mode of interpretation, could read off of the same nature and with regard to the same phenomena, rather the tyrannically inconsiderate and relentless enforcement of claims of power." Given the fact that the same set of phenomena is open to more than one description, it follows that no one description can claim an unconditional authority over any other. Such a claim would, in Nietzsche's view, fall into the trap that philosophers since Plato have stumbled into, namely, the trap of dogmatism, which begins "as soon as any philosophy begins to believe itself" (BGE, 9). This explains why Nietzsche is more than willing to grant the physicists' objection near the end of section 22 that his account of nature is also "only interpretation."

The significance of this admission should not escape us, for it has important implications for the way in which Nietzsche understands the concepts of will to power and nature. The concession that his account of nature as will to power is interpretation rather than explanation precludes the possibility of an essentialist account of either nature or the will to power. We have already noted that nature does not, in itself, unconditionally constrain the ways in which it can be described and interpreted; two opposed interpretations can be based on the same set of phenomena. If there is no single essence of nature that constitutes a norm against which interpretations can judged, or if the essence of nature consists in the fact that it can be interpreted in a variety of ways none of which can claim unconditional authority over the other, then any attempt to uniquely determine nature either as a set of phenomena that obeys certain observable laws or as will to power can be exposed as dogmatic, that is, an interpretation that has begun to believe in itself.

The same sort of conclusions apply equally to the concept of will to power. That Nietzsche was well aware of this can easily be seen from the fact that the expression will to power appears in section 22 within quotation marks. It is used in the context of Nietzsche's description of his own art of interpretation, which we cite here for a second time:

> and somebody might come along who, with the opposite intention and mode of interpretation, could read off of the same nature and with regard to the same phenomena, rather the tyrannically inconsiderate and relentless enforcement of claims of power—an interpreter who could picture the unexceptional and unconditional aspects of all 'will to power' so vividly that almost every word, even the word 'tyranny' itself, would eventually seem unsuitable, or a weakening and attenuating metaphor—being too human—but he might, nevertheless, end by asserting the same about this world as you do, namely, that it has a 'necessary' and 'calculable' course, *not* because laws obtain in it, but because they are absolutely *lacking* [. . .].

The appearance of the expression will to power within quotation marks functions to disrupt its literality and amounts to an admission that even this expression is "only interpretation." The ambiguous status of the will to power, the need to enclose it within quotation marks, is not a consequence of anything peculiar to this concept, but is a coded recognition—perhaps not entirely conscious—of the irreducible suspension of language as such between its literal and figurative modes. Certainly it cannot be regarded as either an innocent or an isolated gesture, since it was Nietzsche's habit, from the very beginning, to bracket the fundamental concepts of Western metaphysics in this way, inaugurating what Derrida has termed "the epochal regime of quotation marks which is to be enforced for every concept belonging to the system of philosophical decidability."[20] Moreover, if we read this section with the rhetorical awareness provided by Nietzsche's theory of language and rhetoric, we find that there is a striking parallel between it and that theory's emphasis on the intra-linguistic resources of language, rather than its referential function, as a determinant of linguistic meaning. The emphasis in section 22, as in the texts we considered previously from the early 1870s, is shifted away from reference as a determinant of meaning towards the constitutive roles played by language and interpretation.

This is reflected in the way in which Nietzsche introduces the will to power into this passage. At first glance this description appears to assume a rigid distinction between the literal and the figurative in order to affirm the foundational status of the will to power. However, a closer reading reveals that this description turns back on itself in such a way as to suspend this very distinction. The sentence in question runs as follows: "An interpreter could picture [*vor Augen stellte*] the unexceptional and unconditional aspects of all 'will to power' so vividly that almost every word, even the word 'tyranny' itself, would eventually seem unsuitable, or a weakening and attenuating metaphor." This sentence appears to assert the literality and primacy of the will to power in contrast with the whole of language as such, implying that the will to power derives it significance and authority from an extra-linguistic referent situated beyond the limits of language. However, if we read closely we find that the passage also says the opposite of this. Nietzsche's use of the conditional tense in describing the possibility of picturing the will to power in such a way so that almost every other word would eventually seem to be a weakening and unsuitable metaphor, and his use of quotation marks around the expression itself, testify not to the possibility of exceeding the limits of the figural in a realm of pure literality, but to the radical undecidability of the concept of will to power. What the passage actually describes is how an interpreter, one schooled in ancient rhetoric perhaps, could be so clever as to make it seem as if the will to power were not a metaphor at all, but a source of literal truth against which almost every word would seem inadequate.[21]

LIFE AND INTERPRETATION

On the basis of our reading of section 22 we can draw the following two conclusions. First, that no one interpretation can unconditionally claim a privileged position in regard to other interpretations. The fact that the same set of phenomena is in principle open to a multiplicity of diverse, even mutually exclusive interpretations precludes the possibility of a single interpretation which would, in virtue of its having captured the essential nature of an object or set of phenomena, unconditionally exclude all other interpretations. Second, the will to power does not name the essence of nature, but is one way among others of describing nature, a form of description that Nietzsche recognizes as explicitly metaphorical.

These conclusions unavoidably affect the way in which we read section 259. For it is quite clear that Nietzsche's explicit recognition of the rhetorical and perspectival nature of all ontological discourse undermines the literal and straightforward reading of the essentializing rhetoric of section 259. Eric Blondel has captured the characteristic effect of strategies such as the one we have just documented. "If Nietzsche can represent a truly new attempt to 'deny' metaphysics," writes Blondel

> it is to the extent that he does and undoes metaphysics *in the same movement*. It is Nietzsche's very text that *assures* this *construction and destruction* of metaphysics. . . . It would, therefore, be naive to catch Nietzsche red-handed at work on metaphysics: he has an *alibi*, since he is, *at the same time, somewhere else*.[22]

The duplicity characteristic of Nietzsche's writing is underscored in the present case by the internal connections between sections 22 and 259. In addition to the circumstance, to which we have already alluded, that both sections make reference to the will to power, there is the crucial, albeit less obvious fact that section 22 foreshadows the political distinctions that lie at the heart of section 259. We recall that the second of the two objections Nietzsche raises against the physicists' interpretation of nature in section 22 is their willingness to make "abundant concessions to the democratic instincts of the modern soul" by accepting a democratic conception of equality before the law, an acceptance motivated, in Nietzsche's view, by a "plebeian antagonism to everything privileged and autocratic." Against this, Nietzsche suggests that nature be read as an arena for the relentless enforcement of competing claims of power. And it is precisely this juxtaposition of the democratic principle of equality with a conception of nature as an endless struggle for power that we find in section 259, but with a single difference: in section 22 Nietzsche explicitly acknowledges that both the principle of equality and the figure of will to power are interpretations, while in section 259 Nietzsche claims that the struggle for power is the "primordial fact" of all history. While one might be tempted to read this statement ontologically—and the rhetoric of the passage clearly suggests this—the explicit admission, made in section 22, that the struggle for power is not a fact at all but an interpretation, destroys this possibility and forces us instead to seek to trace the complex movements and counter-movements of the text, which concurrently offer and withdraw the possibility of an ultimate synthesis.

LIFE-POWER

While we now have good reason to doubt Warren's contention that, for Nietzsche, "exploitation of one person by another is ontologically rooted in life as such," it remains an open question as to how one is to read descriptions of life such as we find in section 259. Even if we accept that Nietzsche's essentialist rhetoric is deeply ambiguous, simultaneously constructive and destructive, is it not also true that this rhetoric sanctions the most horrific political violence?[23] Putting the question in slightly different terms, we might ask whether it is not the case that the concept of will to power entails not merely the expression of one's own power, a desire to grow, but inevitably also domination, the expression of power over another? This conclusion seems almost unavoidable when one reads passages such as this one from section 258:

> The essential characteristic of a good and healthy aristocracy, however, is that it experiences itself *not* as a function [. . .] that it therefore accepts with a good conscience the sacrifice of untold human beings who, *for its sake*, must be reduced and lowered to incomplete beings, to slaves, to instruments.

There is a great temptation to read passages such as this through the lens of National Socialism and conclude, as one commentator has, that "similar reasoning was used to justify, among other atrocities, the conquest of Poland and the concentration and death camps."[24] However before agreeing that, for Nietzsche, political violence, as an expression of the will to power, is necessary to life, we might ask whether it is not rather the need for conflict and struggle that Nietzsche gives voice to here, much as Heraclitus does when he writes that "War [*polemos*] is father of all and king of all; and some he has shown as gods, others men; some he has made slaves, others free."[25] Some support for this interpretation is to be found in the nature of the conflict opposed by the principle of equality in section 259. Let us recall the opening sentence of the section:

> Refraining mutually from injury, violence, and exploitation and placing one's will on a par with that of someone else—this may become, in a certain rough sense, good manners among individuals if the appropriate conditions are present.

The appropriate conditions to which Nietzsche here refers are conditions of equality existing within a social body; a "healthy aristocracy," as he will put it later in the section. The remainder of the section suggests that Nietzsche's objection to the application of this principle to society as a whole, the reason why he describes it as life denying, is that political violence is rooted in life as such. But it is not entirely clear that the passage can only be read in this way. If we closely attend to wording of the opening sentence, a rather different reading becomes possible. For here Nietzsche does not speak of violence as such, but rather of *mutual* violence, which implies that both parties are capable of inflicting injury and exploitation. The importance of conflict is emphasized by Nietzsche's assertion that a cessation of hostilities within the social body must necessarily be followed by the commencement of hostilities between this body and another. However, these hostilities will not differ demonstrably from those that occur between individual members of the social body. In fact, Nietzsche says they will be exactly the same: the body will have "to do to other bodies what the individuals within it refrain from doing to one another." But if these individuals are engaged in mutual injury and exploitation, then the violence that the social body inflicts on other bodies will also be mutual. It is also important to note that Nietzsche speaks of bodies, not a single body, which implies that the hostilities he describes cannot be understood in terms of a simple political opposition between oppressor and oppressed.

More telling for the thesis that the interests of life are better served by conflict than by political violence as such is the parallel between this section and Nietzsche's account of the origin of bad conscience. In both cases what is at issue is the way in which force—the will to power—is conserved and redirected. In the case of the aristocratic social body, life demands that the body "strive to grow, spread, seize and become predominant" in relation to other bodies. This demand arises not out of the social body itself, its existence as a political body, but rather out of the wills of the individual members of the body. What Nietzsche narrates here is the conservation and subsequent redirection of force from individuals to social bodies required by life. Nietzsche describes a similar movement with a slightly different effect in relation to the origin of bad conscience. Here, too, the starting point of the discussion is a group of individuals who suddenly finds themselves to be members of a single social body. Unlike the members of the aristocracy who choose to align themselves, these individuals are forcibly socialized. The effect of this socialization is, at least with respect to the conservation of the will of these individuals, the same. Rather than releasing the tension that existed between individuals, these hostilities are redirected inward:

> Those fearful bulwarks with which the political organization protected itself [. . .] brought about that all those instincts of wild, free, prowling

> man turned backward *against man himself* [. . .]. The man who, from lack of external enemies and resistances and forcibly confined to the oppressive narrowness and punctiliousness of custom, impatiently lacerated, persecuted, gnawed at, assaulted, and maltreated himself. (GM, II.16)

Nietzsche's reaction to this event leaves no doubt as to whether the interests of life were thereby served:

> the existence on earth of an animal soul turned against itself [. . .] was something so new, profound, unheard of, enigmatic, contradictory, *and pregnant with a future* that the aspect of the earth was essentially altered [. . .]. From now on, man [. . .] gives rise to an interest, a tension a hope, almost a certainty, as if with him something were announced and preparing itself, as if man were not a goal but only a way, an episode, a bridge, a great promise—. (GM, II.16)

What interests Nietzsche in this account of the origin of bad conscience is the way in which conflict, here that of an individual with himself, becomes productive. It is not the expression of violence that Nietzsche celebrates, but rather the relationship between conflict and creativity. His objection to democracy and the principle of equality arises not out of an essentialist conception of life, or out of a commitment to political violence as such, but rather out of a conviction that conflict is an unavoidable and necessary ingredient of higher culture. However, this is not a view which Nietzsche came to hold only in the later writings. It is already to be found in at least two texts from the early 1870s. The first and most obvious point of reference is *The Birth of Tragedy*, where the richness of the relationship between Apollo and Dionysus is linked to its fundamentally agonistic character, "just as procreation depends on the duality of the sexes, involving perpetual strife with only periodically intervening reconciliations" (BT, 1). Nietzsche expresses this same thought in more general terms when, paraphrasing Heraclitus, he describes "the eternal contradiction" in the primal unity as "the father of things" (BT, 4). An equally important though lesser known text is the short essay "Homer's Contest," one of the five forewords for five unwritten books written for Cosima Wagner in the winter of 1872. In this essay Nietzsche describes the contest as "the eternal foundation of the Hellenic state" (KSA 1, 787), and suggests that the Greeks honored the contest because they recognized that "the 'natural' qualities and those actually called 'human' are inseparably bound up with one another." In a remark that foreshadows ideas that will be central to the texts of the 1880s, Nietzsche goes on to suggest that the "frightful abilities, those considered to be inhuman, are perhaps even the terrible foundation out of which alone all humanity, in feelings, deeds and and works, can grow" (KSA 1, 783).

These passages contain the seeds of the critique of democracy and socialism which Nietzsche will develop in the writings of the late 1880s. It is well known that a large part of this critique will grow out of Nietzsche's conviction that human beings are essentially unequal and that any attempt to equalize these differences will necessarily have pernicious effects on the health of individuals and the culture at large. Equally important, however, is the manner in which both democracy and socialism, as Nietzsche understood them, strive to eliminate all traces of conflict within society.[26] This, and not equality in itself, must be regarded as Nietzsche's most basic objection to the acceptance of the principle of equality as the fundamental principle of society. His conviction that conflict is essential to the health of any given society is, I suggest, the basis for his vituperative remarks against those who proclaim that exploitation and other like processes will be lacking in societies of the future.

Identifying strife rather political violence as the key to Nietzsche's understanding of the relationship between life and different forms of social-political organization grants us a deeper appreciation of why Nietzsche praises, in crucial moments in each of the three essays of the *Genealogy*, precisely those actions that either lead to the downfall of the ruling aristocracy, or in the case of the third essay, perpetuate and secure the rule of the ascetic priests. If exploitation—understood as the rule of the strong over the weak—is ontologically rooted in life as such then we would expect Nietzsche to unreservedly condemn events such as the slave revolt in morals because it produced a reversal not merely of values, but of substantive power relations as well. But Nietzsche's account of the slave revolt in the first essay of the *Genealogy* fails to confirm this expectation. On the contrary, like the description of the origins of bad conscience cited above, Nietzsche describes the slave revolt in the most affirmative of terms:

> it is clear from the whole nature of an essentially priestly aristocracy why antithetical valuations could [. . .] become dangerously deepened, sharpened and internalized [. . .]. For with the priests *everything* becomes more dangerous [. . .] it was on the soil of this *essentially dangerous* form of human existence, the priestly form, that man first became *an interesting animal*, that only here did the human soul in a higher sense acquire *depth* and become *malevolent* [Böse]—and these are the two basic respects in which man has hitherto been superior to other beasts! (GM, I.6)

The slave revolt in morals, engendered by the "most impotent" of all enemies, the priests, is responsible for man becoming an interesting animal.

How was this deed perpetrated? The answer should be familiar by now: by transforming the human soul into a battleground. Whereas the healthy and noble type of man affirms himself spontaneously through action, the priests "turn away from action and alternate between brooding and emotional explosions" (GM, I.6). In a similar manner to those beasts described by Nietzsche in the second essay whose instincts turned inwards against them as a result of their being imprisoned within the walls of society, the priests' instincts, "denied the true reaction, that of deeds," "compensate themselves with an imaginary revenge" (GM, I.10). It is precisely this internalization of the instincts that triggers the slave revolt in morality, which "begins when *ressentiment* becomes creative and gives birth to values" (GM, I.10).[27] The process of internalization thus transforms the most impotent of all foes into the most formidable and powerful of enemies, capable of triumphing "again and again over all other ideals, over all *nobler* ideals—" (GM, I.8).

Nietzsche's recognition of the importance of the slave revolt for the subsequent development of the human soul indicates that his understanding of society goes further than merely affirming a permanent state of domination by one social group over another. If Nietzsche's conception of politics were limited in this way, he could not recognize the positive consequences of the slave revolt in the way he does. The same holds true for his understanding of the formation of bad conscience and, as we shall subsequently see, for his view of the ascetic priest, who he considers to be "among the greatest *conserving* and yes-creating forces of life" (GM, III.13). If Nietzsche asserts that exploitation is rooted in life as such, it is not because he endorses or affirms political violence, but rather because he was convinced that strife, whether in the individual or society at large, is the essential sign of nobility. Nietzsche says this explicitly in the penultimate section of the first essay:

> One might even say that [the struggle between the values 'good and bad' and 'good and evil'] has risen ever higher and thus become more and more profound and spiritual: so that today there is perhaps no more decisive mark of a 'higher nature,' a more spiritual nature, than that of being divided in this sense and a genuine battleground of these opposed values.[28]

In the passages we have surveyed strife—within oneself and between one group and another—is regarded as a means to power. And while it is true that Nietzsche did not recognize any external, moral constraints on the behavior of an individual or group, there are clear indications in the later writings that power need not always express itself violently, that, on the contrary, a genuinely powerful community will, as a sign of its power, refrain from imposing its will on its own, less powerful members. In one of the most lyrical passages from the *Genealogy*, Nietzsche goes so far as to suggests that there is an inverse relationship between the power of a community and its willingness to use violence:

> As the power [*Macht*] and self-confidence of a community increase, the penal law always becomes more moderate; every weakening or imperiling of the former brings with it a restoration of the harsher forms of the latter [. . .]. The justice which began with, 'everything is dischargeable, everything must be discharged,' ends by winking and letting those incapable of discharging their debt go free—it ends, as does every good thing on earth, by *overcoming itself* [sich selbst aufhebend]. This self-overcoming of justice: one knows the beautiful name it has given itself—*mercy*. (GM, II.10)

While it would be clearly futile to suggest that Nietzsche's positive evaluation of strife and the account of mercy offered in the *Genealogy* somehow neutralize the invocation of slavery cited at the head of this section, these passages strongly suggest that, for Nietzsche, political violence is neither the only, nor necessarily the most affirmative, expression of strength.

PHYSIOLOGY

Like the concept of life, the term physiology represents a moment of deep paradox for the reader of Nietzsche. Here, as before, Nietzsche's texts seem to pull in two opposed, even contradictory, directions. On the one hand, Nietzsche's theory of interpretation, his sustained critique of materialism and of the domination of Western thought by the concepts of cause and effect, all seem to preclude the possibility that physiology and physiological characteristics could function as a norm or criterion against which types of morality and social organization could be measured and judged. On the other hand, Nietzsche's use of the concept of physiology seems to demand precisely this kind of reading, in a manner that both echoes and reinforces the logic and rhetoric of the concept of life.

One of the most striking examples of this use of the concept of physiology is to be found in the note Nietzsche attaches to the first essay of the *Genealogy*, where he underscores the need for a physiological analysis of values to be followed by a medical critique:

> On the other hand, it is equally necessary to engage the interests of physiologists and doctors in these problems (of the *value* of existing evaluations)[. . .]. Indeed, every table of values, every 'thou shalt'

> known to history or ethnology, requires first a *physiological* investigation and interpretation, rather than a psychological one; and every one of them needs a critique on the part of medical science. (GM, I.17)

Nietzsche had expressed similar views in a number of passages from *Beyond Good and Evil*, where he uses the term physiology and physiological criteria in a seemingly reductive manner. The first of these passages is from section 20, where Nietzsche argues that individual philosophical concepts must be understood not as the capricious or autonomous creations of individual philosophers, but rather as members of a system, like "all the members of the fauna of a continent," whose resemblances can be traced back to the unconscious influence of a common grammar. Nietzsche pushes the analysis one step further, suggesting that grammar, too, lacks every element of caprice and autonomy, for "the spell of certain grammatical functions is ultimately also the spell of *physiological* valuations and racial conditions."

Taken by itself, Nietzsche's reduction of grammar to physiological and racial conditions does not seem particularly pernicious. The type of correspondence described in this passage is, on the face of it, quite neutral with respect to physiology and race; no preference is given to one particular grammatical-philosophical system or the particular conditions that produced it. Moreover, reductive tendencies of this type have a long history, most notably perhaps in political thought, where writers of diverse persuasions and periods have long sought to establish causal relationships or correspondences between different climates and forms of political organization.[29]

However, Nietzsche's references to physiology and physiological criteria are not uniformly neutral, but seem intended to affirm and endorse theories of race and heredity of the crudest kind. In several passages Nietzsche traces the rise of herd morality, skepticism, and democracy back to physiology causes. In one such passage, he describes the ascendancy of the instincts of the "herd animal man" to a predominant position in Europe as having proceeded "according to the growing physiological approximation and assimilation of which it is a symptom" (BGE, 202). This process of physiological assimilation mirrors the rise of "a democratic order of things," whose cause Nietzsche identifies as "the blood mixing [*Blutvermischung*] of masters and slaves" (BGE, 261). These two passages illustrate Nietzsche's belief that the rise of mediocrity as a social value can be traced back to a growing physiological mediocrity and the resulting physiological destruction of the master class. The belief that the predominance of one set of values over another can be ascribed to physiological causes assumes, on the most basic level, that values can be passed on physiologically from one generation to another. Nietzsche endorses this very possibility when, in the context of an analysis of skepticism, he traces the origins of this "illness" to effects of crossing discrete races and classes:

> skepticism is the most spiritual expression of a certain complex physiological condition that in ordinary language is called nervous exhaustion and sickliness; it always develops when races or classes that have long been separated are crossed suddenly and decisively. In the new generation that, as it were, has inherited in its blood diverse standards and values, everything is unrest, disturbance, doubt, attempt[. . .]. But what becomes sickest and degenerates most in such hybrids is the *will.* (BGE, 208)

The theory of heredity assumed by this passage is articulated in some detail by Nietzsche in the opening sections of the chapter entitled "What Is Noble." In one section, Nietzsche claims that "the problem of race" needs to be understood in terms of the necessary transmission of characteristics from parent—and forefather—to child:

> It is simply not possible that a human being should *not* have the qualities and preferences of his parents and ancestors in his body, whatever appearances may suggest to the contrary. This is the problem of race. If one knows something about the parents, an inference about the child is permissible; any disgusting incontinence, any nook envy, a clumsy insistence that one is always right—these three things together have always constituted the characteristic type of plebeian—that sort of thing must as surely be transferred to the child as corrupted blood; and with the aid of the best education one will at best *deceive* with regard to such a heredity. (BGE, 264)

Taken together, these passages appear to confirm Bertrand Russell's claim that Nietzsche "regards conquering aristocracies and their descendants as biologically superior to their subjects, as men are superior to domestic animals."[30] However, the matter is more complex than Russell's statement suggests. At least two of the passages cited above raise questions as to how literally Nietzsche's use of this physiological vocabulary should be understood.

The first of these is the diagnosis of skepticism Nietzsche offers in section 208. At first glance, this section gives expression to Nietzsche's conviction that there is a strict correlation between values and physiological characteristics. One consequence of this view is that characteristics and qualities that are present in parents must of necessity be transferred to their children; which is to say, that a translation of sorts takes place between parent and child. However, on closer inspection this section fails to affirm the possibility of a literal transference of characteristics (and values), and instead says that this transference takes place only figuratively. For at the precise moment when Nietzsche correlates the crossing of diverse races and classes with a dissolution of values, the literality of the passage is irrevocably disrupted. The sentence in question reads as follows: "In the new generation that, as it were [*gleichsam*], has inherited in its blood diverse standards and values, everything is unrest, disturbance, doubt, attempt." On the terms of this passage there can be no literal transference of values from parent to child, because the correspondence between physiology and values on which this transference is based is not a literal correlation at all, but a figure of its very impossibility.[31]

Although one might be tempted to dismiss this as a stylistic idiosyncrasy, the ambiguity of Nietzsche's conception of "blood" is confirmed in a passage from the same text where he considers what it means to be a philosopher:

> For every high world one must be born; more clearly said, one must be *bred* [gezüchtet] for it: a right to philosophy—taking the word in its great sense—one has only by virtue of one's origins, one's ancestors; one's 'blood' ['*Geblüt*'] decides here, too. (BGE, 213)

This passage is notable for two reasons. First, Nietzsche's use of quotation marks around the term "blood" underscores the ambiguity of the term, the impossibility of reducing its import to a single, literal meaning. Second, the use of quotation marks around blood affects the meaning of the term "bred." If Nietzsche's conception of blood cannot be read in a strictly literal manner, which is to say in a strictly biological or materialistic manner, then breeding must also be understood otherwise than on the model of Russell's "domestic animals."[32]

The need for an alternate reading of the concepts of heredity and breeding is further underscored by the constellation of the terms *heredity*, *appearance*, and *deception* in section 264 cited above. The section begins with a reference to the necessary course of heredity. "It is simply not possible," writes Nietzsche, "that a human being should *not* have the qualities and preferences of his parents and ancestors in his body, whatever appearances [*Augenschein*] may suggest to the contrary." Such characteristics are transferred to the child "as surely [. . .] as corrupted blood." Since one cannot avoid what is handed down from one's parents, in the case that one is the heir to undesirable characteristics, the only possibility that remains is to use education to "*deceive* [täuschen] with regard to such a heredity." Taken at face value, this passage opposes the necessary course of inheritance, the characteristics transferred as surely as corrupted blood, with the potentially deceptive force of appearance and education. If we are to believe the rhetoric of this passage, the inherited self is the essence of a person, that which can be neither denied or destroyed. However, such an interpretation can stand only if this passage is read in isolation from the rest of *Beyond Good and Evil* and the texts contemporary with it. For as we have noted, these texts represent a sustained critique of the very distinction between appearance and essence on which this interpretation depends. Moreover, the conception of truth Nietzsche articulates in these texts depends crucially on a positive evaluation of appearances; a fact reinforced by Nietzsche's approbation of deception, together with its figure, the mask.

In a frequently quoted passage Nietzsche speaks of the need that every profound spirit has for a mask:

> Every profound spirit needs a mask: even more, around every profound spirit a mask is growing continually, owing to the constantly false, namely *shallow*, interpretation of every word, every step, every sign of life he gives—. (BGE, 40)

Later in this same text Nietzsche once more praises the mask as a form of defense. In its readiness

> to deceive other spirits and to dissimulate in front of them [. . .] the spirit enjoys the multiplicity and craftiness of its masks, it also enjoys the feeling of its security behind them: after all, it is surely its Protean arts that defend and conceal it best. (BGE, 230)[33]

The utility of deception is not limited to its role as as a defensive strategy against others, it can also serve as a means of preservation in relation to one self. In *Ecce Homo*, for example, Nietzsche undermines the conditions for autobiography as such by underscoring the irreducible multiplicity of the *autos* or self that constitutes the subject of the text. One of the strategies Nietzsche employs to make this point is to show how becoming what one is depends on an absolute ignorance of oneself, a need to deceive oneself about what one is:

> At this point the real answer to the question, *how one becomes what one is*, can no longer be avoided[. . .]. To become what one is, one must not have the faintest notion *what* one is. From this point of view even the *blunders* of life have their own meaning and value[. . .]. All this can express a great prudence, even the supreme prudence: where *nosce te ipsum* would be the recipe for ruin, forgetting oneself, *misunderstanding* oneself, making oneself smaller, narrower, mediocre, become reason itself. (EH, II.9)[34]

As this passage illustrates, deception and the mask are not merely self-conscious strategies of self-defense, but are constitutive of identity as such. This conclusion undermines the distinction between essence and appearance, between what is given in one's blood and one's public persona, presupposed by the theory of heredity described in section 264.

In a passage belonging to the first chapter of *Ecce Homo*, but until recently presumed lost, Nietzsche articulates a very different theory of heredity:

> And here I touch on the question of race. I am a Polish nobleman *pur sang*, in which also not one drop of bad blood is mixed, least of all German blood. When I seek my most profound antithesis, the incalculable commonness of instinct, I always find my mother and sister. . . . All dominant concepts of heredity are, physiologically speaking, nonsense[. . .]. One is least of all related to one's parents: it would be the most extreme sign of commonness, to be related to one's parents. The higher natures have their origins infinitely further back[. . .]. I don't understand it but Julius Caesar could be my father—*or* Alexander, this Dionysus personified. (EH, I.3)[35]

In place of a purely genealogical conception of heredity, Nietzsche here proposes a "typological" order in which the question of race can no longer be decided by physiological criteria.[36] Indeed, by emphasizing the disjunction in the last sentence of this passage, Nietzsche suggests that questions of race and genealogy might not avail themselves of a definite answer at all. This is consistent with a typological, as opposed to a physiological, conception of heredity, where more than a single figure might be paradigmatic of a particular type.

The displacement of the question of heredity from a physiological to a typological basis is consistent with Nietzsche's critique of the logic of the proper name in *Ecce Homo*, which undermine the possibility of conceiving of identity in strictly biological terms.[37] Moreover, it is also consonant with the manner in which Nietzsche conceives of master and slave morality, neither of which can be reduced to a biological basis. In fact when he introduces the concepts of master and slave morality in *Beyond Good and Evil*, Nietzsche goes to pains to stress that they should be understood as "basic types," which in higher cultures and individuals can appear together:

> There are *master morality* and *slave morality*—I add immediately that in all the higher and more mixed cultures there also appear attempts at mediation between these two moralities, and yet more often the interpenetration and mutual misunderstanding of both, and at times they occur directly alongside each other—even in the same human being, within a single soul. (BGE, 260)[38]

This sentiment is echoed in the passage from the first essay of the *Genealogy* cited in the previous section, where Nietzsche writes that having both types of morality within oneself is a "decisive mark" of a higher nature.[39]

SICKNESS AND HEALTH

In the opening paragraphs of section seven we cited Nietzsche's call for a "physiological investigation and interpretation" of values and their subsequent "critique on the part of medical science" (GM, I.17), as evidence of the normative role played by the concept of physiology. More precisely, this passage suggests that Nietzsche holds an essentialist conception of physiological health or purity that could be applied as a standard against which particular tables of values can be measured and judged. The reading of the concept of physiology—and the related concepts of race and heredity—undertaken in the preceding section suggests that this is in fact not the case. Like the term *life*, the concept of physiology is suspended between the literal and the figurative, the biological and the semiological. This reading is in large measure affirmed by tracing the logic of the concepts of sickness and health as they appear in Nietzsche's later writings. On this logic, sickness is a necessary supplement to health, which cannot be thought without it. Hence sickness and health are not, as an essentialist interpretation would suggest, binary opposites.

Nietzsche's later writings are a particularly rich source of reflections on sickness and health. This is, no doubt, in large part due to the poor condition of Nietzsche's own health during much of the 1880s. Aside from those brief periods in which he was able to consistently work, these years were filled with terrible bouts of illness and depression. In a letter dated June 30, 1887, that is typical of this period, Nietzsche writes to Franz Overbeck:

> my health is improving only slowly, and in the main remains the same. There is some kind of deep physiological inhibition, whose cause and locus I am unable to verify, thanks to which my mean state ('the general feeling,' as the physiologists say) is consistently less than zero; —without exaggeration, in the past year I have not had a single day where I have been fresh and cheerful in spirit and body. This constant depression (day and night) is worse than those violent and extremely painful crises which I so often fall victim to. (KSAB, 8/870)

The timing of this letter is in itself quite interesting. On the basis of Nietzsche's correspondence we know that it was written just eight days before he began writing the *Genealogy*. In addition, the year of illness and depression Nietzsche refers to in this letter includes the period in which he composed the fifth book of *The Gay Science*, as well as the retrospective prefaces of 1886. It is, of course, no mere coincidence that it is precisely these texts that contain some of the most sustained reflections on sickness and health, and it is here that we find the clearest articulation of their supplementary relationship.

The years directly preceding Nietzsche's resignation from the University of Basel in 1879 were, as is well known, a time of severe ill health. In the 1886 Preface to *Human All-Too-Human* Nietzsche reflects back on these years and on how his illness arose out of necessity, as a cure:

> And to speak seriously, all pessimism [. . .] is thoroughly *cured* by falling ill in the way these free spirits do, staying ill for a good while, and then, for even longer, even longer, becoming healthy—I mean 'healthier.' There is wisdom in it, practical wisdom [*Lebens-Weisheit*], in prescribing health to oneself over a long period of time in only small doses. (HH, P.5)

If illness can be a cure and health itself an obstacle to convalescence, this is because even the great health has need of illness:

> From this diseased isolation, from the desert of such years of experiment, the path is still far to that enormous, overflowing certainty and health, which cannot dispense with illness itself as a means and fish hook of knowledge. (HH, P.4)

Part of the catch Nietzsche's illness procured for him was the text of *The Gay Science.* In the Preface to the second, expanded edition, Nietzsche describes the meaning of the expression "gay science" as

> the saturnalia of a spirit who has patiently resisted a terrible, long pressure [. . .] and who is now all at once seized by hope, by the hope for health, by the *intoxication* of a convalescence. (GS, P.1)

But health, as Nietzsche understands it, is not a condition that can be absolutely separated from illness and its effects. In the same Preface Nietzsche describes the difficulty with which he takes leave of his illness, "whose profits I still have not yet exhausted even today" (GS, P.3).[40] Although one might be tempted to read these statements as romantic embellishments on a difficult period now safely in the past, Nietzsche expressed these same sentiments five years earlier in section 120 of the first book of *The Gay Science*. This section, entitled "Health of the soul," ends with the following remark:

> Finally, the great question would still remain open, whether we can *dispense* with illness [. . .] and whether our thirst for knowledge and self-

> knowledge in particular does not require the sick soul as much as the healthy; in short, whether the will to health alone is not a prejudice, cowardice, and perhaps a bit of very subtle barbarism and backwardness.

The logic of the relationship between sickness and health which Nietzsche describes in these passages, a relationship of supplementarity not mutual exclusivity, plays an important, though to a large degree unrecognized, role in the three essays of the *Genealogy*. This text is often read as a plea for a return to a time dominated by an essentially aristocratic morality untainted by the forces of asceticism. To achieve this goal it would be necessary to overcome or eliminate those forces responsible for the demise of aristocratic morality: the slave revolt, bad conscience, and the ascetic ideal. This line of though is expressed most directly near the end of the second essay, where Nietzsche's prose takes on an almost messianic tone:

> This man of the future, who will redeem us not only from the hitherto reigning ideal but also from what which was bound to grow out of it, the great nausea, the will to nothingness, nihilism; this bell-stroke of noon and of the great decision that liberates the will again and restores its goal to earth and his hope to man; this Antichrist and anti-nihilist, this victor over God and nothingness—*he must come one day*—. (GM, II.24)

However persuasive this line of interpretation might be, the assumption on which it is based, that Nietzsche condemns the slave revolt, the formation of bad conscience and the ascetic ideal, ignores the fact that these phenomena are described as illnesses and obey the logic of sickness and health elucidated above. The condemnatory manner in which Nietzsche characterizes these phenomena must be read against the supplementary logic of sickness and health.

Earlier in this chapter, while considering Nietzsche's account of the origins of bad conscience, we noted the contrast between Nietzsche's description of the event that resulted in the formation of bad conscience, the forcible turning of instincts against man himself, and his evaluation of this phenomenon. Although the process by which bad conscience was formed is described in the most frightful terms—"this animal that rubbed itself raw against the bars of its cage"—Nietzsche's commentary draws attention to the possibilities opened up by this frightful event: "From now on [. . .] he gives rise to an interest, a tension, a hope [. . .] as if man were not a goal but only a way, an episode, a bridge, a great promise—" (GM, II.16). The significance of the words bridge and promise cannot be lost on any reader familiar with *Zarathustra*, where these figures are among those most central to this text and to Nietzsche's conception of the *Übermensch*.[41] The differences between Nietzsche's description of the origins of bad conscience and his evaluation of this event appear inexplicable unless one reads bad conscience as an illness which, rather than being thought in opposition to health as something that exerts a degenerative and corrosive influence, is considered to be an essential part of health, as a force that can open up new and ever greater possibilities for health. Nietzsche says precisely this when, at the beginning of section 19, he writes that "bad conscience is an illness, there is no doubt about that, but an illness as pregnancy is an illness."

The same logic also applies to Nietzsche's account of the slave revolt in morality in the first essay. Like bad conscience, the slave revolt in morals represents a triumph of the weak over the strong. Nietzsche goes to some lengths to emphasize this fact by juxtaposing the "knightly aristocratic value judgments" and their presuppositions, "a powerful physicality, a flourishing, abundant, even overflowing health" with the priestly mode of valuation, which constitutes the valuations of those who "are the most impotent." Does it not follow then that for Nietzsche the triumph of the priests and that most priestly of all people, the Jews, over the nobles represents one of the most calamitous events in the history of the earth? To be sure, but it would be a mistake to conclude from this that the meaning of the slave revolt can be reduced to a sum of its harmful and destructive effects, for Nietzsche's evaluation of the slave revolt is more subtle and ambiguous than this description suggests. Earlier in this chapter we remarked on this ambiguity where, in the course of considering the role of strife in Nietzsche's thinking, we cited his evaluation of the priestly form of existence. At the risk of redundancy, part of the passage is here cited a second time:

> it is only fair to add that it was on the soil of [. . .] the priestly form [of existence] that man first became *an interesting animal*, that only here did the human soul in a higher [*höher*] sense acquire *depth* and become *malevolent* [Böse]. . . . (GM, I.6)

This assessment of the precisely form of existence is highly paradoxical. Having described the priests as the most impotent of all men, Nietzsche goes on to say that they are responsible for a transformation of the human soul of the greatest significance. The reasons behind Nietzsche's evaluation of the priests become clearer if we note that it comes at the end of a reflection on the effects of the priestly aristocracy on health, more precisely, on the illness engendered by their form of life and the remedies that the priests devise against these afflictions. The connection between this reflection on sickness and health and Nietzsche's evaluation of the priestly form of existence is far from meaningless, for the priestly remedies are partly responsible for the increased depth and malevolence of the human soul alluded to above. In fact, it is not the remedies themselves that have produced these effects, but rather the *illness* brought on by the priestly medicine—from which "mankind itself is still ill"—which has resulted in making man a more interesting and profound animal. In the Preface to *The Gay Science*, Nietzsche describes the relationship between illness and profundity as follows: "Only great pain," he writes "compels us philosophers to descend into our ultimate depths [*Tiefe*] [. . .]. I doubt that such pain makes us 'better'; but I know that it makes us more *profound* [*aber ich weiß, daß er uns* vertieft]" (GS, P.3).

The third essay extends the pattern we have observed in the first two essays. In contrast with these essays, which emphasize a particular moment of pain and suffering caused by the imprisonment of the human animal within the walls of society and the priestly medication, the third essay focuses exclusively on the suffering of mankind as such and the priests' (ascetic) response to it. Nietzsche's argument begins from two central assumptions, namely, that man is the suffering creature par excellence, and that it is not suffering itself that burdens him but that suffering that cannot be justified in some way. Nietzsche clearly formulates these assumptions in the final section of the essay:

> Man, the bravest of animals and the one most accustomed to suffering, does *not* repudiate suffering as such; he *desires* it, he even seeks it out, provided he is shown a *meaning* for it, a *purpose* of suffering. The meaninglessness of suffering, *not* suffering itself, was the curse that lay over mankind so far—*and the ascetic ideal offered man meaning!* (GM, III.28)[42]

Much of the third essay is devoted to recounting precisely how it is that the ascetic ideal accomplishes this. For our purposes it will be sufficient to consider section 13 of the third essay, for it is here that the logic of asceticism is most clearly articulated.

This section begins by reiterating the conclusion reached at the end of section 11, namely, that the ascetic ideal is highly paradoxical for it seems to represent a form of life that, in order to maintain itself, turns against life. How is this possible? The answer is to be found within life itself:

> *the ascetic ideal springs from the protective instinct of a degenerating life* which tries by all means to sustain itself and to fight for its existence; it indicates a partial physiological obstruction and exhaustion against which the deepest instincts of life [. . .] continually struggle with new expedients and devices. The ascetic ideal is such an expedient; the case is therefore the opposite of what those who revere this ideal believe: life wrestles in it and through it with death and *against* death; the ascetic ideal is an artifice for the *preservation* of life. (GM, III.13)

The turn against life which the ascetic ideal embodies arises out of a protective instinct of life. Like the priestly medication of the first essay, the remedies offered by the ascetic priest produce a greater amount of pain than the infirmities themselves. Whereas the former produced an unprecedented development in the human soul, the pain caused by the ascetic priest is nothing less than a prophylactic and stimulus to life, "a tool for the creation of more favorable conditions for being here and being man."

NATURE

One of the central foundations of Kantian ethics is the claim that the way the world actually is can never be used to determine how it ought to be: "The ground of obligation," writes Kant, "must not be sought in the nature of man or in the circumstances in which he is placed, but sought a priori solely in the concepts of pure reason.[43] Kant's denial that the world and life as such can ever have normative force arises out of his desire to ground morality in the immutable and unquestionable structure of reason itself. Nietzsche's critique of morality and his own ethics of affirmation proceed from the opposite assumption. In Nietzsche's view, almost all previous philosophy has fallen into the trap of seeking a foundation for morality outside of the world as such, be it in the idea of the Good, in God or in the a priori structure of reason. Because they begin from a position outside or beyond the world and the immanence of all experience of world and life as such, every attempt to ground morality in this way can only result in a denial of the world and of life. In the *Genealogy* Nietzsche describes the problem as follows:

> Man has all too long has an 'evil eye' for his natural inclinations, so that they have finally become inseparable from his 'bad conscience.' An attempt at the reverse would *in itself* be possible [. . .] to wed the bad conscience to all the *unnatural* inclinations, all those aspirations to the beyond, to that which runs counter to sense, instinct, nature, animal, in short all ideals hitherto, which are one and all hostile to life and ideals that slander the world. (GM, II.24)

Nietzsche's critique of morality thus begins by rejecting the possibility of an extra-worldly moral standard, the likes of which all morality hitherto has sought to impose. However, as the above passage illustrates, Nietzsche's critique is not without pitfalls of its own. For his desire to remedy the traditional rejection of sense, instinct, nature, and animal, leads to the appearance that he merely inverts the structure of morality and adopts nature as a standard for a new moral ideal. In the words of one recent commentator, "in forging a naturalist identity of nature—the idea of a preconventional nature—Nietzsche determines a natural criterion of truth . . . a natural criterion of justice . . . and a natural criterion of beauty."[44]

The suggestion that Nietzsche replaces one form of metaphysics with another is, of course, not new. In one of his less charitable evaluations of Nietzsche's thought, Heidegger criticizes Nietzsche for having simply inverted traditional metaphysical oppositions without calling into question the oppositional nature of metaphysical thought itself: "from within metaphysics he was unable to find any other way out than a reversal of metaphysics. But that is the height of futility."[45] There is, of course, much prima facie evidence that supports this interpretation. In the passage cited above Nietzsche appears not to problematize the notion of "natural inclinations" and implies, moreover, that it is in principle possible to return to nature and instinct; as if all that were required in order to effect a critique of morality is to lift the veil that it has imposed on existence and simply reclaim what has hitherto been obscured.

This possibility is explicitly mooted by Nietzsche in section 230 from *Beyond Good and Evil*:

> we hermits and marmots have long persuaded ourselves [. . .] that under such flattering colors and make-up [. . .] the frightful basic text of *homo natura* must again be recognized [*der schreckliche Grundtext homo natura muß wieder heraus erkannt werden*]. To translate man back into nature [*Den Mensch nämlich zurückübersetzen in die Natur*]; to become master over the many vain and overly enthusiastic interpretations and connotations that have so far been scrawled and painted over that eternal basic text of *homo natura* [. . .].

The meaning of this passage seems almost indisputable. Nietzsche's description of *homo natura* as an eternal basic text and the opposition he posits between this text and the metaphysical interpretations that have been inscribed upon it, all point towards the conclusion that the concept of nature is here being employed in an uncritical and explicitly metaphysical manner. The appellation "eternal basic text" expresses a conviction that there is an essence of man that exists outside of history and is immune to temporal permutations. The conjunction of this description with *homo natura* identifies this essence as that which man is by nature. In contrast with this eternal *Grundtext*, the metaphysical interpretations that have been inscribed upon it are nothing more than seductions or temporary obfuscations. Nietzsche characterizes metaphysics here as a force that does not merely misunderstand man as such, but obscures and veils who and what he is by nature. Nietzsche's critique of metaphysics appears at this point to be self-contradictory, employing the very essentializing discourse he elsewhere eschews as a means of critique. In Heideggerian terms, one could say that Nietzsche here replaces the essence of man as *animal rationale* with that of *homo natura.*

Although the logic of this interpretation seems to be incontrovertible, there are reasons to be suspicious of its simplicity and neatness. In light of our earlier inquiries into Nietzsche's use of the concepts of life, physiology, race, and heredity, we have good reason to be wary of any interpretation that would conclude too quickly that Nietzsche falls into the trap of replicating in critique precisely those structures and modes of thought that he seeks to criticize. If anything, one might suspect that Nietzsche here self-consciously employs the most explicit of metaphysical vocabularies as a means of a critique, whose logic and limits are initially—and perhaps intentionally—obscure.

To pursue this line of thought we might begin by examining the rhetoric and logic of the passage more closely. The first point to make is that Nietzsche characterizes the essence of man as a text. Although his use of the adjectives 'eternal' and 'basic' to describe this text imply that it is both ahistorical and immutable, the passage assumes a different meaning when read in light of the arguments Nietzsche advances in section 22. There, as we recall, Nietzsche contrasts his own interpretative method with that of the physicists. While the physicists dogmatically insist on the objective truth of the claim nature is uniformly nomological, Nietzsche argues that this, like his own claims about nature and the will to power, is only interpretation. If contrasting and mutually exclusive interpretations can be read off of the same nature, it is pointless to speak of a nature in itself, or to speak of the essence of nature, for any such claims to have identified the one true nature will capriciously and dogmatically exclude other interpretations. Since any given text is in principle open to an infinite number of interpretations, no one interpretation can unconditionally be privileged over all others.

Taken by itself this argument would be enough to arouse suspicions about the explicitly metaphysical vocabulary of section 230. However, in this case the grounds for suspicion are redoubled by the fact that the subject of section 22 is nothing other than the interpretation of nature. Consequently, this section can be read as an anticipation and a response to the kinds of the objections raised above in regard to section 230.

Returning to the text, we find that the argument advanced above against the essentialist interpretation has already been written into the passage itself. There, as we recall, Nietzsche asserts that the "basic text of *homo natura* must again be recognized." The means by which this recognition is to take place is a translation of man "back into nature." The rhetoric of this section implies a return to an original meaning or sense and is consistent with an essentialist interpretation of the concept of nature. However, if we read more closely another possibility opens up. This second possibility turns on the relationship Nietzsche establishes in this passage between the "basic text" and the means by which it is to be again recognized, namely, retranslation. At the very minimum, translation requires the existence of a text and two languages: the language of the original text and that language in which the text is to be translated. Although this is a necessary condition of translation, it is by no means sufficient for translation to take place. There must also be a translator, who, since there is no reliable means of correlating sentences in one language with those of another, must read the text in question and decide on the best possible translation. But if translating a text is not simply a matter of correlating its sentences with those of another language, then translation itself must be a form of interpretation. Consequently, the same constraints that apply to interpretation apply to translation as well. This means, however, that translation can be no more certain and make no more claims to correctness and decidability than interpretation can. Moreover, if translation is a form of interpretation, it follows that a text can only be known to a translator by means of an interpretation, which is to say, *as* an interpretation. There can be no unmediated access to a text, for either translator or interpreter.

The "eternal basic text" which Nietzsche refers to in section 230 cannot, then, be understood as something akin to the Kantian thing-in-itself, whose qualities and characteristics are entirely independent of human cognitive and linguistic capacities. For on the basis of the foregoing, one cannot speak of a text-in-itself, because a text is nothing more than the sum of its interpretations and translations. As Kofman has observed, "for Nietzsche interpretation is not a commentary on a preexisting text; what exists before the interpretation is not text but chaos."[46] Hence there is no "eternal basic text"—understood metaphysically—to which one could return; indeed there is, literally speaking, nothing to which one could return other than a palimpsest whose cycles of inscription and erasure preclude all possible reference to an original, true text. In *Human All-Too-Human*, Nietzsche criticizes the philosophers' tendency to project historical characteristics of human beings back to an originary and fixed eternal form:

> the philosopher see 'instincts' in present-day human beings and assumes that they belong to the unchangeable facts of humanity, that they can, to that extent, provide a key to the understanding of the world in general. This entire teleology is predicated on the fact that we speak about about human beings [. . .] as if they were *eternal*, as if the natural direction of all things in the world is given from the beginning. But everything has evolved; there are *no eternal facts*, nor are there any absolute truths.— Thus *historical philosophizing* is necessary henceforth and the virtue of modesty as well. (HH, 3).

Even if one were to presuppose that humanity had a fixed origin, the arbitrariness and inherent senselessness of history destroys any possibility of recognizing this eternal form once more. The history of a thing, Nietzsche will write some ten years later, is

> a continuous sign-chain of ever new interpretations and adaptations whose causes do not even have to be related to one another but, on the contrary, in some cases succeed and alternate with one another in a purely chance fashion. (GM, II.12)

The foregoing reading of the concept of nature is supported by a number of passages from both published and unpublished texts in which Nietzsche explicitly rejects the possibility of a return to nature in the sense required by the essentialist interpretation of section 230. One of the most important of these passages is from *Twilight of the Idols*, where Nietzsche writes that

> a reversion [*Rückbildung*], a return in any sense or degree is simply not possible. We physiologists at least know that. Yet all priests and moralists have believed the opposite—they wanted to take mankind back [. . .]. But no one is free to be a crab. Nothing avails: one must go forward [. . .]. (TI, IX.43)

The same sentiment is expressed in two unpublished fragments from the autumn of 1887.[47] The first passage begins with a characteristically negative description of Rousseau:

> Rousseau, this typical 'modern man,' idealist and canaille combined in one person [. . .] preached the 'return to nature'—to what did he actually want to go *back*? I also speak of a 'return to nature' although it is not actually a 'return back' [*Zurückkehren*], but an 'advance towards' [*Hinaufkommen*] the strong, bright frightful nature and naturalness of men who can play with great tasks, because they would become tired with small ones and feel disgusted. (KSA 12, 9.116)

In the second passage, Nietzsche reiterates the fact that there is no preexisting nature to which one could return, but rather one that is constructed and created over time:

> *Not* 'return to nature' for there has never been a natural humanity. The scholastic unnatural and *anti*-natural values is the rule, the beginning. Man comes to nature after a long fight—he never 'returns' [*er kehrt nie 'zurück'*]— Nature, i.e., to dare to be amoral like nature. (KSA 12, 10.53)

The impossibility of a return to nature is also one of the underlying themes of the second essay of the *Genealogy*. Here Nietzsche describes the origins of bad conscience as a product of the imposition of organized society on creatures who until then had lived as "semi-animals, well adapted to the wilderness" (GM, II.16). We recall that the forced socialization of these creatures has one outstanding consequence: it forced their instincts, which could no longer remain unfettered within the walls of society, to turn against the creatures themselves. The effects of this "internalization of man" were not, however, limited to the formation of bad conscience, for the phenomenon of internalization itself represents a fundamental change in the human animal. Their "entire inner world [. . .] expanded and extended itself, acquired depth, breadth and height, in the same measure as outward discharge was *inhibited*" (GM, II.16). Part of this change in the inner world of these animals was a transformation of those drives and instincts that had heretofore guided them in life. Enclosed within the walls of society, these creatures "no longer possessed their former guides, their regulating, unconscious and infallible drives." The drives that were driven inward did not, therefore, remain intact, waiting for the moment where they could express themselves freely, rather conditioned by the new circumstances, they were transformed by new, less harmful, forces.

The depth of the transformation in the inner life of these creatures is illustrated by a comparison Nietzsche draws between their situation and that faced by sea animals when they were compelled to become land animals. This comparison is appropriate because it demonstrates the degree to which the changes produced by interiorization are irreversible. At first these animals seek to use their fins for navigation, but on learning that they are ineffectual on land they learn to rely on their legs. Gradually their fins become weaker and weaker until, several generations in the future, they disappear entirely, much like the human tail. Once completed, this process cannot be reversed. If an animal whose species once lived in the sea were suddenly tossed into the ocean some distance from land, it would likely drown, its legs being of considerable less utility than the fins of its ancestors. A similar process can be imagined to have occurred within the human "semi-animals" enclosed within society, as well as the relevant parallels to drowning at sea.[48]

The foregoing affirms the conclusion reached above, namely, that the concept of nature does not denote an ahistorical essence to which one could in principle return. The recovery of *homo natura* to which Nietzsche refers in section 230 does not express a romantic desire to return, in literal fashion, to a natural state or condition of humanity, but rather functions as a strategic element in Nietzsche's critique of metaphysics and revaluation of values. In the spirit of this assertion, one could argue that in the texts of the late 1880s Nietzsche is practicing what, in the second of his *Untimely Meditations*, he had described as "critical history," the "attempt to give oneself, as it were, a posteriori a past out of which one would like to originate in opposition to that from which one did originate." Such an attempt, Nietzsche continues, is always dangerous

> because it is so hard to find a limit to denial of the past and because second natures are usually weaker than first [. . .]. But here and there a victory is nonetheless achieved, and for the combatants, for those who employ critical history for the sake of life, there is even a noteworthy consolation: that of knowing that this first nature was once a second nature and that every victorious second nature will become a first— (UM, II.3).

Rather than being understood thetically, as essentialist or ontological suppositions that replace one metaphysical interpretation of existence with another, the essentialistic form of the concepts of the concepts of nature, life, physiology, and the will to power, serves to turn the logic of traditional metaphysics against itself, revealing the illusory nature of all such narratives of origins and final ends and, at the same time, offers an interpretation of the past that creates the possibility of a future devoid of those qualities of traditional metaphysics and morality that Nietzsche regards as pernicious and nihilistic.

There is an additional benefit to be gained by viewing Nietzsche's naturalism as strategic rather than ontological, namely, it allows us to reconcile his critique of truth and morality. The seemingly irreconcilable conflict between these two aspects of Nietzsche's thought is resolved because the pseudo-normative concepts of nature, life, and the will to power are revealed to be contingent interpretations of existence, rather than unconditional expressions of a single, eternal truth. As a writer, Nietzsche was guided by the need to view the world from as many perspectives and with as many eyes as possible. The foregoing investigation demonstrates that we, as readers, must endeavor to do the same.

Appendix

Nietzsche's Apocrypha: *The Will to Power* and Contemporary Scholarship

The philologically exact transcripts, virtually free of omissions, which now constitute the basis for this publication, were only produced after a process of verification and reexamination which extended over a period of years.

—Elisabeth Förster-Nietzsche, Foreword to the first edition of The Will to Power *(1901)*

Besides, I've known for a long time that she won't have any peace until I am dead.

—Nietzsche, on his sister Elisabeth, from a draft of a letter to his mother, January, 1888

THE MYTH OF A MAJOR WORK

Commenting on the state of Nietzsche scholarship in the early 1970s, Curt Paul Janz observes that "the entirety of the vast literature on Nietzsche and Nietzsche interpretation rests on the deceptive foundation of inaccessible or even false documents."[1] The documents Janz is referring to here fall into two categories: Nietzsche's literary remains, that is, the book manuscripts, notebooks, drafts, fragments, poems, and lecture notes that remained unpublished at the time Nietzsche became incapacitated in January, 1889; and Nietzsche's voluminous correspondence. The first category of documents, which are usually referred to as Nietzsche's *Nachlaß*—literally, what was left behind—includes a wide variety of different kinds of texts. In addition to the working notebooks which Nietzsche kept during his entire creative life, which contain outlines, ideas and titles for possible books, notes, prescriptions, drawings, train timetables, and outlines of letters, there are seemingly complete but never published texts, perhaps the most famous of which is the essay "On Truth and Lie in the Extra-Moral Sense" (1873), and numerous notes for lecture courses Nietzsche gave on topics such as: "Introduction to the Study of Platonic Dialogue" (1871), "The Pre-Platonic Philosophers" (1873), "Introduction to the Tragedies of Sophocles" (1870), and "Description of Ancient Rhetoric" (1872). Also belonging to this category are three book manuscripts, *Ecce Homo*, *The Antichrist*, and *Nietzsche Contra Wagner*, which Nietzsche prepared for publication, but which either his breakdown prevented him from seeing through the publication process (the first two) or he decided not to publish at the time of his breakdown (the third).[2] The second category of texts, Nietzsche's correspondence, consists of letters to friends, family members, publishers, colleagues, teachers, and occasional admirers, both welcome and unwelcome.[3]

At the time Janz was writing, examples of both categories of texts were either inaccessible or were accessible only in corrupt or apocryphal form. Not only were there important gaps in Nietzsche's published correspondence, but Janz and Karl Schlechta had by this time proven that a significant number of the letters that had been published were either crude forgeries or had been substantially altered.[4] In addition, Nietzsche's notebooks had yet to be published in an accurate, chronological, and scholarly edition. Much of the material from the notebooks was available in the so-called *Großoktavausgabe* of Nietzsche's works published under the auspices of Elisabeth Förster-Nietzsche and the Nietzsche Archive beginning in 1894.[5] However, rather than publishing the notebooks themselves, chronologically and as written, the editors arranged the material systematically according to categories, headings, and plans, some of which were taken from the notebooks themselves, while others were imposed by the editors without any textual basis whatsoever. However well meaning this editorial procedure might have appeared on the surface, it was certainly not innocent. The first consequence of this arrangement was that the notebooks themselves were published in incomplete and haphazard form. Instead of producing a complete, albeit rearranged edition of the material collected in the notebooks, the editors of the various *Nachlaß* volumes of the *Großoktavausgabe* only saw fit to publish selections or excerpts, with the result that much of the notebooks remained inaccessible. Mazzino Montinari recalls his horror in reading one of the Nietzsche biographies written by Förster-Nietzsche and "coming across decisive passages by Nietzsche cited in the text accompanied by comments made by [the editor] Richard Oehler such as 'apparently (!) not printed in the works' or 'cited from the manuscript, not printed in the Nachlaß' or 'apparently not published in the

Nachlaß'" (KSA 14, 14). More crucially in the present context, a significant portion of the material culled from the notebooks was presented as if it constituted a book written and largely prepared by Nietzsche, rather than by the editors. This was the case with the text published under the title *The Will to Power*, which Förster-Nietzsche describes in the Foreword to the first edition (1901) as Nietzsche's "theoretical-philosophical magnum opus" [*theoretisch-philosophisches Hauptwerk*].[6]

The extent to which the previous editions of Nietzsche's *Nachlaß* and letters were inadequate was only fully realized with the publication of the critical edition of Nietzsche's writings edited by Giorgio Colli and Mazzino Montinari. This edition, which was begun in 1967 and is still in progress, aimed to do the following: (1) to produce critical editions of the books Nietzsche published or prepared for publication, as well as the unpublished texts written during Nietzsche's tenure as professor of classical philology at Basel University; (2) to publish, for the first time, a faithful edition of the working notebooks kept by Nietzsche from the winter of 1869, when he became assumed his professorship, until his breakdown in early January, 1889;[7] and (3) to produce a definite, critical edition of Nietzsche's correspondence (1850–1889), his juvenilia, his philological writings, and the lecture courses Nietzsche gave while at Basel (1869–1879). At this point in time, the first two parts of the edition are complete, as is the correspondence and the volume devoted to Nietzsche's philological writings. The texts of Nietzsche's lecture courses have only recently begun to appear.

Although there have been important discoveries with respect to the books Nietzsche himself did not see through publication—in 1969 Montinari stumbled upon a section of *Ecce Homo* that had been suppressed by Förster-Nietzsche amongst Heinrich Köselitz' papers in the Nietzsche Archive[8]—by far the most important achievement of the new critical edition is the fact that all of Nietzsche's notebooks are available in an edition which, both in bulk and in scholarly terms, far exceeds anything previously published. Not only has the amount of material from the notebooks been increased by almost fifty percent,[9] but it is now possible to follow the path of Nietzsche's thought and compare the notes, plans, and drafts from a specific period of time to the published texts, allowing scholars to gain important insight into how these texts developed and achieve a greater understanding of the often complicated relationship between Nietzsche's different books.

One of the most important consequences of the publication of Nietzsche's notebooks is that it has allowed definitive answers to be given to two questions which have occupied Nietzsche studies since the appearance of the first edition of the collected works: first, did Nietzsche, at the time of his collapse, leave behind the unfinished manuscript of a major work, which, as late as the fall of 1888, he describes as still being in progress;[10] and second, is the text published under the title *The Will to Power* a reconstruction of that major work? Readers familiar with the critical apparatus to the new critical edition know that Montinari presents compelling evidence against the claim, which until recently was widely accepted among scholars, that at the time of his breakdown Nietzsche was in the process of completing such a major work. Although the prime facie evidence in favor of the conventional view is quite strong—between the years 1886 and 1888 Nietzsche makes reference to a major work no less than three times in print and many more times than that in his correspondence[11]—the philological evidence shows quite clearly that by the time of his breakdown Nietzsche had renounced the very idea of such a project. It will suffice to briefly summarize the main points in the rise and fall of Nietzsche's major work, since Montinari has published two detailed accounts of the relevant evidence.[12]

In the spring of 1884 Nietzsche writes to Overbeck and others of his plans to spend the subsequent years constructing his philosophy for which *Zarathustra* is a "vestibule." Although the title *The Will to Power* first appears in Nietzsche's notebooks one year later (KSA 11, 39.1), it is not until the summer of 1886 that Nietzsche composes a detailed plan of a text with this name. The full title runs: "The Will to Power. Attempt at a Revaluation of all Values. In Four Books" (KSA 12, 2.100). It is at this time that Nietzsche announces, on the back cover of *Beyond Good and Evil*, that *The Will to Power* is in preparation. In the spring of 1887, after completing a series of prefaces for the new editions of his earlier publications and the Fifth Book of *The Gay Science*, Nietzsche makes a list of 53 notes (KSA 12, 5.50), without any obvious connection to the plan for a major work. Montinari describes this list as "not a plan or an outline, but rather quite simply a index of notes which could eventually be used" (KSA 14, 390). On June 10, 1887, while at Lenz Heath, Nietzsche writes a short text on "European Nihilism" in 16 parts (KSA 12, 5.71). Shortly thereafter he composes *On the Genealogy of Morals*. From the fall of 1887 Nietzsche works intensively on *The Will to Power*. The most significant result of this period of work is a second index of 372 fragments made in February, 1988 (KSA 13, 12.1), the first 300 of which are divided into four books, indicated by the Roman numerals I–IV.[13] In conjunction with the index, Nietzsche copies the 372 fragments into a new notebook, however he is not at all satisfied with his work. In a letter to Köselitz dated February 13, 1887, Nietzsche expresses his dissatisfaction with this compilation: "I have completed the first draft of my "Attempt at a Revaluation": it was, all in all, a torture. Moreover, I don't yet have the strength for such a project. In ten years I'll be in a better position to do it" (KSAB, 8/991).[14]

With the exception of a brief period in the spring of 1888 when he writes *The Case of Wagner*, Nietzsche continues to work intensively on *The Will to Power*. During this period he composes a number of different plans for the text, some containing as many as twelve chapters, rather than the four chapters that was typical of the earlier plans. In March, 1888, Nietzsche makes another index of notes, according to an eleven-part plan composed during this period (KSA 13, 14.169).[15] However, this effort was to prove just as provisional and inconsequential as the previous one: "Nietzsche's attempt to organize the fragments according to this plan is just as significant as the attempt of February, 1888. It is also equally fragmentary, because it is limited to a single set of notes of what is otherwise a rather bulky notebook, and was, like the earlier compilation, later abandoned" (KSA 14, 395).[16] This was to be Nietzsche's final attempt to organize his notes with a view to his major work. Although he is still occupied by the idea of *The Will to Power*, this period of work produces no obvious results. On August 22, a little over a month after sending *The Case of Wagner* to the printer, Nietzsche writes to his friend Meta von Salis that this summer has "come to nothing [. . .]. This pains me very much indeed [. . .] because everything had been prepared for a great and quite specific task" (KSAB, 8/1094). Four days later Nietzsche writes what was to prove to be the last plan for *The Will to Power* (KSA 13, 18.17). Writing to his mother on August 30, Nietzsche reiterates his belief that this project, "which should have been completed this summer has literally come to nothing" (KSAB, 8/1098). Acting upon this realization, Nietzsche decides to publish an "excerpt" of his philosophy. He calls the book *Indolence of a Psychologist*, a title that was later to be dropped in favor of *Twilight of the Idols*.[17] At the same time he writes a plan for a new major work, consisting of four books, entitled *The Revaluation of All Values*.[18] The first book of this new work would bear the title *The Antichrist*.[19] During this period Nietzsche collates the material for *Twilight of the Idols*—the so-called "excerpt"—and puts aside 24 paragraphs of material on religion and Christianity that would eventually constitute the first third of *The Antichrist*. Although Nietzsche still considered *The Antichrist* the first book of the *Revaluation* as late as November 13 (KSAB, 8/1143), in a matter of days he would come to identify the two works completely. While this change is expressed obliquely in a letter to Brandes of November 20,[20] it is explicitly announced by Nietzsche in a letter to Deussen from November 26, 1888: "My *Revaluation of All Values*, which bears the title *The Antichrist*, is finished" (KSAB, 8/1159).[21] This was not, however, to be the last word. On the second of two title pages that stood at the beginning of the manuscript for *The Antichrist*, the subtitle *Revaluation of All Values* was crossed out by Nietzsche, thus ending the story of the major work (KSA 14, 435). On the basis of the available evidence, Montinari draws the following unequivocal conclusion: "From the notes for *The Will to Power* arose *Twilight of the Idols* and *The Antichrist*; the remainder is—*Nachlaß*" (KSA 14, 400).[22]

The foregoing evidence, which for years was inaccessible, should put an end to all debates on the subject of whether Nietzsche left behind an unfinished manuscript of a major work, and whether the text published under the title *The Will to Power* can be considered a reconstruction of that work. For it is clear that, whether due to the nature of the revaluation itself or to his way of doing philosophy, Nietzsche was never able to bring the project of a major work to fruition, be it under the title *The Will to Power* or *Revaluation of All Values*.[23] The two compilations of notes he made for the major work were, in his own view, quite clearly inadequate, and for this reason were abandoned; and in light of his subsequent decision to publish *Twilight of the Idols* and *The Antichrist*, these early compilations should be regarded as nothing more than false steps, rather than as genuine indications of a book which might have been. Even if one were to regard *The Antichrist* as the entire *Revaluation*, it is clear that this is far from the "major work" which Nietzsche had been planning since 1884.[24]

The resolution of the debate over Nietzsche's "major work" has had important consequences for Nietzsche studies. Rather than using the old *Nachlaß* compilations such as *The Will to Power* and *The Innocence of Becoming*,[25] most scholars now use the edition of the notebooks made available by Colli and Montinari, which were published simultaneously in German, French, Italian, and Japanese. The one exception to this is scholars working in the English-speaking world, many of whom continue to use the English translation of *The Will to Power* published in 1967.[26] One reason for this is that not all scholars working on Nietzsche have sufficient language skills to tackle the German edition of the *Nachlaß*, and if the present progress is any indication of the future, the English translation of the complete works will still be underway well into the next century.[27] However, even scholars such as Alexander Nehamas, whose German appears to be more than adequate, obstinately continue to use *The Will to Power*. In fact, although Nehamas says that he relies on the Colli and Montinari edition for Nietzsche's texts (NLL, 237), out of the scores of citations and references to Nietzsche's notes, not a single one is taken from any source other than *The Will to Power*. This is not a mistake of omission, but a conscious hermeneutical decision. "Some justification," writes Nehamas,

> for my relying on *The Will to Power* may be considered necessary. I am aware that these notes do not constitute a 'work' in any traditional sense: the idea to publish them and even their very arrangement, which has necessarily imposed some initial (but in my view *ultimately defeasible*) interpretations of their sense came not from Nietzsche himself but from Elisabeth Förster-Nietzsche after her brother's death. But this collection has become, for better or worse, an integral part of Nietzsche's literary and philosophical work, and it has been instrumental in forming our reactions to him over the past eighty years. . . . Nietzsche is an author, a public figure, and all his writings are relevant to his interpretation. (NLL, 9–10; emphasis added)

Nehamas' justification raises two questions. First, is the arrangement made by Förster-Nietzsche and Köselitz as innocent—and defeasible—as Nehamas assumes? Second, is Nehamas' decision to accept *The Will to Power* as "an integral part of Nietzsche's literary and philosophical work" and to rely (exclusively) upon it when consulting Nietzsche's notebooks defensible in light of what we now know about this text's history, or in so doing does one remain upon the "deceptive foundation of inaccessible or even false documents" described by Janz almost twenty-five years ago? To put this second question more directly and in slightly different terms: Is the text of *The Will to Power* a "philologically exact transcript"[28] of notes taken from Nietzsche's notebooks, as Förster-Nietzsche claims, or have the notes themselves been abridged, rearranged, or otherwise tampered with? In order to answer these questions, we shall have to consider the genesis of *The Will to Power* more closely.[29]

THE CREATION OF *THE WILL TO POWER*

When Nietzsche collapsed in Turin in early January, 1889, Elisabeth Förster-Nietzsche was in Paraguay, where she and her husband, the anti-Semitic activist Bernhard Förster, had gone almost five years previously to found an "Aryan-German" colony, Neu-Germanian.[30] Partly as a consequence of Bernhard Förster's mismanagement and the poor soil in the area, the colony proved to be a financial disaster, and in early June, 1889, Bernhard Förster committed suicide.[31] In an effort to raise money for the colony, Förster-Nietzsche returned to Germany temporarily in 1892, and, after having broken all ties to the colony, she returned for good a year later. At the time of Förster-Nietzsche's return, Heinrich Köselitz, who had a more intimate knowledge of Nietzsche's work and could decipher his practically illegible handwriting better than anyone else at that time, was in the process of editing an edition of Nietzsche's writings. Förster-Nietzsche demanded that Köselitz cease working on this edition and that he hand over all of Nietzsche's papers that were in his possession to her. Since Förster-Nietzsche had a legal right both to Nietzsche's papers and to the publication rights of his books, Köselitz could do nothing but accede to her demands. In 1894 Förster-Nietzsche founded the Nietzsche Archive and put together an editorial team—of which Köselitz was initially not a member—to begin the task of putting together an edition of Nietzsche's complete works.

The edition, which was eventually published under the auspices of the Nietzsche Archive, the so-called *Großoktavausgabe*, would eventually constitute twenty volumes, of which seven contained material from Nietzsche's *Nachlaß*. One of these seven volumes was *The Will to Power*, first published in 1901 with the help of Heinrich Köselitz, who was asked to join the staff of the Nietzsche Archive in 1899.[32] As is well known, the first edition of *The Will to Power*, 483 sections of notes plus 23 pages of Nietzsche's plans, contained less than half of the material found in the second, canonical edition of 1906.[33] Less well known, however, is the fact that this edition was published in its present form over the objections of the editors, Köselitz and the brothers Ernst and August Horneffer. Originally entitled by the editors "Unpublished Material from the Period of the Revaluation" and presented as a collection of notes, not one of Nietzsche's books, *The Will to Power* was a creation of Förster-Nietzsche, who was unwilling to accept that Nietzsche had failed to write a major work.[34] To this end, Förster-Nietzsche rejected both the title and the editors' introduction and instead presented this collection of notes as the reconstruction of Nietzsche's major work. The best account of the genesis of the first edition of *The Will to Power* is provided by Ernst Horneffer, whose critical exposé, *Nietzsche's Last Work*, appeared in 1907:

> We [the editors] wanted to present our compilation of the preliminary notes for the 'Revaluation' merely as *a collection of material that we had arranged*, which each of knew was the case. In order to correspond to the other [*Nachlaß*] volumes, we wanted to call it "Unpublished Material from the Period of the Revaluation."[35] But Frau Förster-Nietzsche wanted to have a 'Revaluation' itself. For this reason this modestly conceived collection of aphorisms was proudly baptized by her as *The Will to Power*, which naturally could only be to Nietzsche's detriment. . . . The worst thing of all was that Frau Förster-Nietzsche suppressed our Introduction, which contained a precise presentation of Nietzsche's working methods, and put in its place one that was completely vapid. Frau Förster-Nietzsche asked . . . why do people need to learn more about her brother's working methods in connection with the 'Revaluation'? That is completely unnecessary. But only by presenting a *clear exposition of these circumstances* could a systematized collection of the material from the preliminary notes for the 'Revaluation' be justified, if at all. Without this the reader will necessary ascribe to the 'Revaluation' a systematic form, which in fact it never had.[36]

Of course none of this was broached in the Foreword written by Förster-Nietzsche. Obscuring the true process of how the text was manufactured, Förster-Nietzsche describes the task of piecing together Nietzsche's text as having been "extraordinarily difficult" and fraught with worry, feelings that were mitigated by the fact that the editors knew "through Nietzsche's own notes, how he conceived of completing his philosophical-theoretical magnum opus" (GA, XV^{1}, xx). The text concludes with a passage which can only be read as an example of the most malicious form of false modesty: "But I emphasize expressly that I myself am not the editor of this volume but at most a collaborator in the most modest sense of the word. The only circumstance that permits me to write this Foreword is that the collected edition of my brother's works is published at my behest, and hence the heaviest part of the responsibility, with all its cares and fights, has been resting on my shoulders for many years now" (GA, XV^1, xxii).

No such fights took place during the preparation of the second edition some five years later. No longer needing to worry about the brothers Horneffer, who by this time had left the Archive, Förster-Nietzsche assumed the job of editing the new edition together with Köselitz, who was in no position to contradict her wishes. The second edition of *The Will to Power*, which is over twice as large as the first, is an extraordinary achievement, produced by means of naivete, shrewdness, and utter incompetence. Determined to produce the work which Nietzsche himself abandoned, Förster-Nietzsche was forced to resort to quite fantastic justifications for the volume she and Köselitz had prepared. After asserting that the main ideas of Nietzsche's "major theoretical-philosophical prose work" are already present in *Zarathustra* in poetic form, Förster-Nietzsche writes that "it is obvious that the world of new thoughts could not be exhausted in *Zarathustra* and demanded a theoretical-philosophical representation in prose, which became clearer and grew from year to year" (TA IX, vii–viii).[37] Although Nietzsche's conception of a major prose work continued to develop and grow in the years following the composition of *Zarathustra*, he was, Förster-Nietzsche admits, never able to bring the work to fruition. The work itself remains "incomplete" and "it was reserved for us editors of the Nietzsche Archive with our weak powers to conscientiously piece together the precious building blocks according to the existing instructions of the author" (TA IX, xxii). This is not the remark of a humble and well-meaning sister attempting to do justice to the legacy of her misunderstood brother, but a fully conscious distortion of the contents of Nietzsche's posthumous papers. This is sufficiently proven by the following statement of August Horneffer, which was written before the second edition of *The Will to Power* appeared in print: "We have, therefore, no 'Revaluation of All Values,' no 'Will to Power'; we only have preliminary notes and sketches for a number of different works with different titles. We can never achieve a certain and complete picture of these individual works."[38]

It is abundantly clear that, at the same time the second edition was published in 1906, there were a number of people, including the brothers Horneffer and Albert Lamm, who saw through Förster-Nietzsche's attempt to present *The Will to Power* as a veridical reconstruction of Nietzsche's major work.[39] Today, of course, it is well known and accepted as a fact that what has been collected under the title *The Will to Power* are notes, which, as Nehamas puts it, "do not constitute a 'work' in any traditional sense." The question before us now is whether the text can nevertheless be regarded as a "defeasible" arrangement of Nietzsche's notes, as Nehamas claims?

Before turning to the philological evidence, which will prove decisive in this matter, there are a great many indications that one should be highly suspicious of any compilation that was published either by Förster-Nietzsche herself or under her direction. The first such indication is that Förster-Nietzsche understood almost nothing about her brother's philosophy, and seemed incapable of engaging in any sustained and serious philosophical thought.[40] Although one might regard Förster-Nietzsche's reference to the "weak powers" of the editors as respectful humility, the same cannot be said for the following passage from a letter she sent to Nietzsche in early January, 1888: "your last book [*Beyond Good and Evil*] will not probably not become the bible of Neu-Germanian; for us practical people a great deal of it is too subtle. . . ." (KGB III, 6/513). After appointing herself head of the Nietzsche Archive and assuming responsibility for the Archive's publication of Nietzsche writings, Förster-Nietzsche hired the Goethe scholar and later founder of anthroposophy Rudolf Steiner to tutor her in her brother's philosophy. Steiner later described Förster-Nietzsche as "a complete laywoman in all that concerns her brother's doctrine . . . lack[ing] any sense for fine, and even for crude logical distinctions, her thinking is void of even the least logical consistency, and she lacks any sense of objectivity."[41] The degree to which Steiner's lessons failed to help Förster-Nietzsche grasp even the most basic aspects of her brother's thought is reflected in the following passage from the Introduction to the second volume of *The Will to Power*:

> Our pride [those readers of the book who are not 'higher human beings'] will consist in our service to the higher human beings, in being their followers and instruments, or in belonging to a powerful and splendid institution, for example, Germany's officer corps or civil service (the philosopher Nietzsche had continually referred to both organizations and to our justifiable pride in being a part of them). (TA 10, xi–xii)

Passages such as these, which are quite frequent in her writings, suggest that Förster-Nietzsche's understanding of her brother's thought is not simply the best intentioned effort of a philosophically unschooled mind, but rather that it is, in its very foundations, an ideologically colored interpretation. That is to say, an interpretation that is inseparable from the anti-Semitic and National Socialist ideologies that were prevalent in Germany in the late nineteenth and early twentieth centuries and hence antipodal to both the letter and the substance of Nietzsche's thought. Reasons for suspicion are provided by the well-known fact that Förster-Nietzsche courted Hitler and the National Socialists in the early 1930s and that Hitler made several well-publicized visits to the Nietzsche Archive.[42] Here it is not simply a matter of a political innocent getting mixed up in the affairs of state in the hope of winning financial support for the Nietzsche Archive—which was also the case[43]—for Förster-Nietzsche was from early on an enthusiastic convert to National Socialism. In a letter to Oswald Spengler, author of *The Decline of the West* and a longtime acquaintance and supporter who had recently resigned from the academic committee of the Nietzsche Archive, Förster-Nietzsche writes the following:

> To my great concern I hear that you are turning your back on the Nietzsche Archive and want to have nothing more to do with it. I regret that very much and cannot understand the reason at all. It has been communicated to me that you have energetically rejected the Third Reich and its Führer and that your departure from the Nietzsche Archive, which stands in a relationship of deep admiration to the Führer, has something to do with this. Now I myself have experienced how you have spoken out most energetically against our highly esteemed new ideal. But it is precisely this that I cannot understand. . . . However perhaps I am mistaken and there are other reasons besides our close ties to the ideals of National Socialism that separate us.[44]

Förster-Nietzsche's admiration for Hitler and National Socialism is a direct extension of the anti-Semitic ideology preached by her husband, Bernhard Förster, and of which Förster-Nietzsche herself was an enthusiastic adherent. During his first visit to the Nietzsche Archive on November 11, 1932, Förster-Nietzsche gave Hitler Nietzsche's walking stick and a copy of the petition that her husband had sent to Bismark in 1880 urging the government to take steps against the Jews living in Germany. According to an account written in the 1930s by an admirer of Förster's, the petition, which contained 250,000 signatures, "demanded the limitation or cessation of Jewish immigration into Germany, the exclusion of Jews from all governmental offices, the preservation of the Christian character of the primary schools, and the resumption of the recording of statistics on the Jewish population."[45] As she presented a copy of this petition to Hitler, Förster-Nietzsche intoned that "it already contained all the demands of the national circles with respect to the Jewish question, which in recent times have been raised and realized by National Socialism."[46]

Förster-Nietzsche's enthusiasm for the anti-Semitic ideology of her husband was, of course, well known to Nietzsche. Her friendship and eventual marriage to Bernhard Förster produced a serious break in their relationship, which was never fully reconciled.[47] In a series of letters and drafts of letters written in the mid- and late 1880s, Nietzsche describes the toll that his sister's political views and her marriage are having on him. In a letter to Malwida von Meysenbug from 1884, Nietzsche writes of his break with Elisabeth: "In the meantime [Nietzsche is referring to his letter of the previous summer] the situation there has changed, so that I have broken radically with my sister: for heaven's sake do not think of wanting to mediate and reconcile us—between a vengeful, anti-Semitic goose and myself *there is* no reconciliation" (KSAB, 6/509).[48] Shortly before Nietzsche had complained to Heinrich Köselitz that "my sister tortures me as before with letters which I classify under the concept 'Anti-Semitism'—you can guess what the specific contents were" (KSAB, 6/484). More than three years later, the situation seems to have only become worse. In a draft of a letter to his sister, Nietzsche complains that her marriage to Bernhard Förster has caused people in Germany to take him for an anti-Semitic thinker too:

> Now it has come to the point that I need to protect myself tooth and nail against being confused with the anti-Semitic *canaille*; after my own sister, my former sister [. . .] has given impetus to this most wretched of all confusions. After reading the name Zarathustra in "The Anti-Semitic Correspondence,"[49] my patience is at an end—I am now against the party of your husband as a form of *self-defense*. These damn anti-Semitic hooligans *should* not put their hands on my ideal!!
>
> That our name is mixed up with this movement as a result of your marriage, how I have suffered because of this! The last six years you have lost all judgment and all discretion.
>
> Heavens, how difficult this is for me!
>
> I have, as is only fair, never asked you to [understand] the position which I, as a philosopher, have taken towards our age; nevertheless, with a little instinct for love you could have avoided settling down so quickly with my antipodes. (KSAB, 8/968)

These letters demonstrate that there is a strict continuity between Förster-Nietzsche's political views in the 1880s and her political engagement of the 1930s. And it is equally as certain that Nietzsche would have rejected the association of his name with "the ideals of National Socialism," just as he earlier univocally rejected any connection between himself and the anti-Semites of his day. As his correspondence with Förster-Nietzsche, Theodor Fritsch, and others shows, Nietzsche did not merely regret the fact that he was being taken for an anti-Semitic ideologue, he took active steps to prevent this confusion as long as he could.[50] Once his voice was silenced by illness, there was nothing to prevent Förster-Nietzsche from effecting a rapprochement between Nietzsche's thought and her own right-wing political ideology. However, in order to do this she would need to somehow alter or manipulate Nietzsche's texts. It would, of course, be too easy to spot discrepancies between the books Nietzsche himself published and "edited" editions published under the auspices of the Nietzsche Archive. However, there were two other sources of unpublished material that could easily be manipulated, namely, Nietzsche's correspondence and his notebooks, both of which Förster-Nietzsche unscrupulously and mercilessly shaped, altered, and defaced.

This is not the place to undertake a critical reading of *The Will to Power* and demonstrate what political biases were at work in the selection and presentation of the "notes" published in the text. However, there is clear evidence that more was at stake than simply a well-meaning attempt to reconstruct Nietzsche's "major work." Consider the plan, chosen by Förster-Nietzsche, with its infamously titled fourth book "Discipline and Breeding."

[+ + +] of All Values

First Book
European Nihilism

Second Book
Critique of the Highest Values

Third Book
Principle of a New Legislation of Values

Fourth Book
Discipline and Breeding

—written March 17, 1887,
Nice (KSA 12, 7.64)[51]

As Karl Schlechta noted in 1954, this is only one of many plans drawn up by Nietzsche.[52] It is neither the most detailed plan, nor is it the last plan Nietzsche wrote for *The Will to Power*. It is also not one of the two plans employed by Nietzsche when, in early 1888, he made two preliminary arrangements of material for his book. If one were to have attempted to 'reconstruct' the text according to the author's intentions—a highly dubious enterprise in any case—one would think that one of these plans would have been the obvious choice. One could also argue in favor of the last plan, which is also one of the most detailed plans ever written by Nietzsche:

Outline of
a plan to:
The Will to Power.
Attempt
at a Revaluation of All Values

—*Sils Maria* on the last
Sunday of the month
of August, 1888

We hyperboreer.—*laying the foundation stone of the problem.*

First Book: '*What is Truth*?'
First Chapter. Psychology of Error.
Second Chapter. The Value of Truth and Error.
Third Chapter. The Will to Truth (first justified in the affirmative value of life).

Second Book: *Origin of Values*.
First Chapter. The Metaphysicians.
Second Chapter. The homines religiosi.
Third Chapter. The Good and the Improvers.

Third Book. *Conflict of Values*
First Chapter. Thoughts about Christianity.
Second Chapter. The Physiology of Art.
Third Chapter. On the History of European Nihilism.

Diversion of a Psychologist

Fourth Book. *The Great Noon*.
First Chapter. The Principle of Life 'Order of Rank'
Second Chapter. The Two Paths.
Third Chapter. The Eternal Recurrence. (KSA 13, 18.17)

Comparing the two plans, there seems little doubt about which plan would have been the better template on the basis of which to 'reconstruct' *The Will to Power*. Why then was the plan from March, 1887, chosen? In her attempt to justify the unjustifiable, Förster-Nietzsche lets slip the real motivation behind the choice of plan. This plan, she claims, is the only one

> which gives a rather clear indication of the composition of the work. Moreover, because of the broad, general features of the division, it offers the *most latitude* . . . to meaningfully arrange the rich material. (TA IX, xx; emphasis added)[53]

It is clear, however, from the published text that the latitude offered by this plan was not enough. If the foregoing account of Förster-Nietzsche's politics and editorial principles were not sufficient to convince us that *The Will to Power* is not an innocent selection of Nietzsche notes that affords us a glimpse into the "workshop of a great thinker," as Walter Kaufmann once suggested,[54] there is a plethora of philological evidence which definitively demonstrates that the text we have before us is corrupt and hence should not be counted among Nietzsche's writings at all.

Rather than representing self-standing notes gleaned from Nietzsche's notebooks, the 1067 sections of *The Will to Power* are for the most part fragmentary passages that have been taken out of context, broken-up, edited, and otherwise distorted. For example, of the 374 notes numbered and arranged by Nietzsche in February, 1888, only 270 were included in the second edition of *The Will to Power*, expanded and reworked by Köselitz and Förster-Nietzsche. Of these 270 notes, 137 were published incompletely, that is, "with arbitrary changes in the text," including "the omission of headings, often of complete sentences," and "the chopping up of connected texts."[55] One of the casualties of the editorial process was the short treatise on European nihilism that Nietzsche wrote in June, 1887. Ironically, in the first edition of *The Will to Power* this text was published as a single note, without editorial intervention. In the second edition, however, this note is inexplicably broken up and is printed as four separate aphorisms, numbers 4, 5, 114, and 55, respectively, without the change being indicated anywhere in the text. The gravity of the changes made by the editors can be appreciated by considering the fact that this is longest text Nietzsche composed on the subject of nihilism, and that both in terms of its subject matter and date of composition the text stands in a close relationship to the *Genealogy*, and holds important clues as to the intellectual background of this book.[56]

One would be hard pressed to explain why the text on nihilism was broken up and published as four separate notes. It is less difficult to grasp why certain other texts were manipulated. Consider the following note, published as section 768 of *The Will to Power*:

> The 'ego' subdues and kills: it operates like an organic cell: it is a robber and violent. It wants to regenerate itself—pregnancy. It wants to give birth to its god and see all mankind at its feet.

This passage is notable for the ferocity of the imagery it employs to describe the functioning of the ego, which is here seen as an extension of a violent, amoral nature. However, the note takes on a different meaning if read in its entirety:

> On the Morality of the 'ego'
>
> The difficulty of making oneself *understood*. To be understood by many is impossible.
>
> *Every* action is misunderstood. And one must have one's *masks* in order *not* to be crucified continually. Also in order to *seduce* . . .
>
> It is better to associate with those who lie intentionally, because only they are able to be true intentionally. The usual way of being true is to have a mask *without being conscious of it*.

> The 'ego' subdues and kills: it operates like an organic cell: it is a robber and violent. It wants to regenerate itself—pregnancy. It wants to give birth to its god and see all mankind at its feet.
>
> The liberated egos struggle for domination. (KSA 10, 1.20)

Whereas the note on nihilism was published in its entirely, albeit in a fragmentary manner, over half of this note was simply excised—without editorial comment.[57] The parts of the note not published as part of section 768 of the *The Will to Power*—the first three and the final sentences—appear no where else in the text. It is, however, rather obvious that these excised sentences radically alter the sense of the passage. Read as an extension of the idea that the mores of society are grounded in an ethics of dissimulation, the violent imagery of the published passage takes on a different meaning. The subduing and violent actions of the ego are not directed towards others, but are part of that process that unconsciously produces a mask for the individual. Having acquired a mask, the egos are no longer prisoners of this process, and they struggle for domination by pitting their own contrived exteriors against those with whom they come in contact with in society. One interpretation of this passage might proceed along such lines. It is, however, an interpretation that is only possible if one reads the note as written, rather than in the edited and exaggeratedly violent form published in *The Will to Power*.

As a third and final example of Köselitz' and Förster-Nietzsche's lack of editorial probity and utter disregard for the integrity of Nietzsche's notebooks, it may be worthwhile to consider a more complicated and lengthy note. The notebook designated as WII.1, a quarto of 142 pages used by Nietzsche in the fall of 1887, contains a number of the passages included in the index compiled by Nietzsche in February, 1888.[58] One of these passages, identified in the index as note 27 of the first book, is a long note on nihilism. Unlike the text from June, 1887, this note is rather fragmentary. Many of its sentences are unpolished and are clearly not well thought out statements, but rather are the kinds of preliminary jottings Nietzsche characteristically made in his notebooks. The fact that this text was never polished and yet was included in the index of February, 1888, tells us a great deal about just how far Nietzsche had progressed with this project. In the canonical edition of *The Will to Power* this text was divided up and published as four separate notes, numbers 2, 13, 22, and 23. In what follows I have translated the note as it appears in the Colli-Montinari edition of the *Nachlaß*, indicating the divisions made by the editors of *The Will to Power*. The numbers in parentheses refers to the the sections of *The Will to Power* in which these passages can be found.

[23] I. *Nihilism a* **normal** *condition.*

[2] *Nihilism*: the goal is lacking; the answer to the question 'Why?' is lacking what does nihilism mean?—*that the highest values devalue themselves.*

[22] It is **ambiguous**:

A)) Nihilism as a sign of the *increased* power *of the spirit*: as **active nihilism**:

[23] It can be a sign of *strength*: the power of the spirit may have grown so strong that the goals which it has held *hitherto* ('convictions,' articles of faith) are inadequate to it

—a faith, namely, generally expresses the constraint of *conditions of existence*, submission to the authority of circumstances under which a being *flourishes, grows gains power . . .*

On the other hand, a sign of *insufficient* strength, to productively *posit* once more a goal, a why?, a faith.

It reaches its **maximum** of relative strength as a violent force of **destruction**: *as active nihilism.* Its opposite would be the weary nihilism which no longer *attacks*: its most famous form, Buddhism: as *passive* nihilism.

[13] Nihilism represents a pathological *transitional stage* (pathological is the tremendous generalization, the conclusion that there is *no meaning at all*): be it that the productive powers are not yet strong enough: be it that the decadence still hesitates and has not yet invented its remedies.

[22] B)) Nihilism as *decline and downward movement of the power of the spirit*: **passive nihilism**:

[23] as a sign of weakness: the strength of the spirit may be worn out, *exhausted*, so that the *previous* goals and and values are inadequate and are no longer believed—

that the synthesis of values and goals (upon which every strong culture rests), dissolves, so that the individual values fight against each other: disintegration

that everything which refreshes, heals, calms and numbs, emerges in the foreground in different *disguises*, religious or moral or political or aesthetic etc.

[13] **2. Presupposition of this hypothesis**

That there is no truth, that there is no absolute of things, no 'thing-in-itself'

> —*this is itself a form of nihilism*, and *the most extreme form*. It places the *value* of things precisely in the fact that *no* reality corresponds and has corresponded to this value, but rather only a symptom of strength on the part of *those who posit values*, a simplification for the *sake of life*. (KSA 12, 9.35)

This diagram allows us to see exactly how the text was manipulated. Whereas the previous note we examined was edited so as to accentuate the violent, militaristic imagery of one part of the passage, the division of this text is utterly capricious, and seems to aim at undermining, rather than preserving, the sense of the passage. Although the passage is unpolished and somewhat fragmentary, the numbers and letters inserted by Nietzsche, which indicate three specific divisions within the text, give it a certain continuity, which the editorial manipulations completely undermine. Moreover, the coupling together of different parts of the passage in discrete sections of *The Will to Power* creates a false sense of continuity and argument. For example, section 13 of *The Will to Power* joins part 2, entitled "Presuppositions of this hypothesis," with the last paragraph of division A of part I, which begins with the assertion that "nihilism represents a pathological transitional stage." The juxtaposition of these two passages makes it appear as if the hypothesis referred to in the second paragraph of section 13 is this claim that nihilism is a transitional stage. However, this is far from clear. The fragmentary form of the note makes it impossible to say with certainty which hypothesis Nietzsche is making reference to. By dividing and rearranging the text, by constituting coherent paragraphs and grammatical sentences where none are to be found, the editors of *The Will to Power* have created a note which has no correlate whatsoever in Nietzsche's notebooks.[59]

TEXTUAL SHADOWS

Nehamas is, of course, quite right in claiming that "Nietzsche is an author, a public figure, and all his writings are relevant to his interpretation" (NLL, 9–10), but as these three examples amply demonstrate, the simple fact is that many, if not most, of the notes assembled in *The Will to Power* cannot genuinely be ascribed to Nietzsche.[60] Even if we assume, as one must, that an author's intentions cannot be said to constitute or exhaust the meaning of his or her work, this assumption can never constitute a reason for ascribing legitimacy to a collection of notes that have been tampered with to such a degree so as to make it, in the words of Montinari, "editorially indefensible and at bottom materially questionable" (KSA 12, 8). On the basis of this evidence there is only one possible conclusion: the compilation and arrangement of *The*

Will to Power cannot in any sense of the word be regarded as defeasible.

Although nearly two decades have passed since the publication of the last of Nietzsche's notebooks, scholars, particularly in the English-speaking world, continue to make uncritical use of *The Will to Power*. One reason for this is undoubtedly the ease of reference afforded by the compactness and the systematic arrangement of the text prepared by Köselitz and Förster-Nietzsche.[61] However, by continuing to rely on this text scholars run the risk of having their own interpretations of Nietzsche influenced by readings of passages that have been edited, broken up, or otherwise corrupted. There is a further, more general and perhaps more pernicious danger, namely, that by using *The Will to Power* we allow ourselves to be influenced, however subtly, by the view of Nietzsche that Förster-Nietzsche was so eager to promote and whose ideological foundations we have briefly explored. We should ask ourselves whether the time has not come to break the last vestiges of the hold that she has, for so long, had over Nietzsche.

Notes

INTRODUCTION

1. Martin Heidegger, *Nietzsche* (Pfullingen: Neske, 1961), vol. I, pp. 13–14; *Nietzsche*, trans. J. Stambaugh, D. F. Krell and F. A. Capuzzi (San Francisco: Harper-Collins, 1991), vol. 1, p. 5. Henceforth cited as N, with volume and page references to the German and English editions.

2. Arthur Danto, *Nietzsche as Philosopher* (New York: Columbia University Press, 1980), p. 9.

3. Danto, *Nietzsche as Philosopher*, p. 13. Since the initial publication of his book, Danto has significantly revised his view of style. See his presidential address to the American Philosophical Association (1985), reprinted in *The Philosophical Disenfranchisement of Art* (New York: Columbia University Press, 1986). It should be noted, however, that while Danto's view of style may have changed, the first set of remarks cited above, which were written in 1979, suggest that his understanding of philosophy itself has not. For a discussion of Danto's views, see Bernd Magnus, Stanley Stewart and J. P. Mileur, *Nietzsche's Case: Philosophy And/As Literature* (New York Routledge, 1993), pp. 7–11.

4. For a general, though not particularly philosophical account of Nietzsche's influence in Germany in the years immediately following his collapse, see Steven Aschheim, *The Nietzsche Legacy in Germany 1890–1990* (Berkeley: University of California Press, 1992), especially pp. 17–50.

5. The journal, *Nietzsche Forschung*, is the annual publication of the *Förder- und Forschungsgemeinshcaft Friedrich Nietzsche* based in Halle, in the former East Germany. *Nietzsche-Studien*, the first journal devoted exclusively to Nietzsche, was founded in 1972.

6. Karsten Harries, "The Philosopher at Sea," in *Nietzsche's New Seas*, ed. Michael Allen Gillespie and Tracy Strong (Chicago: University of Chicago Press, 1988), p. 23. For a particularly egregious example of such translation, see M. S. Silk and J. P. Stern, *Nietzsche on Tragedy* (Cambridge: Cambridge University Press, 1981), chapter 4, which presents a section by section paraphrase of the "argument" of Nietzsche's text.

7. Although we have made no attempt to demonstrate this, the criticism of Danto could equally be made of Heidegger, whose definition of philosophy, though radially different from Danto's, is no less limited. See, for example, Heidegger's frequently quoted statement that a thinker is one who, in contrast with the writer and the researcher who have many thoughts, is "destined to think one single thought, a thought that is always 'about' *beings as a whole*. Each thinker thinks only one *single* thought," N I, p. 475/N 3, p. 4. An important, albeit condensed discussion of this question is to be found in Jacques Derrida, *Spurs*, trans. Barbara Harlow (Chicago: University of Chicago Press, 1979) pp. 109–123.

8. This is not meant to suggest that the Greeks "invented" philosophy or that the influence of Egyptian and, more particularly, Near Eastern thought on Greek culture was negligible. Having said this, what distinguishes Plato from his philosophical predecessors, Greek and non-Greek alike, is his determination of philosophy and the resulting sundering of philosophical discourse from the religious and artistic milieu in which it had hitherto subsisted. For Nietzsche's views on the origins of philosophy, see PTA, 1.

9. Plato, *Republic* trans. Allan Bloom (New York: Basic Books, 1968). Further references will be given parenthetically in the text.

10. Martha Nussbaum has argued that in the *Phaedrus* Plato reconsiders the mutual exclusivity of poetry and philosophy argued for in the *Republic* and ends up arguing for a conception of philosophy that incorporates poetic mania. See *The Fragility of Goodness* (Cambridge: Cambridge University Press, 1986), chapter 7 "Madness, reason and recantation in the *Phaedrus*." This is not the place to consider the merits of Nussbaum's argument. However, even if she is right in thinking that there is a shift in Plato's understanding of the relationship between philosophy and poetry, this would not affect the substance of my claim. For it is quite clear from the subsequent development of philosophy in the West that the arguments in the *Republic* were, rightly or wrongly, considered to be definitive. Whether this means that the traditional interpretation of Plato is mistaken is a question that needs to be pursued in another context.

11. This question and the problem of style in recent interpretations of Nietzsche will be considered in chapter 1.

12. See Wolfgang Schadewaldt, *Die Anfänge der Philosophie bei den Griechen: Die Vorsokratiker und ihre Voraussetzungen* (Frankfurt: Suhrkamp, 1978), chapter 1.

13. There is, of course, a complicated and oftentimes heated debate about the relationship between Plato and Socrates, and how much of what Socrates says is actu-

ally attributable to him, and how much to Plato himself, the details of which cannot be summarized in a footnote. However, I take it to be relatively uncontroversial that whatever Socrates may have thought about philosophy and poetry, the ideas expressed in the *Republic* are ones that Plato himself endorses. There is, I believe, no other way of explaining why so much of the *Republic* is devoted to a discussion of the relationship between philosophy and poetry. If one assumes that this issue is peripheral to the text or that the conclusions reached are not ones that Plato would agree with, then the burden of proof is on those who endorse this view to demonstrate that it is the case. A good summary of the Socrates-Plato debate can be found in the first chapter of Günter Figal's book *Socrates* (Munich: Beck, 1995). See also Gregory Vlastos' influential study, *Socrates*: *Ironist and Moral Philosopher* (Cambridge: Cambridge University Press, 1991).

14. Both Nietzsche and Heidegger identify Plato as the founder of the Western philosophical tradition, which they regard as inherently metaphysical, insofar as the character and parameters of philosophical discourse as articulated by Plato were to become exemplary for the West. For both thinkers, the decisive innovation made by Plato is the postulation of a supersensible mode of being that is the cause and ground of the "empirical" world. Two of the most obvious reference points for Nietzsche are the Preface to BGE and the well known text from TI, "How the 'True World' Became a Fable." For a relatively clear statement of Heidegger's view, see "Platons Lehre von der Wahrheit," in *Wegmarken* (Frankfurt: Klostermann, 1978), especially pp. 228–236.

15. In the *Republic*, Socrates refers to Homer as "the first teacher" [*prótos didáskalos*] (595c). Cf. 606e–607a. For Socrates' explicit criticisms of Homer, see 599c–601b.

16. On the political function of tragedy, see Christian Meier, *Die politische Kunst der griechischen Tragödie* (Beck: Munich, 1988).

17. The translation cited is that of Thomas G. West and Grace Starry West, *Four Texts on Socrates* (Ithaca: Cornell University Press, 1984). For a description of the best possible soul, see *Republic*, 443c-444a.

18. Although the struggle between wisdom and knowledge is a theme in several of Sophocles' extant works, it is most explicitly thematized in *Oedipus The King*, where, in a pivotal speech by the chorus (lines 955–995), the future of the gods is said to depend on Oedipus' oracle being proven true. This speech is a direct response to Jocasta's rejection of prophecy and divine power in lines 945 ff.

19. Schadewaldt, *Die Anfänge der Philosophie bei den Griechen*, p. 13.

20. Schadewaldt, *Die Anfänge der Philosophie bei den Griechen*, p. 13.

21. This distinction between the sophist, one who is paid for making speeches and hence must bend to the will of the market, and the philosopher, who eschews renumeration and is therefore free from such pressures, is one of the central motifs of the *Apology*. In the first of his three speeches Socrates emphasizes that he has never

accepted any money for the conversations he has conducted in Athens (19d–20c). Money is also an issue in the *Republic*, where the sophist Thrasymachus demands payment from Socrates should he lose the argument (337d).

22. Cf. the *Gorgias*, where Socrates describes rhetoric as a form of flattery that consists in knowing how to manage people (463a–b).

23. A point illustrated all too clearly by the *Apology*.

24. See H. G. Gadamer, "Plato und die Dichter" (Frankfurt: Klostermann, 1934), p. 23; reprinted in *Gesammelte Werke* (Tübingen: Mohr, 1986–1995.), vol. 5. Gadamer underscores—perhaps too charitably—the need to consider Plato's critique of poetry within the context of his break with traditional ideas regarding education which emphasized the pedagogic function of epic and tragic poetry.

25. Diels-Kranz fragment 56. The translation cited is that of Charles Kahn, *The Art and Thought of Heraclitus* (Cambridge: Cambridge University Press, 1979), p. 39.

26. The source of this claim is Diogenes Laertius. See his *Lives and Opinions of Eminent Philosophers* trans. R. D. Hicks (New York: Putnam, 1925), p. 281.

27. On the subject of Heraclitus' style, Charles Kahn has suggested that "the true parallel for an understanding of Heraclitus' style is . . . his own contemporaries, Pindar and Aeschylus. . . . I think we can best imagine the structure of Heraclitus' work on the analogy of the great choral odes, with their fluid but carefully articulated movement from image to aphorism, from myth to riddle to contemporary allusion," *The Art and Thought of Heraclitus*, p. 7.

28. Margaret Wilson, *Descartes* (London: Routledge & Kegan Paul, 1978), p. 4.

29. Wilson, *Descartes*, pp. 4–5.

30. Descartes, *Oeuvres philosophiques*, vol. 1 ed. Ferdinand Alquié (Paris: Garnier, 1963) p. 517; *Descartes: Philosophical Writings*, trans. Elizabeth Anscombe and Peter Geach (Sunbury-on-Thames: Thomas Nelson, 1970) pp. 8–9. Although the subject of Wilson's remark is the *Meditations* rather than the *Discourse*, the close temporal proximity of the two works and the similarities in subject and style all speak for the inclusion of the latter work in the category of Descartes' "mature philosophy."

31. Alexandre Koyré has in fact suggested that the *Discourse* "could be called the Cartesian *Confessions*." Alexandre Koyré, Introduction, in Anscombe and Geach, *Descartes: Philosophical Writings*, p. xiv.

32. See *On Free Choice of the Will*, II.3. This passage is cited by Arnauld at the beginning of the fourth set of objections presented to Descartes after the publication of the *Meditations*. I am indebted to Aaron Garrett for bringing Arnauld's reference to this passage to my attention.

33. Although Wilson acknowledges that "many elements in Descartes' arguments have more or less close Augustinian parallels," she hesitates to assess the impor-

tance of this relationship, concluding that it it not "yet clear how recognition of the Augustinian influence should affect our reading of Descartes," *Descartes*, p. 229.

34. Ludwig Wittgenstein, *Philosophische Untersuchungen, Werkausgabe* (Frankfurt: Suhrkamp, 1984), vol. 1, p. 231; *Philosophical Investigations*, trans. G. E. M. Anscombe (Oxford: Blackwell, 1983), p. vii. The English translation of the Preface omits the italicization of the word single [*einer*] contained in the German text.

35. G. P. Baker and P. M. S. Hacker, *An Analytical Commentary on Wittgenstein's Philosophical Investigations* (Chicago: The University of Chicago Press, 1985) vol. 1, p. 8. 'BT' is the abbreviation Baker and Hacker use to refer to the 'Big Typescript,' an unpublished manuscript of Wittgenstein's composed in 1933.

36. That Wittgenstein's later remarks on style apply to his earlier writings as well is suggested by a letter from October, 1919, in which he describes the *Tractatus* as a work that is "strictly philosophical and at the same time literary." Letter to Ludwig von Ficker, cited by Manfred Frank, "Über Stil und Bedeutung," in *Stil in der Philosophie* (Stuttgart: Reclam, 1992), p. 87.

37. It is important to note that Wittgenstein alludes to a connection between his style and the nature of his investigation, not a causal connection, as Baker and Hacker would have it. It is clearly an exaggeration to claim, as they do, that Wittgenstein "blames" his failure to write a more convention book on the nature of his research.

38. Ludwig Wittgenstein, *Vermischte Bemerkungen, Werkausgabe*, vol. 8 (Frankfurt: Suhrkamp, 1984), p. 489.

39. See W.V. Quine, *Word and Object* (Cambridge: MIT Press, 1960) chapter 2, "Translation and Meaning."

40. Donald Davidson, "Belief and the Basis of Meaning," in *Inquiries into Truth and Interpretation* (Oxford: Oxford University Press, 1985), p. 153.

41. Donald Davidson, "What Metaphors Mean," in Davidson, *Inquiries into Truth and Interpretation*, p. 245. Further references will be given in the text.

42. Aristotle, *Poetics*, trans. James Hutton (New York: Norton, 1982). The passage is cited by Derrida in his classic reading of metaphor in the *Poetics*, "White Mythology," in *Margins of Philosophy*, trans. Alan Bass (Chicago: The University of Chicago Press, 1982), pp. 242–243. For the sake of consistency, I sometimes cite Aristotle's text from the translation provided by Bass.

43. Andrzej Warminski, *Readings in Interpretation* (Minneapolis: University of Minnesota Press, 1987), p. lv.

44. See Derrida,"White Mythology," particularly pp. 219–229.

45. Walter Benjamin, "Die Aufgabe des Übersetzers," in *Illuminationen* (Frankfurt/Main: Suhrkamp, 1977), p. 55; "The Task of the Translator," in *Illuminations*, trans. Harry Zohn (New York: Schocken, 1968), p. 74.

46. H. G. Gadamer, *Gesammelte Werke*, vol. I, *Wahrheit und Methode* (Tübingen: Mohr, 1990), p. 191; *Truth and Method* ed. Garrett Barden and John Cumming (New York: Crossroad, 1988), p. 164. Further references will be given in the text to the German edition first, followed by the English.

47. Friedrich Schleiermacher, *Hermeneutik*, ed. Heinz Kimmerle (Heidelberg: Carl Winter, 1959). p. 136.

48. Gadamer is here using the term construe, German *konstruieren*, in a limited sense where it means to analyze the arrangement and connection of words in a sentence, particularly in connection with translation.

49. Derrida, *Spurs*, p. 85.

50. Paul de Man, "The Epistemology of Metaphor," *Critical Inquiry* 5 (1978), p. 14.

51. Paul de Man, "Reply to Raymond Geuss," *Critical Inquiry* 10 (1983), p. 384. Geuss' commentary, "A Response to Paul de Man," appears in the same volume. The target of Geuss' critique is de Man's essay, "Sign and Symbol in Hegel's *Aesthetics*," *Critical Inquiry* 8 (1982).

52. Ludwig Wittgenstein, *Tractatus logico-philosophicus*, trans. D. F. Pears & B. F. McGuinness (London: Routledge Kegan Paul, 1961), propositions 4.021 and 4.023.

CHAPTER 1

1. Cited by Silk and Stern, *Nietzsche on Tragedy*, p. 92.

2. Although the reaction of Ritschl and others took Nietzsche by surprise, it should not have been totally unexpected. As Nietzsche himself reports to Rohde, his lecture "Socrates and Tragedy," given almost two years before the publication of BT, "provoked horror and misunderstanding" in Basel, KSAB, 3/58. Compare Ritschl's letter of February 14, 1872, whose respectful tone fails to disguise its dismissive and censorious content, KGB, II.2/285.

3. R. Hinton Thomas, *Nietzsche in German Politics and Society 1890–1918*, (Manchester: Manchester University Press, 1986). These issues have recently been discussed in greater detail by Aschheim, *Nietzsche's Legacy in Germany 1890–1990.*

4. See *Nietzsche as Postmodernist: Pro and Contra*, ed. Clayton Koelb (Albany: SUNY Press, 1990), *Pourquoi nous ne pas nietzschéens*, ed. Luc Ferry and Alain Renault (Paris: Grasset, 1990), and Thomas Böning, "Literaturwissenscaft im Zeitalter des Nihilismus: Paul de Mans Nietzsche Lektüre," *Deutsche Vierteljahrschrift für Literaturwissenschaft und Geistesgeschichte* 64 (1990).

5. Alexander Nehamas, *Nietzsche: Life as Literature* (Cambridge: Harvard University Press, 1985) p. 9. Further references will be given parenthetically in the text.

6. This is the view of Mazzino Montinari. See his essay "Nietzsches Nachlaß von 1885 bis 1888 oder Textkritik und Wille zur Macht," *Nietzsche lesen* (Berlin: de Gruyter, 1982) which contains a detailed critical history of WM.

7. Nietzsche's references to the will to power in the published texts subsequent to the completion of Za have been documented by James Winchester, *Nietzsche's Aesthetic Turn* (Albany: SUNY Press, 1994), p. 177, note 27.

8. Walter Kaufmann, "Editor's Introduction," *Basic Writings of Nietzsche* (New York: Random House, 1968), p. 439

9. In spite of the great differences which otherwise separate these two texts, there is a striking similarity between GM and Rousseau's discourse "On the Origins of Inequality Among Men." In both cases historical narrative is supplanted by an explicitly allegorical discourse.

10. The dangers of reading Nietzsche too literally are illustrated by the many attempts to show that Nietzsche believed that the doctrine of eternal recurrence could be proven scientifically. See, for example, Walter Kaufmann, *Nietzsche: Philosopher, Psychologist, Antichrist* (Princeton: Princeton University Press, 1974) pp. 326–333. This issue is explored in detail by Nehamas, *Nietzsche: Life as Literature*, chapter 5.

11. As early as 1868 Nietzsche showed a rather emphatic skepticism towards the efficacy of philosophical proofs. See his letter Deussen from mid October, 1868, KSAB, 2/595 as well as KSAB, 3/149.

12. For a discussion of this question see Eric Blondel, *Nietzsche: The Body and Culture*, trans. Séan Hand (Stanford: Stanford University Press, 1991), chapter 2.

13. Gillespie and Strong, *Nietzsche's New Seas*, p. 1

14. Perhaps the most influential of these is Maudemarie Clark's study, *Nietzsche on Truth and Philosophy* (Cambridge: Cambridge University Press, 1990). Clark's interpretation of Nietzsche will be considered in chapters 2 and 3.

15. Henry James, "The Figure in the Carpet," in *The Figure in the Carpet and other Stories*, ed. Frank Kermode (London: Penguin Books, 1986), p. 374.

16. Kaufmann, *Nietzsche*, pp. 94–95. Further references will be given parenthetically in the text.

17. As James Winchester has observed, "When Nehamas writes of Nietzsche's 'vast' varieties of 'styles' he means principally literary genres. . . . Style can be loosely applied to genre, but style is also a designation for what happens within a genre," *Nietzsche's Aesthetic Turn*, pp. 127–128.

18. While it is true that Nehamas rejects what he terms "the problematic distinction between the 'what' and the 'how'" of a text (*Nietzsche: Life as Literature*, p. 39), my contention is that his overly abstract understanding of style leads him into a more subtle, though no less nefarious, version of this distinction.

19. Nehamas' remarks contain clear echoes of Nietzsche's discussion of the pre-Socratics, whose systems have been "refuted" and hence are of little interest in themselves. In such systems "it is only the personal element [*das Persönliche*] that can be of interest to us, for it is this which is eternally irrefutable," KSA 1, p. 803.

20. This passage should be read in conjunction with a parallel passage from GM, I.13: "There is no 'being' behind doing, effecting, becoming; 'the doer' is merely a fiction added to the deed [*hinzugedichtet*]—the deed is everything." Nietzsche's assertion earlier in this section that it is a "seduction of language" and "of the fundamental errors of reason that are petrified in it" that forces us to posit an agent behind every action and effect suggests that subjectivity is itself a linguistic construction and hence a kind of error or fiction.

21. In the following chapter, Nehamas writes that "to be beyond good and evil is to combine all of one's features and qualities, whatever their traditional moral value, into a controlled and coherent whole," *Nietzsche: Life as Literature*, p. 27.

22. "Nietzsche's texts," Nehamas writes, "do not describe but, in exquisitely elaborate detail, *exemplify* the perfect instance of his ideal character. And this character is none other than the character these very texts constitute: Nietzsche himself," *Nietzsche: Life as Literature*, pp. 232–233.

23. Nehamas, following Kaufmann, has the four instances of the word 'one' in the last sentence in italics. In the German text these words are in plain text.

24. The interpretations which Nehamas believes exhibit this tendency are those of Jacques Derrida and Sarah Kofman (see *Nietzsche: Life as Literature*, pp. 15–18). It should be said, however, that Nehamas does not make a genuine attempt to come to terms with views of these commentators; his interest in them is principally as a foil for his own interpretation of Nietzsche. Commenting on Derrida's reading of Nietzsche's sentence "I have forgotten my umbrella," which he argues can never be definitively interpreted, Nehamas writes that Derrida "does not defend his assumption that infallibility and certainty are necessary if interpretation is to be possible," *Nietzsche: Life as Literature*, p. 17, note 13. Such a statement borders on bad faith, since there are numerous texts in which Derrida, vigorously and convincingly, demonstrates the limits of the hermeneutic concept of interpretation. See, for example, "Différance" in *Margins of Philosophy,* trans. Alan Bass (Chicago: University of Chicago Press, 1982) and *Of Grammatology*, trans. Gayatri Spivak (Baltimore: Johns Hopkins University Press, 1976), Part I, Writing Before the Letter.

25. On the errors at work in the formation of character, see M, 115.

26. Gary Shapiro has argued, contra Nehamas, that in the reading of Greek tragedy articulated in BT, Nietzsche "is radically dislocating and de-emphasizing the role of character in drama. . . . Nietzsche's account of Oedipus the character does not suggest any special interest in him as a unified or integrated figure; rather the accent in on the uncanniness of the man whose existence challenges our tendency to see humans (and other things in the world) as individuals," *Nietzschean Narratives*

(Bloomington: Indiana University Press, 1989), p. 155. For Shapiro, Nehamas' tendency to see subjectivity as the product of a conscious strategy of self-construction rather than of forces—linguistic, psychological, and cultural—beyond subjective control is reflected in his failure to recognize the importance of Nietzsche's use of the impersonal "what" [*was*] rather than the personal "who" [*wer*] in the subtitle and elsewhere in EH.

27. This is one reason why Nehamas relies so greatly on WP, which he regards as an essential element of the Nietzschean canon, seeming unaware that the published text is philologically corrupt. Nehamas' view of WP is examined in chapter 5.

28. "I know my fate. One day my name will be associated with the memory of something tremendous—a crisis without equal on earth, the most profound collision of conscience, a decision that was conjured up *against* everything that had been believed, demanded, hallowed so far [. . .]. For when truth enters into a fight with the lies of millennia, we shall have upheavals, a convulsion of earthquakes, a moving of mountains and valleys the likes of which has never been dreamed of. The concept of politics will have merged entirely with a war of spirits," EH, IV.1.

29. John, 19:5. The Latin *ecce homo* is a literal translation of the Greek *idoù ho anthrópos*.

30. Jacques Derrida, "Otobiographies: Teaching of Nietzsche and the Politics of the Proper Name," trans. Avital Ronell, in *The Ear of the Other* (Lincoln: University of Nebraska Press, 1988), p. 15.

31. Pindar's line reads: *genoi' hoios essi mathón*. See *Pindari Carmina*, ed. C. M. Bowra (Oxford: Clarendon Press, 1961), line 73.

32. In the 1886 Preface to HH II, Nietzsche writes: "One should only speak when one cannot be silent, and even then only speak of what one has *overcome*,—everything else is gossip, 'literature,' bad breeding [. . .]. But a few things were necessary—time, convalescence, remoteness, distance—until the desire in me stirred to retrospectively [*nachträglich*] skin, exploit, lay bare, 'represent' (or whatever you want to call it) my experiences, overcomings, some fact or piece of fate for the sake of knowledge. To this degree all my writings—with one single, but essential exception—should be *back dated*; they speak always of something 'behind me,'" HH II, P.1.

33. The movement of deferral described above is one of the central themes of EH. In the first paragraph of the foreword Nietzsche asserts: "I live on my own credit; perhaps it is a mere prejudice that I live." This same idea is taken up later in the text, when he declaims "The time for me has not yet come: some are born posthumously," EH, III.1. See the foreword to A, where Nietzsche writes that it is "only the day after tomorrow that belongs to me. Some are born posthumously."

34. This same dual structure of identity is described by Nietzsche in a note from 1872–1873 entitled "Oedipus. Conversation of the last philosopher with himself": "I call myself the last philosopher because I am the last human being. No one talks with

me but my self and my voice comes to me as the voice of one dying [. . .]. My heart cannot bear the shudder of the loneliest loneliness and compels me to speak as if I were two," KSA 7, 19.131. It is certainly no coincidence that in this note, as in EH, the thematic of identity is explicitly linked with the name Oedipus. One reading of EH could begin by examining the images of the riddle, the absent father, and identity in light of the Oedipal myth. Gary Shapiro has explored some of the connections between EH and the story of Oedipus in a very suggestive way. See *Nietzschean Narratives*, chapter 6.

35. See Nietzsche's letter to Köselitz from December 9, 1888, the day after the manuscript of EH was sent to the publisher: "In *Ecce Homo* you will read about a discovery concerning the *third* and *fourth* untimely ones that will make your hair stand on end—mine, too, stands on end. Both speak only of me *anticipando* [. . .]. Neither Wagner nor Schopenhauer are psychologically present there [. . .] I first *understood* both texts only 14 days ago.—" KSAB, 8/1181.

36. It is interesting to recall that two of the people Nietzsche had extensive contact with during this period, Peter Gast and Georg Brandes, both used pseudonyms. Gast's given name was Heinrich Köselitz, while Brandes was born Morris Cohen.

37. The classical conception of the proper stretches back at least to the *Republic*, where Socrates distinguishes between what is proper to human beings, the soul, the city and what is alien to them. See, for example, 462b–d and 470b–d. For an rich discussion of the proper in relation to Nietzsche, see Sarah Kofman, *Nietzsche and Metaphor*, trans. Duncan Large (Stanford: Stanford University Press, 1993).

38. This conclusion is in fact already announced in the opening lines of the text, where Nietzsche writes that the good fortune of his existence lies precisely in the duality of his identity: "The good fortune of my existence, its uniqueness perhaps, lies in its fatality: I am to express it in the form of a riddle, already dead as my father, while as my mother I am still living and becoming old. [A] dual descent, as it were, both from the highest and the lowest rung on the ladder of life, at the same time a decadent and a *beginning* [. . .]. I know both, I am both—" EH, I.1.

CHAPTER 2

1. The title stems from Ernst Holzer and August Horneffer, editors of GA vol. X, who grouped together the notes for this text under this heading. During the period in which Nietzsche was intensively working on this text—from mid-1872 to late 1873—the titles he considered included "The Philosopher: Reflections on the Struggle between Art and Knowledge," KSA 7, 19 [98], "The Justification of Philosophy Through the Greeks," KSA 7, 19 [316], and "The Philosopher as Physician of Culture," KSAB, 4/298. Daniel Breazeale offers a useful and compact history of *Das Philosophenbuch* in *Philosophy and Truth: Selections from Nietzsche's Notebooks of the Early 1870s* (Atlantic Highlands: Humanities Press, 1979), pp. xviii-xxiii.

2. In a letter to Erwin Rohde from February 21, 1873, Nietzsche expresses the hope that his book will appear after the coming Easter holiday, KSAB, 4/296.

3. In the notebooks from the period extending from the summer to the fall of that year there is a gradual but marked movement away from a concern with the philosopher and the questions of truth and art and a development of an interest in the nature and significance of historical scholarship. The notes devoted to the latter topic will prove to be the basis for the second of the *Untimely Meditations*, "On the Use and Disadvantage of History for Life," which was published in late February, 1874. While it is true that in early 1875 Nietzsche did revisit the subject of early Greek philosophy in his notebooks, the context of this later work was the projected but unwritten meditation "Wir Philologen." Cf. KSA 8, pp. 11–130.

4. On this question, see Magnus, Stewart, and Mileur, *Nietzsche's Case*, pp. 35–46.

5. While "On Truth and Lie" has received a great deal of critical scrutiny, the same is not true of "Philosophy in the Tragic Age of the Greeks," of which relatively few scholars have a positive opinion. See, for example, Eugen Fink, *Nietzsches Philosophie* (Stuttgart: Kohlhammer, 1960), pp. 38–43 and Giorgio Colli, "Nachwort," KSA 1, pp. 916–918. An exception to this tendency is Sarah Kofman, who discusses PTA at some length in *Nietzsche and Metaphor* and chapter 4 of *Socrate(s)* (Paris: Galilée, 1989), which bears the title "Les Socrate(s) de Nietzsche"; trans. Madeleine Dobie, *Graduate Faculty Philosophy Journal*, no. 15–2 (1991).

6. Philippe Lacoue-Labarthe "The Detour," in *The Subject of Philosophy*, ed. Thomas Trezise (Minnesota: University of Minnesota Press, 1993), p. 14.

7. Claudia Crawford, *The Beginnings of Nietzsche's Theory of Language* (Berlin: de Gruyter, 1988), p. 219.

8. In the 1886 preface to HH II, Nietzsche describes TL as a "text that has been kept secret" [*geheim gehaltenes Schriftstück*]. It is significant that here, thirteen years later, Nietzsche mentions TL by name. The fact that he views it as a discrete text that was intentionally held back suggests that he did indeed intend to publish it at one time.

9. See the aforementioned Preface to volume two of HH, where Nietzsche characterizes the time in which he wrote this essay as one in which "I myself was in the midst of a period of moral skepticism and dissolution [*Auflösung*], *that is to say, in the midst of a critique as well as a deepening of all pessimism hitherto.*" Commenting on this passage Claudia Crawford writes that "Nietzsche intensifies pessimism by demonstrating that, because of the nature of human perception and conceptuality, appearance is *all* there is, but his critique of pessimism lies in the . . . complete pleasure in the affirmation of appearance as appearance," *The Beginnings of Nietzsche's Theory of Language*, pp. 218–19.

10. This remark only makes explicit what was already clear from the dedication to Voltaire in celebration of the one hundredth anniversary of his death and the long citation from Descartes' *Discourse*, which was published "In Lieu of a Preface."

11. Clark, *Nietzsche on Truth and Philosophy*, p. 105. Hereafter cited as NTP.

12. This is apparently what is at stake when Nietzsche accuses the Christian theologen of having no facility for philology and therefore being unable "to read off facts without falsifying them by interpretation," A, 52.

13. In addition to Clark, both Alexander Nehamas and Richard Rorty are sympathetic to the view that Nietzsche's early writings on language are relatively unimportant for an understanding of his 'mature' thinking. Although Nehamas doesn't go so far as to assert that both BT and TL are incoherent (as does Clark), he maintains that Nietzsche's view of the distinction between appearance and reality and his understanding of language changed radically as his thought developed. Consequently, Nehamas regards TL as "immensely overrated," *Nietzsche Life as Literature*, p. 246, note 6; cf. pp. 42 ff. Rorty has recently endorsed Clark's view that in the writings of his last two active years Nietzsche develops a pragmatic, that is, common-sense conception of truth. See his "Introduction: Pragmatism and Post-Nietzschean Philosophy," *Essays on Heidegger and Others* (Cambridge: Cambridge University Press, 1991), p. 2. The continuity in Nietzsche's thought has also been questioned, though in a less extreme way, by Winchester, *Nietzsche's Aesthetic Turn*, ch. 5.

14. See Martin Heidegger, *Being and Time*, section 44.

15. Lacoue-Labarthe was perhaps the first to observe that "despite some changes in terminology, Nietzsche's analyses of language will vary little and that he will almost always stick to the knowledge gained in these first years," "The Detour," p. 15. While Lacoue-Labarthe does not defend this assertion in any detail, this task was taken up by Paul de Man in two essays, "The Rhetoric of Tropes" and "The Rhetoric of Persuasion," both contained in *Allegories of Reading* (New Haven: Yale University Press, 1979). More recently Alan Schrift has sought to demonstrate that Nietzsche's "views on language inform many of his later positions, insofar as many of Nietzsche's criticisms of the traditional problems of metaphysics and epistemology appear as consequences of some of his earliest insights into the nature of language and metaphor," Alan Schrift, *Nietzsche and the Question of Interpretation* (New York: Routledge, 1990), p. 123. While these earlier studies might appear to make the present chapter otiose, the approach pursued here is distinct from those cited above in two ways: first, because it takes seriously the challenge posed by Clark's claim that there is a genuine shift in Nietzsche's thinking about truth; second, and more important, because in this chapter I undertake a reading of two key texts from this period, "On Truth and Lie" and Nietzsche's notes for a lecture course on rhetoric, whose close relationship to one another has not previously been explored.

16. A reliable summary of the debate over the dating of the lecture course is provided by Anthoine Meijers in his essay "Gustav Gerber und Friedrich Nietzsche," *Nietzsche Studien*, Vol. 17 (1988). The close parallels between the lecture course and "On True and Lie" and the fact that both texts draw extensively upon Gustav Gerber's *Die Sprache Als Kunst* (see below), suggest quite strongly that the lecture notes were written in the winter of 1872–1873. In spite of this, the editors of the recently published volume of Nietzsche's lectures which contains the notes for the course on rhetoric retain the previously accepted date of 1874. See KGW, II/4: Basler Vorlesun-

gen, 1871–1872/1874–1875, ed. Fritz Bornmann and Mario Carpitella (Berlin: de Gruyter, 1995). However, since the critical apparatus to the lectures has yet to appear, it is unclear why the editors have retained the 1874 date.

17. Anthoine Meijers and Martin Stingelin have produced a concordance of the examples and citations that Nietzsche takes over from Gerber and incorporates in the notes on rhetoric and "On Truth and Lie": "Konkordanz zu den wörtlichen Abschriften und Übernahmen von Beispielen und Zitaten aus Gustav Gerber: *Die Sprache Als Kunst* (Bromberg 1871) in Nietzsches Rhetorik-Vorlesung und in 'Über Wahrheit und Lüge im aussermoralischen Sinne,'" *Nietzsche Studien*, vol. 17 (1988). Although Nietzsche acknowledges that many of the examples he uses in the notes on rhetoric are taken from Gerber, the number and length of many of the citations are quite remarkable. A thoughtful discussion of Nietzsche's liberal use of ideas and material accumulated from his reading can be found in Janz, *Die Briefe Friedrich Nietzsches*, pp. 47–49. Janz argues, correctly I believe, that Nietzsche's genius as a thinker lies not in his originality—his dependence on the work of his contemporaries is quite clear—but rather in his ability to formulate problems in a decisive manner and to pursue them more vigorously and relentlessly than his contemporaries. In so doing, Janz observes, Nietzsche was following in the footsteps of another epochal thinker, namely, Plato.

18. According to Anthoine Meijers, Gerber distinguishes the following phases in the development of language: "(thing-in-itself) - nerve stimulus - sensation - sound - representation - root - word - concept," "Gerber und Nietzsche," p. 377.

19. This does not imply that Nietzsche's other texts from this period, including the rightly famous notebooks from 1872–1873, should therefore be ignored. However, one might be inclined to argue that Crawford takes this principle rather too far when she claims that Nietzsche's theory of language cannot fully be understood without considering its genesis in a series of notes and sketches Nietzsche wrote between 1867–1870 while studying the writings of Schopenhauer, Lange, and Hartmann. The most important of these are a brief text "On The Origin of Language" (1869/70) and two long notes from 1867–1868: "On Schopenhauer" and "On Teleology." While these texts are certainly of historical interest, it is unclear why, if TL does indeed "encapsulates ideas with which [Nietzsche] had been working for years" (*The Beginnings of Nietzsche's Theory of Language*, p. IX), that one should not take this text and the notes for a course on rhetoric contemporaneous with it as one's point of departure.

20. While Schrift argues that there are "numerous examples of genealogical analysis" to be found in Nietzsche writings, the only early "text" he identifies are the notes for "Wir Philologen" penned in 1875, *Nietzsche and the Question of Interpretation*, p. 172. As I argue in this and the following chapter, there are good grounds for regarding TL and BT as genealogical texts.

21. This passage should be compared with the section 2 of *Beyond Good and Evil*, where Nietzsche makes an almost identical claim. This is only one of many parallels between these two texts. That there should be such parallels—one might recall that the second chapter of *Beyond Good and Evil* is entitled "The Free Spirit"—is not

surprising, since shortly before writing the latter text Nietzsche had attempted, unsuccessfully, to revise *Human All-Too-Human* for a new, second edition. A second edition did in fact appear in 1886, but was essentially unchanged with the exception of the addition of two Forewords, one for each of the text's two volumes.

22. This fable first appears in Nietzsche's writings as part of "On The Pathos of Truth," one of the "Five Forewords to Five Unwritten Books" Nietzsche wrote and presented to Cosima Wagner for Christmas, 1872. Interestingly enough, in this fragment the fable is put into the mouth of an "unfeeling demon," KSA 1, p. 759. Since TL only consists of two sections, I have provided pages references to the German text which is found in KSA 7, pp. 875–890.

23. One exception to this tendency is Andrzej Warminski's rigorous and thought provoking essay "Towards A Fabulous Reading: Nietzsche's 'On Truth and Lie in the Extra-Moral Sense,'" *Graduate Faculty Philosophy Journal*, no. 15–2 (1991).

24. Unfortunately, translators of Nietzsche into English have, on the whole, shown a blatant disregard for his punctuation. In the case of "On Truth and Lie," both the Kaufmann translation and that by Gilman, Blair, and Parent do away with the dash. In all fairness it must be said that Gilman et al. do at least translate the entire essay, while Kaufmann, inexplicably and without editorial comment, deletes nearly half of Nietzsche's text thus literally transforming it into a 'fragment.' See *The Portable Nietzsche* (New York: Viking Press, 1954) pp. 42–47.

25. Warminski, "Towards a Fabulous Reading," pp. 114–115.

26. On the Socratic nature of Nietzsche's questions, "What is a word?" "What is truth?" and the very un-Socratic nature of his answers, see Warminski, "Towards a Fabulous Reading," pp. 96–97.

27. As Crawford admirably demonstrates, the development of Nietzsche's views of knowledge and the limits of human cognition owes a great deal to his study of Kant, Schopenhauer, Lange, and Hartmann. And while one might agree with Crawford that "Nietzsche already anticipated all of what he found in Gerber with the exception of the tropological model" (*The Beginnings of Nietzsche's Theory of Language*, p. 212), it is precisely the tropological model—though not the vocabulary of tropes—which is retained by Nietzsche.

28. It is interesting to note that Nietzsche makes use of this same argument in HH, 39, where he compares the error in thinking a particular action "good" or "evil" in itself irrespective of its consequences "with the same error according to which language designates the stone itself as hard, the tree itself as green—therefore, in the same way that we understand the effect as a cause.

29. Paul de Man, "The Rhetoric of Tropes," in *Allegories of Reading*, p. 107. Hereafter cited as RT.

30. Cited by de Man, "The Rhetoric of Tropes," p. 107.

31. A point recently made by Günter Grass with the title of his novel *Die Rattin*, a word that previously did not exist in German.

32. It is worth noting that by stressing the *metapherein* itself, the movement from one sphere to another, rather than the material which is in fact transferred, Nietzsche departs from a long tradition that has understood metaphor as a type of exchange based on similarity. Several times in the course of "On Truth and Lie," Nietzsche emphasizes the arbitrariness of metaphor, and in so doing undermines the usual basis for a distinction between metaphor and metonymy, namely, the distinction between exchange based on perceived similarity (metaphor) and exchange based on contiguity in space and time, without similarity (metonymy). By contrast, Kofman views Nietzsche's use of metaphor in his early writings as essentially metaphysical because the concept of metaphor is still thought in contradistinction to "the proper," *Nietzsche and Metaphor*, p. 16. The ground of Kofman's claim, that in BT and TL Nietzsche "seems precisely to be still accepting an innermost essence of things" seems open to serious question.

33. While Nietzsche denies that words can be true in the sense of providing a mirror image of objects in the world, there is no need to generalize from this to the assertion that truth—in every sense of the word—is a chimera. As we shall see, Nietzsche's move from a correspondence or reference based theory of language to a tropological theory necessitates a rethinking of the structure of truth.

34. As Nietzsche writes in the Epilogue to CW, there are "ways of seeing, immune to reasons and refutations. One cannot refute Christianity, one cannot refute a disease of the eye." Compare GS, 58, where Nietzsche ridicules the idea that a recognition of the errors that lie at the origin of our way of speaking could allow us to simply do away with it.

35. This point is made by Kofman, who writes that the logic of the concept, which requires the forgetting of "individual perspectives," "culminates in the triumph of the collective over the individual The 'proper' is subjected to the social norm just as impressions and images are branded by the concept, subjected and subdued by it," *Nietzsche and Metaphor*, pp. 47–48.

36. Compare GS, 344, where Nietzsche suggests that the will to truth might prove to be a "destructive principle hostile to life [. . .] a concealed will to death."

37. See Warminski, "Towards a Fabulous Reading," p. 99.

38. Warminski, *Readings in Interpretation*, p. 1.

39. Compare BGE, 34: "And if somebody asked, 'But to a fiction there surely belongs an author?'—couldn't one answer simply, why? Doesn't this 'belongs' perhaps belong to the fiction, too? Is it not permitted by now to be a bit ironical about the subject no less than the predicate and object?"

40. De Man, "Tropes," *Allegories of Reading*, p. 49.

41. Warminski, "Towards A Fabulous Reading," pp. 94. Warminski is here following de Man, who characterizes TL as an "ironic allegory," "The Rhetoric of Tropes," p. 116.

42. The basis for the conclusion that Nietzsche rejects literal meaning in toto is often said to be TL's infamous description of truths as illusions. However, there is no need to interpret this description as a denial of either truth or literal meaning. One obvious way in which truths are illusions is that the ostensibly transparent referential structure of language creates the illusion that the relationship between 'truth' and the 'world' is one of correspondence or identity, that is to say, that truths can be directly and unproblematically mapped onto the world.

43. In his lecture course "The Will to Power as Art," Heidegger writes that "one need not penetrate too far into Nietzsche's thought in order to determine without difficulty that his procedure is one of reversal [*Umkehrung*]," N I, p. 39/N 1, p. 30.

44. BT, 14 and GM, III.13, respectively. Nietzsche's description of the ascetic priest in this section raises the complicated question of just how a force which denies life to the extent the ascetic priest does can also be one of life's greatest creators. Nietzsche's attitude to the ascetic priest and the logic he attributes to the ascetic ideal itself bears comparison with Heidegger's evaluation of technology in *The Question Concerning Technology*, in *Martin Heidegger Basic Writings*, ed. David Farrell Krell (New York: Harper & Row, 1977). Heidegger's famous citation from Hölderlin—"Wo aber Gefahr ist, wächst/Das Rettende auch"—could equally well be applied to the third essay of the *Genealogy*. The logic of the ascetic ideal is considered in more detail in chapter 4.

45. One could make the case—as does Warminski in both *Readings in Interpretation* and "Towards a Fabulous Reading"—that language is inherently violent, mutilating both the possessor of language and the phenomena that language itself describes. The existence of such an originary violence does not rule out the possibility of the kinds of linguistic violence described here. On the contrary, the notion of an originary violence only serves to underscore the deceptive tendencies of those forms of romanticism which seek to recover an originary, natural language, free from all forms of violence whatsoever.

46. Nietzsche's critique of Socratism and its belief in the ability of thought to correct existence will become a major part of his critique of Judeo-Christian morality. See, for example, the section of TI entitled "The 'Improvers' of Mankind."

47. The reinterpretation of truth that is explicitly formulated in TL but whose roots can be traced back to BT, represents only the beginning of what will be a lifelong task for Nietzsche. In a famous passage from the third essay of GM written some fourteen years after TL Nietzsche equates the meaning of his entire being with this one task. "What meaning would *our* whole being possess," writes Nietzsche, "if it were not this, that in us the will to truth becomes conscious of itself as a problem," GM, III.27.

48. The same could also be said of the words *täuschen* and *Vertauschung*. In addition to its meaning as 'exchange' or 'substitution,' *Vertauschung* can also be used to denote something taken in mistake, thus a kind of deception.

49. The term *shine* should here be understood in its many senses as appearance, illusion, the glimmer of something "that shines" when it comes in contact with the sun, hence as a kind of "shining forth." For an elucidation of this polysemy and for our literal translation of Nietzsche's *Schein* with its English cognate, see chapter 3.

50. The significance of this trio lies in the fact that it belongs to the essential nature of each, according to Nietzsche, to wear masks, be able to present themselves as other. This becomes especially important when one recalls that woman is one of Nietzsche's favorite figures for truth, something we will have an opportunity to consider below.

51. It is interesting to note that Nietzsche uses the Latin *intuition* and the German *Anschauung* almost interchangeably in TL. The word translated as "intuitions" in the passage cited above is *Intuitionen*, whereas in the following passage Nietzsche uses the German word *Anschauungen* to the same effect: The human being, as a rational being, "no longer lets himself be carried away by sudden impressions [*plötzliche Eindrücke*], by intuitions [*Anschauungen*], but first generalizes all these impressions into less colorful, cooler concepts in order to hitch the wagon of his life and action to them," TL, 250/881. Nietzsche, in contrast to Heidegger, did not have an aversion to using German terms with obviously Latin roots. It would be interesting to consider this difference in greater detail and the extent to which it reflects stylistic and philosophical differences between Nietzsche and Heidegger, particularly since Nietzsche, less than a year before dictating TL, had remarked on the essential "bond which truly connects the innermost recesses of the German spirit and the Greek genius," a view he was later to repudiate, but which Heidegger was to go to great pains to emphasize. For Nietzsche's assertion see "On the Future of Our Educational Institutions," KSA 1, p. 691.

52. BT, with its apparent privileging of music over the image and the concept, has often (mistakenly) been read as a prime example of such phonocentrism. This question is considered in more detail in Chapter 3.

53. Clayton Koelb, "Reading as a Philosophical Strategy," in *Nietzsche as Postmodernist: Essays Pro and Contra*, ed. Clayton Koelb (Albany: SUNY Press, 1990), p. 146.

54. My reading of Nietzsche's references to truth as a woman has been greatly influenced by numerous discussions with Madeleine Dobie.

55. The question of truth and woman in Nietzsche has, since the publication of Derrida's essay *Spurs*, received a great deal of attention, and it is not my intention here to elucidate the main points of Derrida's subtle argument, or to narrate the turns which the debate has taken in response to Derrida's text.

56. The translation is from John Burnet, *Early Greek Philosophy* (London: Adam & Charles Black, 1971), p. 172.

57. This structure is, of course, virtually identical with the one elaborated by Plato in Book VII of the *Republic*. For a discussion of these points, see the Introduction.

58. See Sarah Kofman, *Nietzsche et la scène philosophique* (Paris: Galilée, 1986), pp. 254–259.

59. The intersection of the Greeks and truth unavoidably brings the name Heidegger to mind. Is it not Nietzsche, but Heidegger with whom we associate the project of reinterpreting truth by looking back to the Greeks? The reasons why this element of Nietzsche's thinking has been ignored and why Nietzsche's reinterpretation of truth is most frequently understood as a denial of truth cannot be considered here. Needless to say, this lack in the conventional understanding of Nietzsche owes much to the literary character of Nietzsche's texts. It is, however, worthwhile pointing out that Heidegger's own reinterpretation of truth or *aletheia* has much more in common with Nietzsche's efforts than either he or many readers of Heidegger have recognized. There is, for example, more than a passing similarity between Nietzsche's understanding of truth as a veiled woman and Heidegger's suggestion that the essence of truth is untruth, that is, the essence of truth is concealment, rather than unconcealment (see, for example, sections 204–237 of Heidegger's *Beiträge zur Philosophie* [Frankfurt: Klostermann, 1989]). Nietzsche's emphasis on the structure of the veil and his criticisms of the traditional conception of truth as unveiling can also be read as a critique of the traditional understanding of truth as pure presence, which is a major target of Heidegger's critique of truth. Here, as elsewhere, the similarities between Heidegger and Nietzsche grow greater when one is able to distance oneself from Heidegger's Nietzsche interpretation and from his own self-interpretation, both of which depend in large part on his denial of connections and similarities of precisely this type.

60. Nietzsche's emphasis is excluded by Kaufmann in his translation.

61. "At long last, let us contrast the very different manner in which *we* conceive the problem of error and appearance. (I say "we" for politeness' sake.)"

62. Lest this passage be considered an anomaly in Nietzsche's later writings, a virtually identical passage is to be found in GM, I.13. Here Nietzsche writes that "a quantum of force is equivalent to a quantum of drive, will, effect—more, it is nothing other than precisely this very willing, effecting, and only owing *to the seduction of language (and of the fundamental errors of reason that are petrified in it)* which conceives and misconceives all effects as conditioned by something that causes effects, by a 'subject,' can it appear otherwise" (emphasis added). Similar passages in the *Nachlaß* are to be found in KSA 13, 14.79 and 14.122.

63. This description reiterates a claim Nietzsche makes in HH, 11 where he writes: "Men believed to actually have knowledge of the world in language [. . .]. Long after the fact [*Sehr nachträglich*]—first now—it occurs to men that they have propagated a terrible error by their belief in language. Luckily is is too late for the development of reason, which rests upon this belief, to be reversed."

64. The last sentence is perhaps clearer in the German: "*er hat ja jedes Wort für sich, jeden Satz für sich, den wir sprechen*!"

65. Perhaps the best account of Nietzsche's view of science, which is also consistent with the conclusions of this chapter, is Babette Babich's excellent but challenging study, *Nietzsche's Philosophy of Science* (Albany: SUNY Press, 1994).

CHAPTER 3

1. Otto Ribbeck was a classical philologist and an acquaintance of Rohde's and Nietzsche's.

2. M. S. Silk and J. P. Stern, *Nietzsche on Tragedy* (Cambridge: Cambridge University Press, 1981), p. 349. Hereafter cited as NoT.

3. BT was published on January 2, 1872; Nietzsche dictated "On Truth and Lie" in June, 1873.

4. There is, however, less agreement on this point than on the diminished status of language within BT. See, for example, Fink, *Nietzsches Philosophie*, pp. 32–34, and Clark, *Nietzsche on Truth and Philosophy*, pp. 63–93, each of whom views "On Truth and Lie" as an immature essay written by Nietzsche while he was still under the influence of Schopenhauer.

5. Lacoue-Labarthe, "The Detour," p. 34. Hereafter cited as D. A close reading of Nietzsche's notebooks from this period (1869–1875) seems to confirm Lacoue-Labarthe's suggestion that there is a marked change in Nietzsche's thinking after his discovery of rhetoric. The immediate effects of this discovery, itself limited to Nietzsche's study of two books—Gustav Gerber's *Die Sprache als Kunst* and Richard Volkmann's *Die Rhetoric der Griechen und Römer in systematischer Übersicht dargestellt*—can be seen in a notebook Nietzsche kept between the summer of 1872 and the beginning of 1873 (see KSA 7, pp. 417–520). This notebook contains material Nietzsche hoped to include in the never completed *Das Philosophenbuch*, and is the basis for the essay "On Truth and Lie," which at one time was projected as the introduction to that book.

6. See, for example, Nietzsche's remark in a letter to Carl Gersdorff written in March 1870: "For me, all that is best and most beautiful is associated with the names Schopenhauer and Wagner," KSAB, 3/65.

7. Gilles Deleuze, *Nietzsche & Philosophy*, trans. Hugh Tomlinson (New York: Columbia University Press, 1983), p. 11. Peter Szondi, who recognizes that Schopenhauer's and Nietzsche's views of tragedy are quite opposed, nevertheless concludes that BT "bears the stamp of [Schopenhauer's] system to the last detail," "Versuch Über das Tragische," *Schriften*, vol. I, ed. Wolfgang Fietkau (Frankfurt: Suhrkamp, 1978), p. 214.

8. John Sallis, *Crossings: Nietzsche and the Space of Tragedy* (Chicago: University of Chicago Press, 1991), p. 148. Hereafter cited as CRS.

9. A thorough account of the complicated genesis of BT is given by Silk and Stern, *Nietzsche on Tragedy*, pp. 31–61. They conclude that "the book [is] very largely a composite of earlier extended drafts," i.e from the lectures, essays and fragments Nietzsche wrote between January 1870 and the completion of the book in December, 1871. "It is worth stressing," Silk and Stern continue, ". . . that most consequential points of passages in BT are prefigured, sometimes loosely, sometimes almost verbatim, in one or other of the preliminary versions" (p. 59). Commenting on this state of affairs, Paul de Man has written that "one may feel tempted to [say] . . . that the complex inception of *The Birth of Tragedy* makes the final product into a patchwork of disconnected fragments," "Genesis and Genealogy," *Allegories of Reading*, p. 85. See also Montinari's brief account of BT's genesis in KSA 14, pp. 41–43.

10. However, as Andrzej Warminski has shown, this reinforcement is only apparent. See his reading of Nietzsche's reinterpretation of "Greek cheerfulness" in *Readings in Interpretation*, pp. xxxv–lvi.

11. This is rather clearly articulated in the second book of the first volume of *The World as Will and Representation*, which bears the title "The Objectification of the Will."

12. Nietzsche's description of the primal unity as contradictory marks an important departure from Schopenhauer's understanding of the will. According to Schopenhauer, it is appearance, not the will, that is contradictory. As the thing-in-itself, the will remains indivisible: "We have considered the great multiplicity and diversity of appearances in which the will objectifies itself. We have also observed their infinite and irreconcilable struggle with one another. However, on the basis of our entire presentation up to this point, the will itself, as the thing-in-itself, can in no way be grasped in this multiplicity and variation [*Wechsel*]. . . . Like a magic lantern which shows many different images but is only one and the same flame . . . the will remains unmoved in the midst of that variation," *Die Welt als Wille und Vorstellung* (Zürich: Diogenes, 1977), vol. I, section 28. Nietzsche's thinking here shows a greater affinity with Heraclitus, than with Schopenhauer. In BT, 4 Nietzsche paraphrases Heraclitus when he describes "the eternal contradiction" in the primal unity as "the father of things."

13. See the *Republic*, Book X, lines 595a–602b. The affinities between Platonic and Schopenhaurian thought are not merely accidental, since Schopenhauer explicitly conceives of his own work in Platonic terms, even going so far as to assert that "the stages of the objectification of the will are nothing other than Plato's ideas," *Die Welt als Wille und Vorstellung*, vol. I, section 25. It is also apposite to recall that book three of the first volume bears the subtitle "The Platonic Idea: the Object of Art."

14. *Republic*, 598b. For a critical analysis of this passage, see the Introduction.

15. Nietzsche makes reference to this description again in section 14, in the course of a consideration of Socrates' critique of art and its relationship to the origins of the Platonic dialogue. These passages signal the beginning of an engagement with Plato and 'Platonism' that will extend through many, if not all, of Nietzsche's subse-

quent writings. Although the explicit target of Nietzsche's critique in BT is the Socratic tendency, an often-cited note from late 1870 or early 1871 makes it quite clear that Nietzsche had already begun to see Plato, not Socrates, as his true antipode: "My philosophy an *inverted Platonism*: the further away from true being, the purer, the more beautiful, the better it is. Life in shine as a goal," KSA 7, 7.156.

16. KSA 7, 12.1. Further references to this fragment, often cited in the literature as "On Music and Words," appear in the text under the abbreviation '1871.' The title "On Music and Words" did not originate with Nietzsche and seems to have been the construct of the editors of the *Großoktavausgabe*. On this point, see *Nietzsche and Tragedy*, p. 387.

17. KSA 14, p. 42. As the editors note, Joachim Mette published this manuscript under the title *Socrates und die griechische Tragödie*, "ursprüngliche Fassung der Geburt der Tragödie aus dem Geiste der Musik" (Munich: Beck, 1933).

18. Here I am following Krell, who, in his translation of Heidegger's lecture course "The Will to Power as Art," renders the German *Rausch* as "rapture." For Krell's explanation, see *Nietzsche*, 1, p. 92.

19. The entire citation reads as follows: "Du siehst an mir, wozu sie nützt/ Dem, der nicht viel Verstand besitzt/ Die Wahrheit durch ein Bild zu sagen [In me you see the value of poems/To tell the truth by means of a figure/To those who don't possess a great deal of intelligence]."

20. See, for example, Nietzsche's reference to lyric poetry as "Bilderrede" [figurative speech], BT, 6.

21. It should be noted, however, that Sallis does not recognize that the same argument applies to *Bild*; following Kaufmann, he takes the word almost exclusively to mean visual image.

22. "On the Future of Our Education Institutions," Preface, KSA 1, p. 649.

23. See, for example, Kaufmann's translation and Sallis, *Crossings*, p. 17.

24. Sallis, in a provocative analysis of Dionysian *ecstasis*, argues that this term should be understood as a three-fold movement of transgression, disruption, and reinstatement of the limits of subjectivity. The crucial term in this triad is disruption, which brings about a transformation of the limits of subjectivity. The reinstatement that takes place is not a reinscription of the previous boundaries, but is necessarily a definition of new limits. The complicated logic of the Dionysian precludes that the "opposition between the Apollinian and the Dionysian is . . . a simple binary opposition," *Crossings*, p. 56. Sallis' analysis of Dionysian *ecstasis* should be compared with Heidegger's commentary on "Rapture as Aesthetic State" in his lecture course on "The Will to Power as Art."

25. Here and elsewhere I follow Sallis' practice of rendering *Schein* by its English cognate 'shine.'

26. *Der Plastiker.*

27. That *Bild* and *Bildner* should be read as having overlapping meanings is clear from Nietzsche's use of the adjectival form of both words in the first section as antonyms for "*unbildlich*" or "non-imagistic," which is how Dionysian art is first described. See, for example, the first sentence of the third paragraph, where we read that "the beautiful shine of the dream worlds in the creation of which every human being is truly an artist, is the prerequisite of all plastic art [*bildenden Kunst*]."

28. Lines 527–540, quoted from the translation by Robert Fagles (New York: Penguin, 1977), p. 202. Orestes' skill as a soothsayer should be contrasted with the lack of interpretative acumen attributed to the nurse, whose description of herself as a "prophet" is contradicted by the leader of the chorus who, because she takes the news of Orestes' death at face value, refers to her as "a poor seer," lines 745, 767; translation pp. 210–211.

29. Diels-Kranz fragment 93, quoted from the translation by Charles Kahn, *The Art and Thought of Heraclitus*, p. 43. See also Za, "On the Gift-Giving Virtue": "All names of good and evil are signs [*Gleichnisse*]: they do not declare, but merely hint. A fool is he who wants knowledge from them."

30. Book V, lines 444–452, quoted from the translation by Richmond Lattimore (Chicago: University of Chicago Press, 1961). This passage is cited by John Sallis in an imaginative discussion of Apollo in *Crossings*, pp. 22–25.

31. An indication of the difficulties involved in trying to recover the original Greek experience of tragedy is given by Nietzsche in his warning that the image of tragedy must be sought within the context of the tradition of antiquity, "so that we do not over-hellenize the Hellenic [*das Hellenische überhellenisiren*] and contrive a work of art that never had a home on earth. This is no small danger," KSA 1, p. 518. In 1875 Nietzsche will return to this question in the notes for an never completed essay on philology, "Wir Philologen." Cf. KSA 8, pp. 2–130.

32. Although one might be inclined to regard this comparison as somewhat forced, the similarities between the two texts extend beyond the question of method. This becomes clear if we consider the analysis of the Socratic tendency in BT, which prefigures, in important ways, the discussion of the ascetic ideal in GM, III.

33. I am therefore in complete sympathy with John Sallis' remark that Silk and Stern's interpretation of the opposition between Apollo and Dionysus results in "a reduction of the structure of Nietzsche's discourse, as though it were simply a matter of establishing a philologically complete inventory of the god[s'] features *and then* determining the Apollinian [and Dionysian] on the basis of such an inventory," *Crossings*, p. 23.

34. The German word *Gleichnis*, which, as Lacoue-Labarthe has pointed out (see below), is notoriously difficult to translate, will be rendered in these pages as allegory. Although this is not an unusual or arbitrary translation, it might seem eccentric to some, and thus require an explanation. While it is true that *Gleichnis* could reasonably be rendered by the English words parable, allegory, image or figure, the latter two

terms are too general to be of use in understanding the contrast Nietzsche draws in this text between *Symbol* and *Gleichnis*. Between parable and allegory there is, I believe, little difference in meaning or structure, and I have chosen to use allegory for the following reasons. Parable, in both English and German, has a predominantly religious connotation which seems inappropriate here. Moreover, (perhaps because of its religious connotations) it seems to contradict linguistic practice. We speak quite often of allegorical images or stories, but only rarely of parabolic ones. Thus Nietzsche's description of Raphael's *Transfiguration* as a "*gleichnissartige Gemälde*" (BT, 4) is, I would suggest, correctly rendered by "allegorical painting," rather than by "parabolic painting." This is borne out by Nietzsche's commentary, which indicates that what is significant about Raphael's painting is not that it illustrates a religious or moral principle, but rather that it figures the reciprocal relationship between the Apollinian world of beauty and its Dionysian underground, the terrible wisdom of Silenus.

35. Etymologically the word *Gleichnis* can be traced back to the Greek *parabolé*, from the verb *parallein*, and to the Latin *parabola*, meaning to compare. From these roots, the German noun has acquired two complimentary meanings, denoting either a strictly logical comparison or a broader figurative comparison. The former meaning is certainly the sense of Schopenhauer's translation of the Greek *homoion* (Aristotle: *Poetics*, 22; *Rhetoric*, III, ii) and the Latin *simile* by *Gleichnis* in section 289 of *Parerga und Paralipomena* (Zurich: Diogenes, 1977), while the latter is reflected in the aphorisms Schopenhauer collects in the last chapter of that book, entitled *Gleichnisse, Parabeln und Fabeln*.

36. In section 21 Nietzsche describes the tragic myth as "*ein erhabenes Gleichnis*," which Kaufmann renders as "a sublime parable." Kaufmann's decision to translate both *Symbol and Gleichnis* with the English word *symbol* amounts to a leveling or homogenization of Nietzsche's text. In one case this results in a complete erasure of *Gleichnis* from the text, as when Kaufmann renders the phrase "*so spricht bereits die Symbolik des Satychors in einem Gleichniss jenes Urverhältniss zwischen Ding an sich und Erscheinung aus*" as "the symbolism of the satyr proclaims this primordial relationship between the thing-in-itself and appearance," BT, 8.

37. Ironically, Lacoue-Labarthe's assertion is contradicted by his translation of BT in which the distinction between these two terms is maintained. In section 5, for example, Lacoue-Labarthe renders Nietzsche's description of the lyric poet cum world genius Archilochus as one who "seinen Urschmerz in jenem Gleichnisse vom Menschen Archilochus symbolish ausspricht" as follows: "Archiloque . . . exprime symboliquement sa douleur originaire dans ce substitut analogique," *La naissance de la tragédie*, trans. P. Lacoue-Labarthe (Paris: Gallimard, 1977), p. 45. Lacoue-Labarthe's translation should be compared with that of Kaufmann, who collapses this distinction by rendering *Gleichnis* and *symbolisch* with symbol and its adjectival cognate: "Archilochus . . . expressing his primordial pain symbolically in the symbol of the man Archilochus."

38. Two passages in particular, on pages 359 and 366, respectively, foreshadow the use of *Gleichnis* which we find in BT. The second of these passages is cited and discussed below.

39. It follows from this that one ought to be more circumspect than has hitherto been the case about blurring the distinction between BT and the hundreds of pages of notes, essays and lectures that were composed prior to its publication. This distinction has generally not been respected (see, e.g., the work of Lacoue-Labarthe and Kofman), and while it is quite common for commentators to blur the distinctions between Nietzsche's published and unpublished writings, it is especially important to be conscious of this boundary in cases such as this, where there appear to be significant differences between the published text and the prefatory material collected in the *Nachlaß*.

40. In accordance with Nietzsche's practice in BT, I assume that image and language are, ontologically considered, equivalent means of expression. This implies that both image and language are (1) necessarily subordinate to music and its semiological power, and (2) come into existence by imitating appearance. Both of these claims are implicit in Nietzsche's consideration of naive art, in which both Homer, the epic poet, and Raphael, the painter, are called naive artists.

41. According to Sallis, the Apollinian and Dionysian artists imitate the natural artistic forces themselves, which are the true objects of art: "The artist—every artist—produces an imitation of one or the other of these impulses, these art-states of nature," *Crossings*, p. 21. But the Apollinian artist does not imitate one of these natural states, but rather produces an imitation of appearance which takes these states as its model. If Apollinian art were an imitation of the dream state itself, it would not be the shine of shine, but would have to be regarded as twice removed from an originary shine. For it would then be imitating something—the dream state—which is itself already imitation; although the impulse to dream arises from nature, the dream state is itself a mimetic state whose object is the world of appearance, which must be regarded not as an imitation of the will, but rather, as its *manifestation*. On my interpretation, Apollinian art is a "mirror image" of the dream state in that it imitates appearance in the same manner as the dream state and is therefore, like this state, the shine of shine. Apollinian and Dionysian art imitate their "archetypes" to the extent that the exact nature of their imitation is determined by these archetypes; their objects, that which they imitate, are to be found elsewhere, that is, in appearance and the will. Nietzsche says this explicitly in the 1871 fragment: "The 'will,' as the most originary form of appearance, is the object of music: in which sense it can be called imitation [*Nachahmung*] of nature, but of the most universal form of nature," 1871, p. 365.

42. That is, in sections 2, 5 and 16.

43. This definition is implied by the etymology of the Greek word *allegoria*, which is derived from the verb *allegorein*, meaning to speak figuratively.

44. On Apollo as the god of distance, see book I of the *Iliad*.

45. Walter Benjamin, "Goethes Wahlverwandtschaften," *Illuminationen* (Frankfurt: Suhrkamp, 1977) p. 89.

46. Paul de Man, "The Rhetoric of Temporality," Blindness and Insight (Minneapolis: University of Minnesota Press, 1983), p. 207.

47. It is in this sense that myth, too, is allegorical. In BT, 21 Nietzsche writes the following: "myth protects us against the music, while on the other hand it alone gives music the highest freedom. In return, music imparts to the tragic myth an intense and convincing metaphysical significance that word and image without this singular help could never have attained." And further in the section, Nietzsche describes tragic myth as an "allegory of the most universal facts, which music alone can communicate directly." Cf. BT, 16.

48. My reading of this passage is indebted to Andrzej Warminski, who calls attention to its (and its translation's) problematic character in *Readings in Interpretation*, pp. xliii–xlv. Further references will be given in the text.

49. Kaufmann's translation reads as follows: "Now, however, under the Apollinian dream inspiration, this music reveals itself to him again as a *symbolic dream image*."

50. Cf. the Introduction, particularly the section "The Rhetoric of Truth."

51. See Nietzsche's discussion of Greek cheerfulness (BT, 9) and section 11 below.

52. Given Nietzsche's account of this distinction, his description of the tragic drama—as opposed to the chorus—as the "Apollinian manifestation of Dionysian insights and effects" [*Erkenntnisse und Wirkungen*] is, literally speaking, quite impossible. An Apollinian image qua image can never produce a Dionysian effect.

53. Nietzsche says precisely this further on in the same section: "But insofar as the subject is the artist, he has already been released from his individual will and has become, as it were, the medium through which the one truly existing subject celebrates its redemption in shine.

54. Jacques Derrida, *Of Grammatology*, p. 145. For a further elucidation of this concept, see pp. 144–164.

55. Compare Nietzsche's remark in section 21: "I have only to appeal to those, who, immediately related to music, have, as it were, their maternal womb in it, and relate to things almost exclusively through unconscious musical relations.

56. De Man, "The Rhetoric of Tropes," *Allegories of Reading*, p. 117.

57. Cf. EH, 'BT.'4.

58. In light of this conclusion it is difficult to agree with Lacoue-Labarthe's assertion, cited at the outset of this chapter, that Nietzsche's discovery of rhetoric causes the theory of language he had held up to that point to "fall apart." Cf. "The Detour," p. 26.

59. For a more extensive consideration of the relationship between syntax and semantics along the lines sketched here, see de Man, "Semiology and Rhetoric," *Allegories of Reading*, pp. 3–26.

60. "Und wir dürfen wohl sagen, daß selbst der 'Wille' nichts als die allgemeinste Erscheinungsform eines uns übrigens gänzlich Unentziffbaren ist." Compare the letter to Deussen cited at the head of this chapter.

61. In this case it is Silk and Stern, not de Man, who are "not always scrupulous." Their desire to read BT on the most literal of levels leads them, as we have seen, to interpret Nietzsche's text in ways which show little or no awareness for the complexity of Nietzsche's style and rhetorical strategies, including irony. See their resume of sections 22–23 of BT, *Nietzsche on Tragedy*, pp. 375–377.

62. See Sallis, *Crossings*, pp. 31–32 and 60–68. Sallis concludes that "in the wake of Nietzsche's massive critique of Schopenhauer prior to 1872, which poses again and again the collapse of the fundamental distinction of Schopenhauer's metaphysics [between essence and appearance], there can be no question of a reading that would begin by assimilating BT to that metaphysical axis," *Crossings*, p. 67. The fragment "On Schopenhauer" [*Zu Schopenhauer*] in included in HKGW, vol. 3, pp. 352–361. Among the criticisms Nietzsche formulates in this fragment is that the thing-in-itself is "only a hidden category" and that "the will, which Schopenhauer puts in place of the Kantian X, is produced only with the help of a poetic intuition," p. 354. This text is reproduced, with English translation, in Crawford, *The Beginnings of Nietzsche's Theory of Language*, pp. 226–238.

63. The text Nietzsche cites in this section is Wagner's *Beethoven* (1870), which contains an enthusiastic account of Schopenhauer's philosophy of music, particularly his views on the relationship of music and language. Wagner's renewed enthusiasm for Schopenhauer seems to have made a strong impression on Nietzsche, who was presented with a copy of the book by the author in November, 1870 (KSAB, 3/108). According to Silk and Stern, Nietzsche's writings on tragedy after having read *Beethoven* are more strongly marked by Schopenhauer's "influence," *Nietzsche on Tragedy*, pp. 58–59. However, given Nietzsche's skepticism regarding Schopenhauer, it is difficult to view this influence as anything more than strategic.

64. Nietzsche's relationship to Schopenhauer is considered in more detail in the final section of this chapter.

65. Maudemarie Clark, "Language and Deconstruction: Nietzsche, de Man, and Postmodernism," in *Nietzsche as Postmodernist*, ed. Clayton Koelb (Albany: SUNY Press, 1990), pp. 75–90. Hereafter cited as LD.

66. See, for example, sections 7 and 17.

67. Compare the following remark from the same notebook: "There is no natural beauty [. . .] pain is therefore productive; it produces the beautiful as a related complimentary color," KSA 7, 7. 116.

68. Socratism arises out of another type of misreading, namely, a misreading of the structures of knowledge, which are, at root, figurative. Nietzsche's analysis of science and the process by means of which science is revealed to itself as illusion should be compared with the analysis of science and truth in the second essay of GM.

69. See, for example, the following passage from section 20: "For to us who stand on the boundary line between two forms of existence, the Hellenic prototype retains this immeasurable value that all these transitions and struggles are imprinted upon it [. . .] except that we, *as it were*, pass through the chief epochs of the Hellenic genius, analogically in reverse order, and seem now, for example, to be passing backward from the Alexandrian age to the period of tragedy" (emphasis added). Once again, Nietzsche's use of the phrase "as it were" disrupts the literalness of the passage and hence the genetic-historical claims for a return to the period of tragedy.

70. If, as we suggested earlier, Nietzsche's enthusiasm for Schopenhauer's and Wagner's ideas had waned long before he wrote BT then we would expect to find evidence of this in those sections of the book which most explicitly concern them. This is the case, as we earlier noted, with regard to Nietzsche's analysis of the relationship between music and image, which must be read as a critique, not a reinscription, of Schopenhauer's metaphysics. I would suggest that the same logic is at work in the latter sections of the book in regards to Wagner and his cultural program, expressed in the idea of a rebirth of the tragic.

71. "It seems clear that I can use language metaphorically only if I use it literally as well," LD, 86. See also *Nietzsche on Truth and Philosophy*, chapter 3.

72. This is illustrated quite nicely by a a notebook entry devoted to BT written in 1885 or 1886. The last sentence of the entry reads as follows: "The anti-natural element of wisdom reveals itself in its hostility to art: wanting to know, when shine is precisely the redemption—what a reversal, what an instinct to nothing!" KSA 12, 2.119. For additional notebook entries on BT see, for example, KSA 12, 2.106 and 110–114 (1885–1886) and KSA 13: 14.14–26 and 33–36, and 17.3 (1888). The concepts of the Apollinian and the Dionysian are discussed, with approval, in TI, IX.10. See also the Preface to the 1886 edition of BT, the "Attempt at a Self-Critique," and the resume of the book in EH, where Nietzsche refers to the interpretations of the Dionysian and of Socrates as "the two decisive *innovations* of the book," EH, 'BT.'1. Hardly a fitting description for a book one had rejected.

CHAPTER 4

1. Fink, *Nietzsches Philosophie*, p. 7

2. Elaine Pagels, *The Origin of Satan* (New York: Random House, 1995).

3. See Winchester, *Nietzsche's Aesthetic Turn*, pp. 153–154.

4. In a note from the same period Nietzsche puts this point more directly: "The same text allows countless [*unzählige*] interpretations: there is no 'correct' interpretation," KSA 12, 1.120. Contrary to what some commentators have deduced, the denial that there is a single correct interpretation does not imply that all interpretations are therefore equally good. Rather, the point, as Kofman has elegantly put it, is that "life is enigmatic and allows an indefinite questioning, an indefinite multiplicity of hypotheses," *Nietzsche and Metaphor*, p. 142.

5. As noted above, the problems raised by Nietzsche's naturalism have largely been ignored by most commentators. It is tempting to view this tendency as an overreaction to the Nazi appropriation of Nietzsche and the attempt to wed crude biologistic theories of race together to Nietzsche's own idiosyncratic discussion of race and use of naturalistic concepts. However, it is more likely that the difficulties this vocabulary poses for the reader are themselves the greatest incentive to turn a blind eye to it. Heidegger, a vocal opponent of the Nazi appropriation of Nietzsche, was nevertheless aware of the need to confront the problem: "Now, it would actually be a a very forced and even vain endeavor if one wanted to conceal Nietzsche's obvious use of biological language, or even to play it down; if one wanted to bypass the fact that this use of language contains a biological way of thinking and is thus not an external covering," N I, p. 519/N 1, p. 41. However, rather than attempting to come to terms with Nietzsche's use of biological language, Heidegger reads it ontologically, as an expression of "what was preserved unspoken in the primordial essence of being as *physis*," N I, p. 526/N 1, p. 46. Another notable attempt to address the issues raised by Nietzsche's naturalism is Malcolm Pasley's essay "Nietzsche's Use of Medical Terms," in *Nietzsche—Imagery and Thought*, ed. Malcolm Pasley (Berkeley: University of California Press, 1978). Pasley, like Heidegger, fails to sufficiently problematize Nietzsche's naturalistic rhetoric by interpreting it solely in biographical terms as an expression of Nietzsche's struggle with his chronically poor health. For a recent and more theoretically informed discussion of Nietzsche's naturalistic rhetoric, particularly that of the body, see Blondel, *Nietzsche: The Body and Culture*.

6. This passage should be compared with the discussion, in the first two books of the *Republic*, of the idea that justice is the advantage of the stronger. Glaucon, playing devil's advocate, describes the origin of justice as a mean between "what is best—doing injustice without paying the penalty—and what is worst—suffering injustice without being able to avenge oneself" (359a). While it is the case that laws restrict an individual's ability to perform injustice, they also prevent him or her from suffering at the hands of others. The one exception Glaucon admits to this scheme is the truly powerful man, for whom it would be madness to agree to such restrictions.

7. Compare BGE, 23, where Nietzsche suggests that "even the affects of hatred, envy covetousness, and the lust to rule [are] conditions of life [. . .] factors which, fundamentally and essentially, must be present in the general economy of life and must, therefore, be further enhanced if life is to be further enhanced."

8. Reiner Schürmann, *Heidegger on Being and Acting*, trans. Christine-Marie Gros with Reiner Schürmann (Bloomington: Indiana University Press, 1989), pp. 97–105.

9. Compare this passage from the *Nachlaß*: "NB. one *drives nature out* of morality when one says 'Love your enemies': for then the *natural* 'Thou shalt *love* thy neighbor and *hate* thy enemy' in the law (in instinct) has become meaningless; then this *love of one's neighbor* must also find a new basis (as a *kind of love of God*). Everywhere *God* is inserted and '*utility*' withdrawn; everywhere the real origin of morality

is denied; the *veneration of nature* [Naturwürdigung] which lies precisely in the *recognition of a natural morality*, is *destroyed* at its roots [Natur-Moral . . . *in Grund und Boden* vernichtet]," KSA 12, 10.157.

10. One example among many is Bertrand Russell's interpretation of Nietzsche. See the entry on Nietzsche in Russell's *The History of Western Philosophy* (London: George Allen & Unwin, 1961), pp. 735 ff.

11. Mark Warren, *Nietzsche and Political Thought* (Cambridge: MIT Press, 1988), pp. 227–228. Henceforth cited as NPT.

12. For a more complete elaboration of Warren's interpretation of the will to power, see *Nietzsche and Political Thought*, pp. 111–158. A similar criticism is voiced by Fink, who argues that Nietzsche's conception of the will to power is afflicted by an unresolved tension between its ontological and ontic senses. See *Nietzsches Philosophie*, p. 128.

13. The importance of the concept of interpretation in Nietzsche's later writings is argued at length by Kofman in the appendix to *Nietzsche and Metaphor*, "Genealogy, Interpretation, Text." See also Schrift, *Nietzsche and the Question of Interpretation*, pp. 144–168 and Blondel, *Nietzsche: The Body and Culture*, pp. 88–133.

14. Compare the second essay of GM, particularly Nietzsche's critical examination of the concepts of origin and purpose in section 12, where the following remark is to be found: "the cause and origin of a thing and its eventual utility, its actual employment and place in a system of purposes, lie worlds apart; whatever exists, having somehow come into being, is again and again interpreted [*immer wieder . . . ausgelegt*] to new ends, taken over, transformed, and redirected by some power superior to it." What is at issue here is Warren's understanding of what it means to give a "textual account." If one believes that there is a decidable difference between the world and our way of speaking about it, as Warren does, then a purely textual account will seem necessarily impoverished. However, Warren's objection appear less compelling if we adopt a broader, Nietzschean, concept of the text. See, for example, Derrida, *Of Grammatology*, pp. 157–164, and Blondel, *Nietzsche: The Body and Culture*, pp. 22–41.

15. Compare Nietzsche's critique of mechanistic interpretation in GS, 373. Here Nietzsche asserts that "an essentially mechanistic world would be an essentially *meaningless* world [. . .]. Assuming that one assessed the *value* of a piece of music according to how much of it could be counted, calculated, and expressed in formulas [. . .]. What would one have comprehended, understood, grasped of it! Nothing, really nothing of what is 'music' in it!" This same argument could, by analogy, be made with regard to dreams and intoxication.

16. This is consistent with the conclusions reached in chapter 3 regarding the essentially—and necessarily—figurative relationship between music and the will.

17. Arthur Danto has expressed the rather injudicious opinion that Nietzsche's "writings may be read in pretty much any order," *Nietzsche as Philosopher*, p. 19. More recently Richard Schacht has argued that the form of Nietzsche's published writ-

ings is no different from that of WP, writing that the latter is "of course . . . a 'non-book,' at least in the sense of something attributable to Nietzsche himself in terms of its selection of material, organization, and publication as a book—though in form it is as much a 'book' as many of the things he himself did publish, "Nietzsche as Colleague," *International Studies in Philosophy* XXII/2 (1990), p. 65. For a more considered view of Nietzsche's writing, see Babette Babich, *Nietzsche's Philosophy of Science*, pp. 15–32.

18. This strategy is utilized elsewhere in BGE, for example, in sections 15 and 36.

19. Cf. KSA 13, 14.79, where Nietzsche characterizes our entire way of speaking about actions and effects as "a mere semiotic [that] designates nothing real [*nichts Reales bezeichnet*]." The critique of causality articulated in these passages was first mooted in BT, 15, where Nietzsche questions the Socratic belief that the world can be comprehended by means of the "thread of causality."

20. Derrida, *Spurs*, p. 107.

21. Nietzsche employs a similar strategy in section 36 of the same text, where he emphasizes that the will to power constitutes his own way of putting things, not the only or true way: "Suppose, finally, we succeeded in explaining our entire instinctive life as the development and ramification of *one* basic form of the will—namely, of the will to power, as *my* proposition has it [. . .] then one would have gained the right to determine *all* efficient force univocally as—*will to power*. The world [. . .] would be 'will to power' and nothing else—" (BGE, 36). Here, too, Nietzsche brackets the concept of the will to power in the final sentence. This section is the published version of the infamous last section of WP (KSA 11, 38.12).

22. Blondel, *Nietzsche: The Body and Culture*, p. 76. Although Blondel does not acknowledge the work of Derrida or de Man, their influence is clearly evident in this passage and throughout much of this study.

23. This is the implicit assumption of Karl Löwith's remark that while "an abyss separates Nietzsche from his unscrupulous prophets . . . he prepared a way for them which he himself did not take," *Mein Leben in Deutschland vor und nach 1933* (Stuttgart: Metzler, 1986), p. 5.

24. Winchester, *Nietzsche's Aesthetic Turn*, p. 153. Observing that passages such as this "are the exception rather than the rule," Winchester concludes that "even though his rhetoric might lead us to think otherwise, Nietzsche's higher or noble individual is not primarily an exploiter of others, but more often an individualist showing little social concern," p. 155. While it is difficult to argue with this conclusion, it remains true that the motif of violence in Nietzsche has a clear social dimension.

25. Diels-Kranz, 53; the translation is that of Kahn, *The Art and Thought of Heraclitus*, p. 67.

26. In his recent study *A Nietzschean Defense of Democracy: An Experiment in Postmodern Politics* (Chicago: Open Court, 1995), Lawrence J. Hatab has attempted to

show that conflict is essential to democracy and that Nietzsche's social philosophy, which emphasizes conflict, is less antithetical to democracy than has usually been supposed.

27. Although Nietzsche's description of the essence of ressentiment as a "*need* to direct one's view outward instead of back to oneself" (GM, I.10) appears to contradict this point, this need develops, I suggest, as a result of the inability of the instincts to be discharged outwards. *Ressentiment* does not make the priests weak, rather their weakness—the inability to act—produces *ressentiment.*

28. In a passage from the manuscript of section 257 of BGE but struck from the printed version, Nietzsche describes the conditions of a higher culture in remarkably similar terms: "The 'humanization' [*Vermenschlichung*] of such barbarians [. . .] is essentially a weakening and attenuating process and takes place precisely at the expense of those drives to which they owe their victory and property; and while they take possession of the more 'humane' virtues in this way [. . .] an inverse process occurs gradually on the side of the oppressed and enslaved. To the degree in which they are kept more subdued and more humane, and hence grow physically stronger, the barbarian, the fortified human being, the half-animal with wild cravings, develops in them:— the barbarian who one day senses he is strong enough to ward off his masters who have become more humane, that is to say, weaker. The game begins anew [*Das Spiel beginnt vom Neuem*]: the elements of a higher culture are once again present," KSA 14, pp. 371–372.

29. Rousseau, for example, asserts that "there are, then, for each climate natural causes on the basis of which it is possible to assign the form of government toward which the force of the climate leads it, and even to say what type of inhabitants it should have," *On the Social Contract*, trans. Judith Masters (New York: St. Martin's Press, 1979), Book III, ch. viii, p. 92. In addition to Montesquieu, who Rousseau cites at the beginning of the chapter, Aristotle makes similar claims in the *Politics*.

30. Bertrand Russell, *The History of Western Philosophy*, p. 736.

31. One could in fact draw a parallel between passages such as this and those in BT which, in the process of describing a translation or transference end up by inscribing its very impossibility, cf. chapter 3.

32. The question of breeding has taken on an unnecessarily important role in some interpretations of Nietzsche due to the decision taken by Förster-Nietzsche and Köselitz to arbitrarily privilege one of the many plans Nietzsche drew up for WP as the template for their compilation. According to this plan, the fourth and final book of WP was to bear the title "Discipline and Breeding" [*Zucht und Züchtung*] (cf. KSA 12, 7.64). However, this plan from March 17, 1887, bears little resemblance to many of the other plans Nietzsche composed during this period, including the last plan from late August, 1888, which makes no mention of either discipline or breeding. In this plan the fourth book bears the title "The Great Noon," KSA 13, 18.1.

33. In *Parerga und Paralipomena* Schopenhauer writes that "it is unconsciously fitting that in all European languages the word *Person* is usually used to designate a

human individual. For the true meaning of *persona* is actor's mask, and no one shows themselves as they really are, rather everyone wears a mask and plays a role." *Parerga und Paralipomena*, vol. 2, section 315.

34. Nietzsche expresses an analogous thought in the Preface to HH, where he writes as follows: "Life is not devised by morality, it *wants* deception, it *lives* from deception—right? There I go again and begin to do what I have always done—I, an old immoralist and bird catcher—to speak amorally, extra-morally, 'beyond good and evil'?—" (HH, P.1). The conjunction of life and deception together with Nietzsche's use of the expression 'extra-moral' recalls "On Truth and Lie," where the theme of deception figures most prominently.

35. In their commentary on the textual history of EH, Colli and Montinari recount the discovery of a sheet of paper that contained the hitherto lost text of section three of "Why I am so wise." This sheet, discovered among the unpublished papers of Heinrich Köselitz in the Goethe and Schiller Archive in Weimar in July, 1969, was one of several short texts written by Nietzsche in late December, 1888, almost all of which were destroyed by Nietzsche's mother and sister because of their unflattering portraits of some of Nietzsche's closest relatives and friends, themselves among them. According to the testimony of Nietzsche's publisher Naumann and Köselitz' correspondence, this sheet was sent by Nietzsche to his publisher along with instructions for further additions and changes on December 29, 1888, several days before his final breakdown. In spite of this, Kaufmann dismisses this text as inferior in "style and content," *Nietzsche*, p. 455, and accordingly declined to include it in his translation of EH or to make any mention of it in his notes or the variants published as an afterword to the text. For a more detailed account of the discovery and history of this sheet see KSA 14, pp. 459–463.

36. Sarah Kofman, *Explosion I, De l' "Ecce Homo" de Nietzsche* (Paris: Galilée, 1992) p. 209. Nietzsche's inclination toward typological thinking goes back to his lecture course "Die vorplatonischen Philosophen" (1872), where he classifies the philosophers from Pythagoras to Socrates as pure types [*die Einseitigen*], and those from Plato onwards as hybrid philosophers [*Mischphilosophen*]," GA, vol. XIX, pp. 129–130. In addition, see the lecture "Socrates and Tragedy" (1870), where Nietzsche distinguishes the Socratic tendency from Socrates the man: "Socratism is older than Socrates; its disintegrating influence on art makes itself known already much earlier," KSA 1, p. 545.

37. This question is considered at greater length in chapter 1.

38. In the rejected version of BGE, 257 cited in note 19 above, Nietzsche writes that "being a master has its instincts, just as being a slave: 'nature' is in both,—and 'morality,' too, is a part of nature."— KSA 14, p. 372.

39. This remark should be compared with an unpublished note contemporaneous with BGE: "NB. With respect to Aryan and Semitic. Where races are mixed, the source of great culture," KSA 12, 1.153. Compare the discussion of the anti-Semitic activist Theodor Fritsch in chapter 5.

40. Nietzsche continues in the same section: "And as for sickness: are we not almost tempted to ask whether we could get along without it? Only great pain is the ultimate liberator of the spirit, being the teacher of *the great suspicion* that turns every U into an X[. . .]." Nietzsche initially intended this section to appear as aphorism number 372 of the fifth book under the title "To the credit of illness." Cf. KSA 14, p. 233.

41. "Man is a rope tied between beast and *Übermensch*—a rope over an abyss. A dangerous across, a dangerous on-the-way, a dangerous looking back, a dangerous shuddering and stopping. What is great in man is that he is a bridge and not an end," Za, P.4.

42. It is worth noting that Nietzsche identifies the causes of this general suffering as illnesses derived from the most various of physiological causes. See sections 13, 15, and 17 of the third essay. Interestingly enough, one of the terms Nietzsche employs to describe these infirmities—"physiological inhibition"—is also used by him to characterize his own physical state in several letters from the period of GM. See KSAB, 8/870 and 878. The latter, a letter to Overbeck from June 30, 1887, is cited above in the body of the text.

43. Immanuel Kant, *Foundations of the Metaphysics of Morals*, trans. Lewis White Beck (Indianapolis: Bobbs-Merrill, 1959).

44. Robert Legros, "La métaphysique nietzschéenne de la vie," in *Pourquoi nous ne sommmes pas nietzschéens*, ed. Luc Ferry and Alain Renaut (Paris: Grasset, 1991), p. 184.

45. Martin Heidegger, "Brief über den 'Humanismus,'" *Wegmarken* (Frankfurt: Klostermann, 1978), pp. 334–35; "Letter on Humanism," trans. Frank A. Capuzzi and J. Glenn Gray, in *Martin Heidegger: Basic Writings*, ed. David Farrell Krell (New York: Harper & Row, 1977), p. 218.

46. Kofman, *Nietzsche and Metaphor*, p. 138.

47. These two fragments were among the 374 passages Nietzsche numbered and arranged in the middle of February, 1888, while working on an early—and ultimately abandoned—draft of WP. This plan is discussed by Montinari in KSA 14, pp. 391 ff.

48. This text should be read in conjunction with "Morality as Anti-Nature," where Nietzsche contrasts the practice of spiritualizing destructive passions with the priest's practice of extirpation or castration. Unlike extirpation, which simply condemns the offending drives and seeks to ablate them, spiritualization recognizes the economic value of these drives to the living organism, and consequently strives to transform, rather than destroy, them. It has an open eye to "that economy which needs and knows how to use everything which the [. . .] *diseased* reason of the priest rejects," TI, V.6. The same logic is at work in the process of internalization described in the second essay of GM where the force of the untamed instincts is exploited and utilized, not removed and discarded. A more thorough consideration of internalization and spiritualization would also include an elucidation of the concept of self-overcoming, which is a central theme of Za.

APPENDIX

1. Curt Paul Janz, *Die Briefe Friedrich Nietzsches* (Zürich: Theologischer Verlag, 1972), p. 152.

2. On Nietzsche's decision to delay publication of NCW, see KSA 14, pp. 520–522 and the letter of January 2, 1889, to his publisher, C. G. Naumann, KSAB, 8/1237.

3. Unwelcome admirers included people such as the prominent anti-Semitic writer and agitator Theodor Fritsch, editor of "The Anti-Semitic Correspondence," a small privately circulated journal that had attempted to make use of Nietzsche's work in support of its cause. Fritsch was later to achieve a certain degree of fame for editing the *Handbuch der Judenfrage. Die wichtigsten Tatsachen zur Beurteilung des jüdischen Volkes*, 47th ed. (Leipzig: Hammer, 1942). Nietzsche, who is discussed briefly in this text, is cited as one of a series of "philosophers of Aryan blood" who are contrasted with cosmopolitan and dissolute Jewish philosophers such as Edmund Husserl and Georg Simmel, pp. 391–393. Significantly, Nietzsche's bother-in-law, Bernhard Förster, is praised as one of the founders of the modern anti-Semitic movement in Germany, p. 14. For Nietzsche's response to Fritsch's entreaties, see KSAB, 8/819, 823.

4. Friedrich Nietzsche, *Werke in drei Bänden*, ed. Karl Schlechta (Munich: Hanser, 1965), "Philologischer Nachbricht," vol. III, pp. 1408–1432; and Janz, *Die Briefe Friedrich Nietzsches*, esp. chapter VIII, "Die Briefe an Mutter and Schwester im besonderem."

5. The *Großoktavausgabe* was the first attempt at a complete edition of Nietzsche's writings. For an overview of its contents, see KSA 14, pp. 7–11. The best account of the checkered history of the Nietzsche Archive is David Marc Hoffmann's comprehensive study *Zur Geschichte des Nietzsche-Archivs* (Berlin: de Gruyter, 1991).

6. Elisabeth Förster-Nietzsche, "Foreword," GA, XV[1], p. vii. This volume, containing the first edition of WM, appeared in 1901 and was supplanted, in 1911, by volumes XV–XVI of the revised edition of the *Großoktavausgabe*, which reproduces the expanded and reedited version of WP, which was published in 1906 as part of the *Taschenausgabe*. These two volumes will be cited as GA, XV[1] and GA, XV[2], respectively.

7. For an elucidation of the principles which guided the publication of the notebooks, see the "Editorische Grundzüge der Kritischen Studienausgabe," KSA 14, pp. 18–20.

8. For an account of the rather complicated textual history of EH, see KSA 14, pp. 454–470. The suppressed section is discussed in pp. 459–464. See also Montinari's essay, "Ein neuer Abschnitt in 'Ecce homo,'" *Nietzsche lesen*, pp. 120–168. Kaufmann's translation of EH, which first appeared in 1967, was never revised to include

this passage. In an appendix to his *Nietzsche* written in 1974, Kaufmann explains his decision as follows: while the handwriting shows "no signs of insanity . . . the style strikes me as far less sane than that of any other passage of equal length in EH or in any of his other books, and it is arguable how much weight one should give to Nietzsche's momentary wish to substitute this page for a section that contains some splendid formulations and is clearly, I think, superior in style as well as content," *Nietzsche*, p. 455. While Kaufmann is no doubt correct in his assessment of the text, the feelings Nietzsche expresses here are, as some of the letters cited in the present chapter demonstrate, quite genuine and not at all "insane." Cf. Shapiro, *Nietzschean Narratives*, chapter 6.

9. In contrast to the *Großoktavausgabe*, which was the most comprehensive edition of Nietzsche's works hitherto and contained 3,500 pages of material from the notebooks, the new critical edition contains approximately 5,000 pages of such material, KSA 14, p. 17.

10. See the Preface to TI, where Nietzsche describes September 30, 1888, as "the day that the first book of *The Revaluation of Values* was completed." The text Nietzsche is referring to here is *The Antichrist*. As we shall see, within a short time Nietzsche was to regard this text as the whole of the *Revaluation*, and then, soon thereafter, as not part of this project at all.

11. A major work bearing the title *The Will to Power* is first mentioned in print on the back cover of BGE, where it is listed as being "in preparation" (the cover itself is reproduced in KGW, VI/2). The text is next mentioned one year later in GM, III.27, where it is again described as being in preparation. The final published reference to WP is to be found in section 7 of CW—completed in August, 1888—where Nietzsche promises the reader to return to the subject of decadence and art "in a chapter of my major work [*Hauptwerk*], which carries the title 'On The Physiology of Art.'" The references to this project in the correspondence are too numerous to list. Some of the more important letters are: KSAB, 6: 499, 504, 509, and 529.

12. The following two paragraphs are largely based on Montinari's commentary, "Nietzsches Nachlaß 1885–1888 und der 'Wille zur Macht,'" KSA 14, pp. 383–400. Montinari's argument is repeated in a somewhat different form in "Nietzsche's Nachlaß von 1885–1888 oder Textkritik und 'Wille zur Macht,'" *Nietzsche lesen*, pp. 92–119.

13. In fact, there are 374 fragments; Nietzsche used numbers 46 and 71 twice (cf. KSA 13, 12.1).

14. See the draft of a letter to Overbeck from the same day in which Nietzsche describes the "total conception" of the work as "by far the longest torture I've experienced, a genuine illness," KSAB, 8/990.

15. This explicitly contradicts Förster-Nietzsche's claim that the plan on which her edition of WP is organized, dated March 17, 1887, is "the *only* [plan] on the basis of which Nietzsche himself began to classify and organize the material for his major work," GA, XV^1, p. x.

16. In his critical monograph, *Nietzsche als Moralist und Schriftsteller* (Jena: E. Diederichs, 1906), August Horneffer, one of the editors of the first edition of WP (1901), writes that the index of 374 fragments was "only a provisional arrangement, which cannot be considered authoritative for the material which came before or for that which followed," p. 82.

17. This was done on the suggestion of Köselitz, who found the first title too tame. See Köselitz' letter from September 20, 1888, KGB, III, 6/580, and Nietzsche's response one-week later, KSAB, 8/1122.

18. In Montinari's view, the plans for the *Revaluation* do not represent a parallel project to that of WP but its "negation," KSA 14, p. 400. The fact that the title of this new work was taken from the subtitle of the previously planned major work, the division into four books, and lack of any mention of WP after August 26, 1888, all support Montinari's conclusion.

19. The transition from WP to the *Revaluation* is very clear in the two letters to Meta von Salis of August 22 and September 7, 1888. In the first letter, which is cited above, Nietzsche describes the collapse of WP. In the second, he announces the project of the *Revaluation* and the title of its first book, *The Antichrist* (KSAB, 8/1102).

20. Here Nietzsche describes the *Revaluation* as a work that "lies finished before me," KSAB, 8/1151.

21. This change does not seem to have been noticed by Kaufmann, whose translation still carries the title "*Revaluation of All Values. First Book: The Antichrist. Attempt at a Critique of Christianity*," *The Portable Nietzsche*, pp. 568–569. According to Montinari, this title appears in the earlier of two title pages Nietzsche prepared for A (cf. KSA 14, p. 434).

22. It is a sad commentary on the mischief caused by Förster-Nietzsche that this same argument had been made over 60 years earlier by Albert Lamm in a review of WP and the other "posthumous works" published by the Nietzsche Archive in the *Taschenausgabe* of 1906: "It is possible that at one time Nietzsche had the idea [of writing a major work]. . . . But Nietzsche himself, while reworking this material, found more important things to do with it, and the work which his fate interrupted is *not* what we have before us; what lies before us here, Nietzsche himself had *put aside*," "Friedrich Nietzsche und seine nachgelassene 'Lehren,'" *Süddeutsche Monatshefte* (1906), p. 275.

23. Janz considers the very idea of a major work utterly foreign to Nietzsche's thought, and hence from the very beginning a project that could not succeed, *Die Briefe Friedrich Nietzsches*, pp. 149–151. See also Lamm, "Friedrich Nietzsche und seine nachgelassene 'Lehren,'" pp. 263f.

24. The significance of this last point should not be underestimated. Even if one were to consider Nietzsche's decision to cross out the subtitle *Revaluation of Values* from the title page of A as an impulsive act that should be given less weight than the textual evidence which identifies A as the *Revaluation*, it is difficult to see what

impact, if any, this should have on the way in which we regard A and the other texts Nietzsche composed in 1888. It seems almost perverse to suggest that, bearing the subtitle *Revaluation of Values*, A should thus be regarded as Nietzsche's magnum opus. For a thoughtful discussion of the *Revaluation* and its relationship to EH, see Shapiro, *Nietzschean Narratives*, pp. 144–147.

25. This selection from Nietzsche's notebooks from the mid and late 1880s was edited by Alfred Baeumler and published as part of an edition of Nietzsche's writings published by Kröner Verlag in 1931.

26. For a discussion of role WP has played in recent American Nietzsche scholarship, see Magnus, Stewart, and Mileur, *Nietzsche's Case*, pp. 35–36. The material contained in this chapter is reprinted from Magnus' influential essay "The Use and Abuse of *The Will to Power*," in *Reading Nietzsche*, ed. Robert Solomon and Kathleen Higgins (New York: Oxford University Press, 1988).

27. The English edition is being published by Stanford University Press under the direction of Ernst Behler. To date only the first two volumes have appeared.

28. GA, XV^1, p. xiv.

29. In a recent essay Richard Schacht claims that "the campaign to discredit the so-called 'non-book' WP . . . is a red herring. . . . Regarded as nothing more than a sample of material from the notebooks . . . I see nothing wrong with making use of it," "Nietzsche as Colleague," *International Studies in Philosophy* XXII/2 (1990), p. 65. However Schacht, like Nehamas, conflates two related but ultimately quite separate issues: the question of whether WP is a book as, for example, TI is a book, and the more important question of whether the text as published is philologically reliable. It is the latter question which Schacht, Nehamas and most other Anglo-American scholars fail to ask. See also Schrift, *Nietzsche and Question of Interpretation*, p. 124.

30. Janz, *Nietzsches Biographie*, vol. III, p. 125. For a description of the colony, see pp. 125–128. For a recent discussion of the failed colony, see Ben Macintyre, *Forgotten Fatherland: The search for Elisabeth Nietzsche* (New York: HarperPerennial, 1993).

31. Janz, *Nietzsches Biographie*, vol. III, p. 126. As Janz notes, Förster's mismanagement of the colony was so great that it was the subject of an exposé, *Enthüllungen über die Dr. Bernhard Förstersche Ansiedlung Neu-Germaniien in Paraguay*, Julius Klingbeil (Leipzig: Kommionsverlag, 1889).

32. Janz, *Die Briefe Friedrich Nietzsches*, p. 33.

33. Although the 1906 edition of WP, volumes IX–X of the *Taschenausgabe* of Nietzsche's works, was eventually superseded by the 1911 edition edited by Otto Weiss, volumes XV–XVI of the revised *Großoktavausgabe*, the bodies of the two texts are identical. While Weiss contributed an introduction and critical apparatus, he did not alter the selection, order or number of notes incorporated in WP.

34. Förster-Nietzsche's belief that Nietzsche had indeed written a major work was so unshakable that she went so far as to accuse Franz Overbeck, who had traveled to Turin under difficult circumstances to retrieve the ill Nietzsche in January, 1889, of losing the manuscript of the text. See Hoffman, *Zur Geschichte des Nietzsche-Archivs*, pp. 61–65, and GA, XV[1], p. xvii.

35. The title of GA XIII, edited by H. Köselitz and A. Horneffer, is *Unveröffentlichtes aus der Umwertungszeit* [Unpublished Material from the Period of the Revaluation].

36. Ernst Horneffer, *Nietzsches Leztes Schaffen: Eine kritische Studie* (Jena E. Diederichs, 1907). See also August Horneffer, *Nietzsche als Moralist und Schriftsteller*, pp. 80–83.

37. This ever increasing clarity was, however, reserved for the notes, which, according to Förster-Nietzsche, allow one "to understand his thoughts so much better" than the published works: "TI is an instructive example of how much misunderstanding can be produced by the brevity of the representation of his ideas," TA IX, p. xxi. This is a consistent theme in Förster-Nietzsche's commentaries. Cf., for example, GA, XV[1], pp. xi, xvi.

38. A. Horneffer, *Nietzsche als Moralist und Schriftsteller*, p. 82.

39. Lamm's review, which was written shortly after the publication of the canonical edition of WP in 1906, is as prescient as it is damning. One passage in particular deserved to be cited as some length: "A pernicious and hopeless confusion results, if, in the belief that his work came to a premature end, older notes, rejected by Nietzsche himself, are pasted together into fraudulent works, and these are then placed behind his last books as their conclusion. It is precisely these last books that go beyond these preliminary studies and make them otiose. It may be the case that these *Nachlaß*-volumes are, as one is in the habit of saying, *more comprehensible* than the major works, but whoever believes to have understood Nietzsche on the basis of these texts hopelessly misunderstands him," "Friedrich Nietzsche und seine nachgelassene 'Lehren,'" p. 278.

40. Janz, *Die Briefe Friedrich Nietzsches*, Chapter VII, "Das Verhältnis der Geschwister," pp. 50–62. See also Janz, *Nietzsches Biographie*, vol. II, pp. 339–341 and Kaufmann, *Nietzsche*, pp. 4–9.

41. Rudolf Steiner, "Zur Charakteristik der Frau Förster-Nietzsche," in *Das Magazin für Litteratur*, February 10, 1900; cited by Kaufmann, *Nietzsche*, pp. 4–5.

42. Hitler visited the Archive at the behest of Förster-Nietzsche on November 2, 1932 and July 20, 1934. One of the earliest critiques of attempts by Förster-Nietzsche and others to enlist Nietzsche for the National Socialist cause is Georges Bataille's essay "Nietzsche and the Fascists," trans. Allan Stoekl, *George Bataille, Visions of Excess: Selected Writings, 1927–1939* (Minneapolis: University of Minnesota Press, 1985).

43. Hoffman, *Zur Geschichte des Nietzsche-Archivs*, recounts how Hitler made money available to Förster-Nietzsche and the Nietzsche Archive for the purpose of purchasing letters of Nietzsche's which were in private hands.

44. Oswald Spengler, *Briefe*, ed. Anton M. Koktanek (Munich: Beck, 1963), p. 749. The letter is dated October 11, 1935. See also the letter of March 13, 1924 (p. 306), where Förster-Nietzsche expresses her admiration for Hitler and her outrage over his ongoing trial.

45. Fritsch, *Handbuch der Judenfrage*, p. 14.

46. "Bericht über die achte ordentliche Mitgliedversammlung der Gesellschaft der Freunde des Nietzsche-Archivs vom 6. Dezember 1933," p. 6; cited by Hoffman, *Zur Geschichte des Nietzsche-Archivs*, p. 110.

47. Janz, *Die Briefe Friedrich Nietzsches*, p. 55.

48. In May 1883, Meysenbug had arranged a meeting between Nietzsche and Förster-Nietzsche in Rome with the intention of effecting just such a reconciliation. At that time the cause of their break was Förster-Nietzsche's campaign against Lou Andreas-Salomé. See Janz, *Nietzsches Biographie*, vol. II, pp. 176–182 and 199–203.

49. See note 3 above.

50. See the letter to Overbeck from late December, 1888, where Nietzsche bitterly complains about Förster-Nietzsche's objections to his association with "Jews, like G. Brandes, who have their finger in every pie [. . .]. At the same time she calls me 'dear Fritz' [. . .]. *This* has gone on for seven years now!— —" KSAB, 8/1210.

51. Montinari notes that part of the page has been cut away, obscuring the beginning of the title. This makes it "highly probable," but not entirely certain, that this plan belongs to WP, KSA 14, p. 391.

52. Schlechta, *Werke in drei Bänden*, vol. III, p. 1396.

53. Otto Weiss, editor of the 1911 edition of WP, does little more than echo this statement when he writes that the March, 1887 plan is "the shortest, clearest and, at the same time, the most pregnant [plan] Nietzsche ever advanced," GA XV^2, p. xxxiv. Although Weiss' hands were clearly tied by the fact that Förster-Nietzsche did not want a genuinely critical edition of WP to appear (cf. her Afterword to GA XV^2, pp. 478–479), one cannot help but rue his complicity in the entire affair. As Schlechta has observed, when one reads the critical apparatus to the text prepared by Weiss, "It becomes clear that the editor is making every effort to gain a foothold where there is no firm ground to be had," Schlechta, *Werke in drei Bänden*, vol. III, p. 1397.

54. *The Will to Power*, trans. Walter Kaufmann and R. J. Hollingdale, edited with commentary by Walter Kaufmann (New York: Vintage, 1968), p. xvi. Perhaps unbeknownst to Kaufmann, Förster-Nietzsche uses the very same metaphor to describe WP. See TA IX, p. xx.

55. Montinari, *Nietzsche lesen*, p. 107.

56. Mark Warren has persuasively argued for the close connection between these two texts. See his *Nietzsche and Political Thought*, chapter 1.

57. This is true for the German and the English editions of WP. Although Kaufmann gives the appearance of being a scrupulous editor, his efforts are seriously hampered and ultimately undermined by the fact that he follows the text of the canonical version of WP. As the following examination aims to demonstrate, no amount of editorial commentary can redeem this text.

58. For a description of the notebooks, their designations, dates and contents, see the "Übersicht der Ausgaben, Erstdrucke und Manuskripte," KSA 14, pp. 26–35.

59. One of the striking features of this note is how fragmentary it is when compared with the notes published in WP. Such "cleaning-up" of the text was, of course, necessary if it was to be presented as a reconstruction of Nietzsche's major work. One of the consequences of this process is that many of the notes read more like complete aphorisms than like unpolished notes. The success of this editorial effort can be gauged by Heidegger incautious remark that the sections of WP are "for the most part not simple incomplete fragments . . . [but] carefully worked out 'aphorisms,' as Nietzsche's individual notations are customarily called," N I, p. 19/N 1, p. 11. Of course Heidegger, who had worked in the Nietzsche Archive until shortly before this lecture course was given, must have known that this was not the case. The reasons behind Heidegger's decision to privilege the WP and how his relationship with Alfred Baeumler, a prominent National Socialist and Nietzsche scholar and editor, might have affected his interpretation of Nietzsche have not, to the best of my knowledge, been adequately explored. It is clear, however, that both Heidegger and Baeumler shared the view that Nietzsche's philosophy proper was to be found in the *Nachlaß* and not in the published texts. See Alfred Baeumler, *Nietzsche der Philosoph und Politiker* (Leipzig: Reklam, 1931), pp. 7–9. For an introductory discussion of this relationship and of Baeumler's influence on Heidegger's reading of Nietzsche, see David Farrell Krell's commentary to the four volumes of the English translation of Heidegger's *Nietzsche*, particularly vol. III, pp. 267–274.

60. For a list of the passages which were tampered with see Jörg Salaquarda, "Konkordanz Der Wille zur Macht: Nachlass in chronologischer Ordung der kritischen Gesamtausgabe," *Nietzsche-Studien*, vol. 39 (1980).

61. Magnus, Stewart, and Mileur, *Nietzsche's Case*, pp. 45–46.

Bibliography

NIETZSCHE'S WRITINGS IN GERMAN

Nietzsches Werke (Großoktavausgabe). Ed. E. Förster-Nietzsche. Leipzig: Naumann/Kröner, 1894–1926.

Nietzsches Werke (Taschenausgabe). Ed. E. Förster-Nietzsche. Leipzig: Naumann, 1906.

Historisch-kritische Gesamtausgabe, Werke. Ed. Hans Joachim Mette and Karl Schlechta. München: Beck, 1933 ff.

Kritische Gesamtausgabe Werke. Ed. Giorgi Colli and Mazzino Montinari. Berlin: de Gruyter, 1967 ff.

Kritische Gesamtausgabe Briefwechsel. Ed. Giorgi Colli and Mazzino Montinari. Berlin: de Gruyter, 1975 ff.

Sämtliche Werke, Kritische Studienausgabe. Ed. Giorgi Colli and Mazzino Montinari. Berlin: de Gruyter, 1980.

Sämtliche Briefe, Kritische Studienausgabe. Ed. Giorgi Colli and Mazzino Montinari. Berlin: de Gruyter, 1986.

TRANSLATIONS CONSULTED

The Antichrist. Trans. Walter Kaufmann. *The Portable Nietzsche*. New York: Viking Press, 1954.

The Birth of Tragedy. Trans. Walter Kaufmann. *Basic Writings of Nietzsche*. New York: Random House, 1968.

La naissance de la tragédie. Trans. Philippe Lacoue-Labarthe. Paris: Gallimard, 1977.

Beyond Good and Evil. Trans. Walter Kaufmann, *Basic Writings of Nietzsche*. New York: Random House, 1968.

The Case of Wagner. Trans. Walter Kaufmann, *Basic Writings of Nietzsche*. New York: Random House, 1968.

"Description of Ancient Rhetoric." Trans. Sander L. Gilman, Carole Blair, and David J. Parent. *Friedrich Nietzsche on Rhetoric and Language*. Oxford: Oxford University Press, 1989.

Ecce Homo. Trans. Walter Kaufmann. *Basic Writings of Nietzsche*. New York: Random House, 1968.

The Gay Science. Trans. Walter Kaufmann, New York: Vintage Press, 1974.

Human All-Too-Human. Trans. Marion Faber and Stephen Lehmann. Lincoln: University of Nebraska Press, 1986.

Nietzsche Contra Wagner. Trans. Walter Kaufmann. *The Portable Nietzsche*. New York: Viking Press, 1954.

On the Genealogy of Morals. Trans. Walter Kaufmann and R. J. Hollingdale. *Basic Writings of Nietzsche*. New York: Random House, 1968.

"On Truth and Lie in the Extra-Moral Sense." Trans. Sander L. Gilman, Carole Blair and David J. Parent. *Friedrich Nietzsche on Rhetoric and Language*. Oxford: Oxford University Press, 1989.

Thus Spoke Zarathustra. Trans. Walter Kaufmann. *The Portable Nietzsche*. New York: Viking Press, 1954.

Twilight of the Idols. Trans. Walter Kaufmann. *The Portable Nietzsche*. New York: Viking Press, 1954.

Untimely Meditations. Trans. R. J. Hollingdale. Cambridge: Cambridge University Press, 1983.

The Will to Power. Trans. Walter Kaufmann and R. J. Hollingdale. New York: Vintage Press, 1968.

SECONDARY TEXTS

Aeschylus. *The Oresteia*. Trans. Robert Fagles. New York: Penguin, 1977.

Aristotle. *Poetics*. Trans. James Hutton. New York: Norton, 1982.

Aschheim, Steven. *The Nietzsche Legacy in Germany 1890–1990*. Berkeley: University of California Press, 1992.

Babich, Babette. *Nietzsche's Philosophy of Science*. Albany: SUNY Press, 1994.

Baeumler, Alfred. *Nietzsche der Philosoph und Politiker*. Leipzig: Reklam, 1931.

Baker, G. P. and Hacker, P. M. S. *An Analytical Commentary on Wittgenstein's Philosophical Investigations*. Chicago: The University of Chicago Press, 1985.

Bataille, Georges. "Nietzsche and the Fascists." Trans. Allan Stoekl. *George Bataille, Visions of Excess: Selected Writings, 1927–1939*. Minneapolis: University of Minnesota Press, 1985.

Benjamin, Walter. "Die Aufgabe des Übersetzers." *Illuminationen*. Frankfurt: Suhrkamp, 1977.

———. "Goethes Wahlverwandtshaften." *Illuminationen*. Frankfurt: Suhrkamp, 1977.

———. "Über den Begriff der Geschichte." *Illuminationen*. Frankfurt: Suhrkamp, 1977.

———. "The Task of the Translator." *Illuminations*. Trans. Harry Zohn. New York: Schocken, 1968

Blondel, Eric. *Nietzsche: The Body and Culture*. Trans. Séan Hand. Stanford: Stanford University Press, 1991.

Böning, Thomas. "Literaturwissenscaft im Zeitalter des Nihilismus: Paul de Mans Nietzsche Lektüre." *Deutsche Vierteljahrschrift für Literaturwissenschaft und Geistesgeschichte* 64 (1990).

Breazeale, Daniel. *Philosophy and Truth: Selections from Nietzsche's Notebooks of the Early 1870's*. Atlantic Highlands (NJ): Humanities Press, 1979.

Burnet, John. *Early Greek Philosophy*. London: Adam & Charles Black, 1971.

Clark, Maudemarie. *Nietzsche on Truth and Philosophy*. Cambridge: Cambridge University Press, 1990.

———. "Language and Deconstruction: Nietzsche, de Man, and Postmodernism." *Nietzsche as Postmodernist: Essays Pro and Contra*. Ed. Clayton Koelb. Albany: Suny Press, 1990.

Crawford, Claudia. *The Beginnings of Nietzsche's Theory of Language*. Berlin: de Gruyter, 1988.

De Man, Paul. "Epistemology of Metaphor." *Critical Inquiry* 5 (1978).

———. "Genesis and Genealogy." *Allegories of Reading*. New Haven: Yale University Press, 1979.

———. "Reply to Raymond Geuss." *Critical Inquiry* 10 (1983).

———. "The Rhetoric of Temporality." *Blindness and Insight*. New York: Columbia University Press, 1981.

———. "Rhetoric of Tropes." *Allegories of Reading*. New Haven: Yale University Press, 1979.

———. "The Task of the Translator." *The Resistance to Theory*. Minneapolis: University of Minnesota Press, 1986.

———. "Tropes." *Allegories of Reading*. New Haven: Yale University Press, 1979.

Danto, Arthur. *Nietzsche as Philosopher*. New York: Columbia University Press, 1980.

———. *The Philosophical Disenfranchisement of Art*. New York: Columbia University Press, 1986.

Davidson, Donald. "Belief and the Basis of Meaning." *Inquiries into Truth and Interpretation*. Oxford: Oxford University Press, 1985.

———. "What Metaphors Mean." *Inquiries into Truth and Interpretation*. Oxford: Oxford University Press, 1985.

Deleuze, Gilles. *Nietzsche & Philosophy*. Trans. Hugh Tomlinson. New York: Columbia University Press, 1983.

Derrida, Jacques. "Différance." Trans. Alan Bass. *Margins of Philosophy*. Chicago: University of Chicago Press, 1982.

———. *Of Grammatology*. Trans. Gayatri Spivak. Baltimore: Johns Hopkins University Press, 1976.

———. "Otobiographies: Teaching of Nietzsche and the Politics of the Proper Name." Trans. Avital Ronell. *The Ear of the Other*. Lincoln: University of Nebraska Press, 1988.

———. *Spurs: Nietzsche's Styles*. Trans. Barbara Harlow. Chicago: University of Chicago Press, 1979.

———. "White Mythology: Metaphor in the Text of Philosophy." Trans. Alan Bass. *Margins of Philosophy*. Chicago: University of Chicago Press, 1982.

Descartes, Rene. *Oeuvres philosophiques*. Ed. Ferdinand Alquié. Paris: Garnier, 1963.

———. *Philosophical Writings*. Trans. Elizabeth Anscombe and Peter Geach. Sunbury-on-Thames: Thomas Nelson, 1970.

Diogenes Laertius. *Lives and Opinions of Eminent Philosophers*. Trans. R. D. Hicks. New York: Putnam, 1925.

Figal, Günter. *Socrates*. Munich: Beck, 1995.

Fink, Eugen. *Nietzsches Philosophie*. Stuttgart: Kohlhammer, 1960.

Fritsch, Theodor. *Handbuch der Judenfrage. Die wichtigsten Tatsachen zur Beurteilung des jüdischen Volkes*. 47th ed. Leipzig: Hammer, 1942.

Gadamer, Hans-Georg. "Plato und die Dichter." *Gesammelte Werke*, vol. 5. Tübingen: J. C. B. Mohr, 1990–1995.

———. *Truth and Method.* Ed. Garrett Barden and John Cumming. New York: Crossroad, 1988.

———. *Wahrheit und Methode. Gesammelte Werke*, vol. 1. Tübingen: J. C. B. Mohr, 1990–1995.

Gillespie, Michael Allen and Strong, Tracy. "Introduction." *Nietzsche's New Seas.* Ed. Michael Allen Gillespie and Tracy Strong. Chicago: University of Chicago Press, 1988.

Harries, Karsten. "The Philosopher at Sea." *Nietzsche's New Seas.* Ed. Michael Allen Gillespie and Tracy Strong. Chicago: University of Chicago Press, 1988.

Hatab, Lawrence J. *A Nietzschean Defense of Democracy: An Experiment in Postmodern Politics.* Chicago: Open Court, 1995.

Heidegger, Martin. *Beiträge zur Philosophie. Gesamtuasgabe*, vol. 65. Frankfurt: Klosterman, 1989.

———. "Letter on Humanism." Trans. Frank A. Capuzzi and J. Glenn Gray. *Martin Heidegger Basic Writings.* Ed. David Farrell Krell. New York: Harper & Row, 1977.

———. *Nietzsche.* Pfullingen: Günther Neske, 1961.

———. *Nietzsche.* Trans. J. Stambaugh, D. F. Krell and F. A. Capuzzi. San Francisco: HarperCollins, 1991.

———. "The Question Concerning Technology." Trans. William Lovitt. *Martin Heidegger Basic Writings.* Ed. David Farrell Krell. New York: Harper & Row, 1977.

———. *Sein und Zeit.* Tübingen: Max Niemeyer, 1986.

———. *Vorträge und Aufsätze.* Pfüllingen: Günther Neske, 1990.

———. *Wegmarken.* Frankfurt: Klostermann, 1978.

Hoffman, David Marc. *Zur Geschichte des Nietzsche-Archivs.* Berlin: de Gruyter, 1991.

Homer. *The Iliad.* Trans. Richmond Lattimore. Chicago: University of Chicago Press, 1961.

Horneffer, August. *Nietzsche als Moralist und Schriftsteller.* Jena: E. Diederichs, 1906.

Horneffer, Ernst. *Nietzsches Leztes Schaffen: Eine kritische Studie.* Jena E. Diederichs, 1907.

James, Henry. "The Figure in the Carpet." *The Figure in the Carpet and Other Stories*. Ed. Frank Kermode. London: Penguin Books, 1986.

Janz, Curt Paul. *Nietzsche Biographie*. Munich: Carl Hanser, 1987.

———. *Die Briefe Friedrich Nietzsches*. Zürich: Theologischer Verlag, 1972.

Kahn, Charles. *The Art and Thought of Heraclitus*. Cambridge: Cambridge University Press, 1979.

Kant, Immanuel. *Foundations of the Metaphysics of Morals*. Trans. Lewis White Beck. Indianapolis: Bobbs-Merrill, 1959.

Kaufmann, Walter. *Nietzsche: Philosopher, Psychologist, Antichrist*. Princeton: Princeton University Press, 1974.

Koelb, Clayton. "Reading as a Philosophical Strategy." *Nietzsche as Postmodernist: Essays Pro and Contra*. Ed. Clayton Koelb. Albany: Suny Press, 1990.

Kofman, Sarah. *Explosion I, De l' 'Ecce Homo' de Nietzsche*. Paris: Galilée, 1992.

———. *Nietzsche et la scène philosophique*. Paris: Galilée, 1986.

———. *Nietzsche and Metaphor*. Trans. Duncan Large. Stanford: Stanford University Press, 1993.

———. *Socrates*. Paris: Galilée, 1989.

Koyré, Alexandre. "Introduction." *Descartes: Philosophical Writings*. Trans. Elizabeth Anscombe and Peter Geach. Sunbury-on-Thames: Thomas Nelson, 1970.

Kuenzli, Rudolf E. "The Nazi Appropriation of Nietzsche." *Nietzsche-Studien* 12 (1983).

Lacoue-Labarthe, Philippe. "The Detour." *The Subject of Philosophy*. Ed. Thomas Trezise. Minnesota: University of Minnesota Press, 1993.

Lamm, Albert. "Friedrich Nietzsche und seine nachgelassene 'Lehren.'" *Süddeutsche Monatshefte* (1906).

Legros, Robert. "La métaphysique nietzschéenne de la vie." *Pourquoi nous ne sommes pas nietzschéens*. Ed. Luc Ferry and Alain Renaut. Paris: Grasset, 1991

Magnus, Bernd. "The Use and Abuse of *The Will to Power*." *Reading Nietzsche*. Ed. Robert Solomon and Kathleen Higgins. New York: Oxford University Press, 1988.

Magnus, Bernd, Stewart, Stanley, and Mileur, Jean-Pierre. *Nietzsche's Case: Philosophy As/And Literature*. New York: Routledge, 1993.

Meier, Christian. *Die politische Kunst der griechischen Tragödie*. Beck: Munich, 1988.

Meijers, Anthoine. "Gustav Gerber und Friedrich Nietzsche." *Nietzsche-Studien* 17 (1988).

Meijers, Anthoine and Stingelin, Martin. "Konkordanz zu den wörtlichen Abschriften und Übernahmen von Beispielen und Zitaten aus Gustav Gerber: *Die Sprache Als Kunst* Bromberg 1871 in Nietzsches Rhetorik-Vorlesung und in 'Über Wahrheit und Lüge im aussermoralischen Sinne.'" *Nietzsche-Studien* (17) 1988.

Montinari, Mazzino. *Nietzsche lesen*. Berlin: de Gruyter, 1982.

Nehamas, Alexander. *Nietzsche: Life as Literature*. Cambridge: Harvard University Press, 1985.

Nussbaum, Martha. *The Fragility of Goodness*. Cambridge: Cambridge University Press, 1986.

Pagels, Elaine. *The Origin of Satan*. New York: Random House, 1995.

Pasley, Malcolm. "Nietzsche's Use of Medical Terms." *Nietzsche—Imagery and Thought*. Ed. Malcolm Pasley. Berkeley: University of California Press, 1978.

Plato. *Apology*. Trans. Thomas G. West and Grace Starry West. *Four Texts on Socrates*. Ithaca: Cornell Univsersity Press, 1984.

———. *The Republic*. Trans. Allan Bloom. New York: Basic Books, 1968.

Quine, W. V. O. *Word and Object*. Cambridge: MIT Press, 1960.

Rorty, Richard. *Essays on Heidegger and Others*. Cambridge: Cambridge University Press, 1991.

Rousseau, Jean-Jacques. *On the Social Contract*. Trans. Judith Masters. New York: St. Martin's Press, 1979.

Russell, Bertrand. *The History of Western Philosophy*. London: George Allen & Unwin, 1961.

Salaquarda, Jörg. "Konkordanz Der Wille zur Macht: Nachlass in chronologischer Ordung der kritischen Gesamtausgabe." *Nietzsche-Studien* 39 (1980).

Sallis, John. *Nietzsche and the Space of Tragedy*. Chicago: University of Chicago Press, 1991.

Schacht, Richard. "Nietzsche as Colleague." *International Studies in Philosophy* XXII/2 (1990).

Schadewaldt, Wolfgang. *Die Anfänge der Philosophie bei den Griechen: Die Vorsokratiker und ihre Voraussetzungen*. Frankfurt: Suhrkamp, 1978.

Schlechta, Karl. "Philologischer Nachbricht." Friedrich Nietzsche, *Werke in drei Bänden*. Ed. Karl Schlechta. Munich: Hanser, 1965.

Schleiermacher, Friedrich. *Hermeneutik*. Ed. Heinz Kimmerle. Heidelberg: Carl Winter, 1959.

Schopenhauer, Arthur. *Parega and Paralipomena*. Zürich: Diogenes, 1977.

———. *Die Welt als Wille und Vorstellung*. Zürich: Diogenes, 1977.

Schrift, Alan. *Nietzsche and the Question of Interpretation*. New York: Routledge, 1990.

Schürmann, Reiner. *Heidegger on Being and Acting*. Trans. Christine-Marie Gros with Reiner Schürmann. Bloomington: Indiana University Press, 1989.

Shapiro, Gary. *Nietzschean Narratives*. Bloomington: Indiana University Press, 1989.

Silk, M. S. and Stern, J. P. *Nietzsche on Tragedy*. Cambridge: Cambridge University Press, 1981.

Sophocles. *The Three Thebean Plays*. Trans. Robert Fagles. New York: Penguin, 1984.

Spengler, Oswald. *Briefe*. Ed. Anton M. Koktanek. Munich: Beck, 1963.

Steiner, Rudolf. "Zur Charakteristik der Frau Förster-Nietzsche." *Das Magazin für Litteratur*. February 10, 1900.

Szondi, Peter. "Versuch Über das Tragische." *Schriften*, vol I. Ed. Wolfgang Fietkau. Frankfurt: Suhrkamp, 1978.

Vlastos, Gregory. *Socrates: Ironist and Moral Philosopher*. Cambridge: Cambridge University Press, 1991.

Warren, Mark. *Nietzsche and Political Thought*. Cambridge: The MIT Press, 1988.

Warminski, Andrzej. "Towards a Fabulous Reading: Nietzsche's 'On Truth and Lie in the Extra-Moral Sense.'" *Graduate Faculty Philosophy Journal* 15.2 (1991).

———. *Readings in Interpretation*. Minneapolis: University of Minnesota Press, 1987.

Wilson, Margaret. *Descartes*. London: Routledge & Kegan Paul, 1978.

Winchester, James. *Nietzsche's Aesthetic Turn*. Albany: SUNY Press, 1994.

Wittgenstein, Ludwig. *Philosophical Investigations*. Trans. G. E. M. Anscombe. Oxford: Blackwell, 1983.

———. *Philosophische Untersuchungen*. Ed. Joachim Schulte. *Werkausgabe*, vol. 1. Frankfurt: Suhrkamp, 1984.

———. *Tractatus Logico-Philosophicus*. Trans. D. F. Pears and B. F. McGuiness. London: Routledge & Kegan Paul, 1974.

———. *Tractatus Logico-Philosophicus*. Ed. Joachim Schulte. *Werkausgabe*, vol. 1.

———. *Vermischte Bemerkungen*. Ed. G. H. v. Wright. *Werkausgabe*, vol. 8.

Index

A

B

H

I

J

K

L

P

Q

R

S

T

V

W

Z